THE FULLNESS OF KNOWING

THE FULLNESS OF KNOWING
Modernity and Postmodernity
from Defoe to Gadamer

Daniel E. Ritchie

BAYLOR UNIVERSITY PRESS

Scripture quotations are from the New Revised Standard Version Bible, copyright 1989, Division of Christian Education of the National Council of the Churches of Christ in the United States of America. Used by permission. All rights reserved.

Cover Design by Pamela Poll
Cover art: A machine "for improving speculative knowledge" from "A Voyage to Laputa" in *Gulliver's Travels* (1726) by Jonathan Swift

Library of Congress Cataloging-in-Publication Data

Ritchie, Daniel E.
  The fullness of knowing : modernity and postmodernity from Defoe to Gadamer / Daniel E. Ritchie.
     p. cm.
  Includes bibliographical references and index.
  ISBN 978-1-932792-17-1 (cloth : alk. paper)
  1. Knowledge, Theory of--History. 2. Philosophy, Modern--History. 3. Enlightenment. 4. Postmodernism. I. Title.
  BD161.R58 2009
  121--dc22
                          2009027672

Printed in the United States of America on acid-free paper with a minimum of 30% pcw recycled content.

To my father, Edgar C. Ritchie

Semper Paratus

CONTENTS

ACKNOWLEDGMENTS

I would like to thank my research assistant, Charity Kroeker, for editing the introduction and first three chapters of this book, and for raising many helpful questions that improved its content. Bethel University provided a summer stipend for our work through its Edgren Scholars program, and for that I am grateful. I thank the reference librarians at Bethel for their expert advice, and Deborah Sullivan-Trainor, Associate Dean of General Education and Faculty Development at Bethel, for help with my translations from French. Hosanna Krienke put the bibliography and footnotes into manageable, consistent form.

Grateful acknowledgment is made to *Renascence*, which published an earlier form of the first chapter as "Robinson Crusoe as Narrative Theologian" (vol. 49, no. 2, Winter 1997, pp. 95–110). Material from that essay is reprinted by permission. Some of the ideas from chapter 6 first appeared in the March/April 2004 issue of *Books and Culture*, and acknowledgment is also made to that publication.

INTRODUCTION
Unenlightened Writers and the Postmodern World

This is a book about knowledge. At many points it agrees with the postmodern critique of the Western approach to knowledge since the Enlightenment. Many Enlightenment promises have proven hollow—the promises to build knowledge on a foundation of certainty, to achieve substantial moral and scientific progress, and to apply scientific methodology to all areas of human knowledge. On the other hand, much of the postmodern critique is itself questionable—the reduction of knowledge to power, the suspicion of natural science, and the instinctive but selective doubt about the ability of language to communicate. Although postmodernism has shown the inadequacies of Enlightenment approaches to knowledge, its alternatives are often unpersuasive.

The word "modernity" in the title refers to the Enlightenment from the time of Daniel Defoe (1660?–1731) through the eighteenth century. It is not a technical term, and I will use various shades of *modern* throughout the book. Its purpose in the title is to begin making connections between the questions raised in our postmodern age with those raised by Defoe, Swift, Burke, and others during the Enlightenment. Each chapter of the book explores one of those connections in depth.

The origin of the book came from my growing recognition as a student of the eighteenth century that many of today's best criticisms of the Enlightenment are not really all that original. Many of the best English minds during the Enlightenment itself had no more confidence in the promises of their age than the postmodern critics of today.

In 1790 the politician Edmund Burke wrote, "You see, Sir, in this enlightened age I am bold enough to confess that we are generally men of untaught feelings."[1] He was explaining his opposition to the French revolutionaries, who saw themselves as the creators of a fully rational, fully just society. In Burke's view, their new political science swept away the sources of knowledge— including "untaught feelings"—that he thought a good society needed. Burke was among the first to see and criticize the revolutionaries' professed link between their political causes and the spread of "science" in its modern, popular connotation of certain, cumulative knowledge. He doubted this link; he believed their overconfidence would have terrible results, amply demonstrated by the Reign of Terror (1793–1794). A century-and-a-half later, the German philosophers Max Horkheimer and Theodor Adorno were arguing much the same theory, only in hindsight: the political science of the Enlightenment had turned into the opposite of rationality and justice—irrationality and domination—during the twentieth century.[2]

This book selects seven major topics that have attracted critiques from both the Enlightenment era and postmodern times. All of these topics have to do with knowledge. Nevertheless, the book is not a formal study of epistemology. Instead, it chooses certain figures and cultural movements for analysis because of their wide-ranging epistemological significance. The book begins with work from the early eighteenth century by Defoe and Isaac Watts, when the challenges raised by Enlightenment modes of knowledge were difficult to recognize. It ends with analyses of Edmund Burke and William Cowper, whose late eighteenth-century works raised objections to specific Enlightenment assumptions and promises. The book's major purpose is to acquaint readers with some ideas for broadening our approach to knowledge beyond the Enlightenment boundaries, without falling into some of the excesses of postmodernism.

————

Near the beginning of the eighteenth century, a critical mass of thinkers began to believe they could create a solid foundation for knowledge through some combination of the rationalism of René Descartes, the science of Sir Isaac Newton, and the empiricism of John Locke. This meant constraining knowledge to what could be proven logically, tested scientifically, or verified empirically. The knowledge that arose from tradition or unmethodical personal intuition was discarded, and knowledge derived from religion or art was severely restricted. At the same time, the prestige of knowledge that met new Enlightenment standards, such as physics, archeology, philology, and other cumulative sciences, expanded greatly.[3] Fueled by the success of this kind of knowledge, faith in progress swelled.

Ever-widening divisions between rationality and feeling, propositional truth and experience, verifiable history and meaning resulted from Enlightenment conflicts over knowledge. In each case, the first term came to count as knowledge, whereas the second term lost prestige. By narrowing the scope of what counted as knowledge, the Enlightenment changed the way in which most Westerners came to understand their world.

Inspired by the predictive and explanatory success of Newtonian physics, many began to think that all knowledge claims should be quantifiable and repeatable or verifiable and empirical. The new physics of Newton had enabled astronomers and physicists to accumulate this kind of knowledge in an unprecedented manner. Its success conferred great prestige on the power of the apparently impersonal methods of modern science, while casting doubt on the authority of knowledge that came from the noncumulative, representational methods of religion, literature, and the arts.

Other Enlightenment thinkers took their cue from the logical reasoning of Descartes and believed that truth could emerge only from a chain of clear and distinct perceptions. For them, knowledge should, in principle, have the form of rational propositions. Descartes supposed that he began by doubting everything except the single, indubitable certainty that he was engaged in thinking. He then had a firm foundation on which to base the knowledge of his own existence, God's existence, and ultimately an entire body of certain knowledge. In Descartes' clear-cut method to achieve certainty, he took much for granted—for instance, his ability to use French and Latin (and translate the same thought from one language to the other) and his reliance on thought patterns inherited from scholastic philosophy.[4] But he believed that he had erected a system of certain knowledge that was not beholden to culture-bound traditions. As the Enlightenment progressed, other thinkers followed his lead, seeking authority in the systematic manner of their thought and discarding customary, historical, or traditional ways of understanding. Human laws, for instance, should be based on universal propositions about human nature, rather than on historical circumstances or culturally significant traditions. Voltaire illustrates the confidence this systematic approach created, when he writes, "in the course of an hour, thirty laws of this description, all of a nature beneficial to mankind, would be unanimously agreed to" by simple farmers.[5]

Many Enlightenment figures expected that knowledge would advance without hindrance. By the late 1700s, they believed they were close to realizing the Enlightenment hope of producing progressively larger areas of knowledge by reducing the hold of superstition, prejudice, and tradition. The virtuous life could then be prized away from its customary roots in religion, which was increasingly seen as irrelevant at best and oppressive at worst. The political revolutions at the end of the century seemed to offer emancipation from intellectual darkness, ecclesiastical bondage, and political despotism and to promise illumination, tolerance, and freedom.[6] Thomas Paine, who thought he saw "a regeneration of man" in the French Revolution, summed up these hopes in the second part of *The Rights of Man* (1792):

> Never did so great an opportunity offer itself to England, and to all Europe, as is produced by the two revolutions of America and France. By the former, freedom has a national champion in the western world; and by the latter, in Europe. . . . The present age will hereafter merit to be called the Age of Reason, and the present generation will appear to the future as the Adam of a new world.[7]

Yet midway into the 1790s, the French Revolution went terribly wrong. Maximilien Robespierre found that terror was necessary to promote the new, revolutionary vision of virtue. At the height of the Reign of Terror, he identified his own policies with the voice of reason and linked his moderate opponents in the ruling Convention with counterrevolutionaries. He warned his audience against becoming the "dupe of words" and stated ominously "whoever doesn't hate crime utterly cannot love virtue."[8] Both friends and enemies of the revolution heard such words as the outcome of a century of Enlightenment. The terror that they attempted to justify destroyed many people's confidence in Enlightenment rationality as a means for even understanding the social order, let alone for reshaping it.

Two centuries later, the confidence of the Enlightenment has been shattered. Blamed by some for making humans incapable of telling right from wrong and by others for elevating so weak a creature as the autonomous individual to the arbiter of morality, the Enlightenment hope of a politics, theology, and morality based on universal reason is a shambles. Horkheimer and Adorno, writing in Germany just after World War II, saw in the Enlightenment the seeds of Fascist state socialism.[9] Friedrich Nietzsche and the Marquis de Sade, they wrote chillingly, realized that it was impossible to derive an argument against murder from Enlightenment reason.

Nearly every leading thinker today realizes the limits of the Enlightenment.[10] The assumption that all rational people could agree on the contours of knowledge has turned out to be false. All knowledge has a genealogy—a particular origin and history—that colors its methods and outcomes. Not even scientific knowledge is impersonal, as many Enlightenment thinkers had assumed. Its paradigms reflect commitments, unspoken assumptions, perspectives, and skills that cannot be objectified or reduced to method. So prevalent is the criticism of "the Enlightenment project," as it is often called, that it is difficult to find a defender.

The most common postmodern solutions, however, seem to offer little hope of reconnecting our fragmented knowledge and experience into a more holistic unity. Some have lost faith in language to represent truth and are interested only in "finding a new and more interesting way of expressing ourselves."[11] The breakdown of aesthetic standards, for others, means that artistic judgments boil down to how spectacular a performance is.[12] Some find refuge in a social or political ideology that shuts out dissenters and creates an atmosphere in which free discussion and participation are absent. On a more popular level, some New Age religionists turn away from science altogether and try to reconnect the heart and the mind by shutting out the outside world and anointing themselves their as own creators.[13]

However skeptical one may be about particular thinkers or movements within postmodernism, they have undoubtedly made us think anew about the shape of knowledge. They have questioned the validity of the Enlightenment's neutral, objective observer and made us see that we cannot abandon our own cultural situation in the quest for truth. They have taught us that if we limit knowledge to empirically testable hypotheses, we will force many important human questions about the universe, society, and human purpose outside the realm of comprehension altogether. By showing us the rickety foundations of Enlightenment epistemology, they have forced us to consider new connections among scientific, aesthetic, and religious forms of knowledge.[14]

All of these insights are useful. But postmodern voices are as deeply divided as pre-Enlightenment thinkers about where to turn for solutions to the problems of the Enlightenment. Sometimes they appeal only to a narrow group of like-minded people committed to a certain method of social change. But what of those who reject the activist's equation of justice with a particular ideology? At other times they offer nothing beyond pointing out the ironies embedded in the language of Western thought. But what of those who cannot share the deconstructionist's reduction of language to a game that changes with each new interpreter? On still other occasions, they turn inward to irrational, subjective experience. But what of those who reject the self-indulgent solipsism of the New Age?

Few believe that the latest version of postmodernity promises a more coherent life. But neither can we return to the Enlightenment trail of trusting that cumulative, objective knowledge will result in a progressively wiser, more humane existence.

People on the wrong trail have three alternatives. Some continue pursuing their way, doggedly insisting that the old map will ultimately prove right after all. Others strike out in an entirely new direction, persuaded that the newest track is the superior one. In this book, I want to take a third path. I will return to the century of Enlightenment—the eighteenth century—and listen to its first critics with our own, more recent questions in mind. I will bring earlier poets, preachers, and politicians into the conversation and ask if their pre-Enlightenment pursuit of truth can help us overcome the fragmentation we experience today.

There are, of course, many other valuable writers and movements from the eighteenth century who are absent from this book. Jean-Jacques Rousseau, Jonathan Edwards, Sir Joshua Reynolds, the gothic novelists, numerous religious poets, the revivers of the folk ballad; all of these Enlightenment-era figures raised epistemological questions about the limits to knowledge, the value of traditional wisdom, the place of beauty, and the significance of emotion. Other significant figures from the nineteenth century could have been chosen as well. My choice of subjects reflects my own interests and abilities. The book is not intended to be exhaustive. Nor is it definitive. Its conclusions are tentative, as the title suggests, urging us toward fuller ways of knowing without pretending to have found an authoritative epistemology.

Revisiting those eighteenth-century landmarks, however, does not mean we should attempt to recreate a pre-Enlightenment world. Jonathan Swift's satire is a wonderful sledgehammer for demolishing the bloated claims of technology but not a fine chisel for creating a more humane approach to information in our day. Hence the need for writers like Wendell Berry and Sven Birkerts. Burke can help us understand tradition, but elements like an established church, which he assumed to be essential to society, are plainly inapplicable to the twenty-first century. Hence the need for Hans-Georg Gadamer's philosophical treatment of tradition. My use of more recent figures, then, is intended to bring our conversation with the Enlightenment and postmodernism into the present. Both my earlier and later figures answer questions raised by the Enlightenment, and I hope to show that their thought responds to postmodernism as well.

By the end of the century, the critics of Enlightenment knew they were on the cultural margins. Every thoughtful person could see the split between rational, empirical approaches to knowledge on the one hand, and more personal, traditional, religious, or aesthetic approaches on the other. Lamenting this split and its consequences for theological truth, the poet Cowper (1731–1800) wrote, "Then truth is hush'd that heresy may preach, / And all is trash that reason cannot reach."[15] He was satirizing modern thinkers who believed they could develop a truly scientific basis for politics, religion, and philosophy. Tradition, personal commitment, beauty, and revelation, they believed, had no place in the Enlightenment mind. The poetic imagination could produce a pleasing flower here and there, but it was useless in the pursuit of knowledge. Yet in an age in which humans were increasingly impressed only with knowledge based on utility or the empirically demonstrable experiment, Cowper asserted the value of tacit, unspoken knowledge. This knowledge came from common sense, from personal experience, and from periods of reflection or (as he would say) "retirement." One of his major poetic themes was that the reigning, impersonal rationalism of the end of the century had narrowed the definition of knowledge.

In the twentieth century, the chemist-turned-philosopher Michael Polanyi expressed parallel concerns in much greater philosophical detail. True scientists do not follow an impersonal, detached scientific method in their effort to understand nature, he argued. Personal intuition and a sense of beauty are essential to the advancement of science, together with a personal commitment to the theory in which the scientist believes. The knowledge one has, Polanyi wrote, means nothing unless one "indwells" it. He meant that knowledge becomes significant only when one somehow orients one's life around it and bases one's decisions on it.

In their response to the epistemological crises of their times, Cowper and Polanyi represent many of the thinkers and movements in this book. These two writers, who close the book, can help us understand and recover the role of personal commitment as we seek to overcome the dichotomy between subjectivity and objectivity. They can help us close the gap that has opened up between what human beings require for a coherent life and what the Enlightenment considered knowledge of the self, nature, and society. Each of the figures in this book is concerned about this gap, yet none is complete in himself. Even the dialogue between Enlightenment and postmodern figures leaves many unanswered questions. It is my hope, however, that the individuals discussed in this book will help us begin a fuller conversation about the contours of a more coherent and humane knowledge for the twenty-first century.

1

LEARNING TO READ, LEARNING TO LISTEN IN *ROBINSON CRUSOE*

> I expected every Wave would have swallowed us up, and that every time the Ship fell down, as I thought, in the Trough or Hollow of the sea, we should never rise more; and in this Agony of Mind, I made many Vows and Resolutions, that if it would please God here to spare my Life this one Voyage, if ever I got once my Foot upon dry Land again, I would go directly home to my Father, and never set it into a Ship again while I liv'd . . . and I resolv'd that I would, like a true repenting Prodigal, go home to my Father. (Daniel Defoe, *Robinson Crusoe*, 8)

At the heart of postmodern theory is the critique of the metanarrative. No explanation outside of a story can give it final authority. All one has is the story.

Enlightenment thinkers, from the eighteenth through the twentieth centuries, approached the truth of narrative from a different angle. These thinkers assumed that truths about the universe and human nature could be reduced to explanations that anyone could accept, regardless of his or her culture and its particular stories. The truth of a narrative, then, depended on its conformity or contribution to these universal explanations—metanarratives—whose authority lay outside the narrative itself.

Buoyed by the success of Sir Isaac Newton and his followers, the prestige of physics soared during the 1700s. After all, everyone could see the truth of the law of gravity, Christian or Jew, Englishman or Turk. Many thinkers hoped that all fields of knowledge, including politics, moral philosophy, and religion, could enjoy the success and apparent certainty of physics. Once national prejudices and political traditions were laid aside, they believed, all people would agree that just government was based on propositions about human equality, consent, and freedom. Moral philosophy would be freed from the stories of particular cultures and be based on Immanuel Kant's categorical imperative, to "act only according to that maxim through which you can at the same time will that it should become a universal law." Religious truths would be based on universal religious experience or on logical propositions about God and the human soul, rather than on the authority of particular Scriptures or the traditions of particular communities. Intellectual authority would come instead from enlightened individuals who took Kant's challenge, and "dared to know" by dint of their own efforts.

Like most pre-Enlightenment figures, Daniel Defoe assumes a unity among various ways of knowing—specifically among theological, historical, and personal knowledge. He illustrates that unity in his first novel, *Robinson Crusoe*, published in 1719.[1] Yet the two sequels to that book illustrate the changes that were taking place during his era, changes that destroyed that unity. Defoe presented Robinson's story as a historical one. The theological and personal meanings that Robinson took from his experience were inseparable from his fictional, personal history. Under pressure from curious readers, however, Defoe was quickly forced to abandon the pretense of a Crusoe who was "historical" in the modern sense. In the sequels, Defoe ultimately separated the fictional "history" of Crusoe from the "meaning" of Crusoe's life. The truth of *Robinson Crusoe* lay in its moral meaning, Defoe eventually maintained, but not in the story. Its truths, he wrote, could be extracted from its fictions.

Defoe's response to his readers mirrors the emerging Enlightenment tendency to see fiction and fact as opposites. That view is apparent in a number of Enlightenment movements, but it emerges with particular clarity in the treatment of Scripture.[2] Biblical critics were beginning to separate the factual, empirically verifiable elements of Scripture from their figural meaning. A biblical story like that of Abraham and Isaac for instance, could still be meaningful as myth or allegory, but one could no longer have true knowledge of its historical veracity. Only a "higher criticism," which adhered to the scientific standards for knowledge, could yield the truth about the Bible. Defoe was by no means self-consciously aware of these cultural shifts or the profound consequences they would have. Even the biblical scholars who contributed to the shift did not appreciate the consequences of their thought.[3] Yet the split between "fiction" and "historical fact," which was beginning to open up in this era, is clearly reflected in Defoe's sequels. I shall try to show that this split between history and meaning is a major cause of the weaknesses of Defoe's later writings. More importantly, I hope to show that a source of the enduring appeal of *Robinson Crusoe* is the profound unity between the story of Defoe's hero and the theological knowledge Crusoe attains.

Robinson Crusoe, Puritan Autobiography, and Narrative Truth

Defoe's *Robinson Crusoe* has fascinated every generation of readers since its publication. Its popularity quickly called forth a sequel, *The Farther Adventures of Robinson Crusoe* (1719) and a collection of essays, *Serious Reflections . . . of Robinson Crusoe*, published in 1720. A large part of the book's historic popularity comes from Crusoe's spiritual quest, especially in countries like Britain and the United States with a strong cultural presence of Congregationalists, Baptists, Presbyterians, and other dissenters from the established Church of England. Late in the nineteenth century, for instance, the British critic John Ruskin reported reading *Robinson Crusoe* and *The Pilgrim's Progress* every Sunday, "my mother having it deeply in her heart to make an evangelical clergyman of me."[4] For many Christian readers (if not for Ruskin himself) Crusoe's growing ability to understand his life through the narratives of Scripture has rung true to the interpretation of their own lives.

At the time when Defoe's three volumes appeared, biblical interpretation was changing, along with other forms of knowledge in the Enlightenment. As described by Hans Frei, one of the founders of "narrative theology," Western reading of the Bible up to the eighteenth century was "strongly realistic, i.e., at once literal and historical, not only doctrinal or edifying."[5] Under the pressure of the emerging higher criticism, however, historical readings of Scripture broke away from "edifying" readings. This split occurred because of an unacknowledged Enlightenment assumption—

only recently questioned by recent narrative theologians—that if Scripture is taken as literally true, it must also be historically verifiable. When higher criticism questioned that identity, liberal theologians began to search for a nonhistorical meaning of the scriptural text, separate from its literal meaning, either in existentialism, myth, or religious experience.[6] Conservative theologians meanwhile set themselves the task of defending the text's historical veracity. Throughout the Enlightenment, both sides tried to keep the Bible from being classified as fiction.

Defoe's three volumes reflect both the earlier, unified reading of Scripture and the Enlightenment split between fiction and fact. In *Robinson Crusoe*, Defoe's hero reflects the earlier way of reading Scripture. Crusoe comes to recognize the truth of the biblical narratives as his own life story unfolds. That is, Crusoe learns to accept the authority of biblical stories and images for the purpose of reinterpreting his past life and for shaping his future life. His life story, futile up to the time of his conversion, begins to make sense as he learns to interpret it with respect to sacred stories. To put it another way, Crusoe learns to "read" his life correctly by orienting his own patterns of experience with the stories of Scripture. Similarly, other readers in the Puritan tradition and its descendants came to see *Robinson Crusoe* as a personal experiment in what has more recently been called narrative theology: as Robinson found his life story answering to the patterns of biblical stories and images, so, too, could the reader reflect on the applicability of Robinson's discoveries for his or her personal life.

The two sequels to the novel, however, show Defoe as a child of the Enlightenment. Under the pressure of his contemporary culture, Defoe grows nervous about the truth of his books. Ultimately, he abstracts the moral truth of Crusoe's experience from the now disposable fictions he had written. In the preface to *Farther Adventures*, he defends *Robinson Crusoe* against those who "reproach it with being a romance, [and who] search it for errors in geography, inconsistency in the relation, and contradictions in the fact," (vii). These searches have proven "abortive," he writes, and he goes on to criticize those who "pretend that the author has supplied the story out of his invention," (viii). By the time of *Serious Reflections*, however, he gives up the pretense that Crusoe is a real person. To defend his achievement, Defoe splits his work into two separable parts, the fable (or story) and the moral. In so doing, Defoe accepts the Enlightenment separation between the meaning of a text and its verifiable history (*Serious Reflections*, ix).

In the first volume, Robinson develops his relationship to the Bible in large part because Defoe took for granted the earlier way of reading Scripture. Defoe came out of a rich Puritan intellectual and literary tradition that shaped the narrative structure of *Robinson Crusoe*. As in Defoe's story, the basic pattern of the spiritual biographies, autobiographies, and pilgrim allegories of Puritan literature involved the work of Providence before conversion, conversion itself, recovery, and the subject's present spiritual state.[7] These works saw the Christian life as a narrative whole, often pictured as a journey, in which the climactic moment was conversion.

Although the focus of such Puritan literature was typically on a particular individual, the individual was not entirely free to shape his or her life story at will. The individual's account had to correspond to the Puritan interpretation of the Bible in some credible way. The individual's self-understanding emerged from reflecting on his or her life in conversation with a text that the community recognized as true. For these readers, the truth of a fictional work like John Bunyan's *The Pilgrim's Progress* (1678) rested on the believable correspondences between the stories of the Bible and the events that entangle Christian and his family—and the readers as well. On its title page, Bunyan's book is said to be "delivered under the similitude of a dream," and its epigraph quotes from Hosea 12:10: "I have used similitudes." Bunyan establishes the authority of his fiction, therefore, on the pattern of a biblical writer. His book was part of a vast Puritan genre of "pilgrim allegories" in the late seventeenth century, which used the genre of the fictional journey to relate typical, biblical truths of alienation from the world, temptation, fall, forgiveness, and the discovery of a new identity. Even a contemporary Puritan work of nonfiction, Mary Rowlandson's account of her captivity among the Indians of New England (1682), validated its truth by finding correspondences between the events she experienced and Old Testament captivity narratives. There was never any doubt that *The Pilgrim's Progress* was fictional or that Mary Rowlandson's *Sovereignty and Goodness of God* was not. But the Puritan audience of these works, living before the appearance of Enlightenment higher criticism, would have considered them both "true" because their accounts corresponded to the patterns found in the Bible.

Puritan divines acknowledged that the Bible itself used fictional stories, especially the parables of the New Testament, to convey truth. They gave limited approval for the didactic usage of nonscriptural material that also used fiction to express truth. Defoe justifies his invention of dialogue between characters in "The Family Instructor" (1715) on these grounds. Bunyan's *The Pilgrim's Progress*, a far more extended fiction, was justifiable because the book's allegorical form adhered to the underlying truth that could be discerned in Scripture. In the metrical *Apology* that precedes his book, Bunyan writes:

> This Book it chaulketh out before thine eyes,
> The man that seeks the everlasting Prize:
> It shews you whence he comes, whither he goes,
> What he leaves undone; also what he does:
> It also shews you how he runs, and runs,
> Till he unto the Gate of Glory comes.

Because it was clearly a parable of the Christian life, *The Pilgrim's Progress* could be accepted by Puritans as true.

Defoe, however, was unable to present *Robinson Crusoe* as a work of fiction at first. Unlike Bunyan, he could never claim that his book was a dream or a parable. He was never fully able to overcome his own suspicion that imaginative fiction was a waste of time and a usurpation of God's unique role as creator.[8] Defoe therefore provides a uniquely interesting case. He was able to write what many would call the first modern novel in large part because his tradition recognized that a fictional work could capture the truthful patterns of a life. That same tradition, however, prevented Defoe from embracing his own achievement.[9]

Puritans like Defoe clearly recognized the distinction between history and fiction. But they did not acknowledge a crucial importance to this distinction as they read Scripture or modern fictional works from their tradition (such as *The Pilgrim's Progress*) which aspired to deliver theological knowledge. It would not have occurred to them to make the later Enlightenment distinction between the Bible's verifiable facts and the personal meanings drawn from its fictional (or fiction-like) elements. When Puritans used fiction, whether in the short dialogues of "The Family

Instructor" or in the extended allegory of *The Pilgrim's Progress*, they believed they had to rise to a level of truth that differed only in degree from that of Scripture. From everything we know about his intellectual and cultural context, Defoe had to regard *Robinson Crusoe* as conveying true knowledge—both literally and morally. There was no alternative.

An example from Psalm 78, which eventually has great significance for Crusoe, may help to clarify this unity. The psalmist begins by explaining why he recounts the words and works of God:

> That the generation to come might know them even the children which should be born; who should arise and declare them to their children: That they might set their hope in God, and not forget the works of God, but keep his commandments. (Ps 78:6-7 KJV)

By rightly hearing the story of Israel's wanderings, the psalmist says, our children may trust in God. Unlike the Israelites of the exodus, they may remember his works and keep his commandments (vv.7-8). It does not occur to the psalmist (or to Crusoe, when he reads this psalm) that the truth of this story rests on certain historically verifiable details while its edifying message about trusting God is kept in a separate sphere. The whole psalm is an imaginative unity whose meaning is inseparable from the story it tells. Psalm 78 will ultimately provide unity for Crusoe's own life, as we shall see, when he recognizes his own life in the terms it supplies.

The unity of truth that bound together personal life and scriptural narrative was rapidly evaporating during the life of Defoe. By the time Defoe wrote his preface to volume three, he realized he had to acknowledge that loss and respond to it. A gap had developed between scriptural truth and personal narrative that the psalmist—and the Crusoe of volume one—would not have recognized. In his preface to the third volume, Defoe defends the first two volumes of *Robinson Crusoe* because of the "moral and religious Improvement" they bring. But this preface, and volume three as a whole, makes a peculiarly modern distinction between the historically dubious tale of Crusoe and its allegedly true meaning, even as Defoe desperately affirms its historicity:

> In a word, there's not a circumstance in the imaginary story, but has its just allusion to a *real story*, and chimes part for part, and step for step with the inimitable Life of Robinson Crusoe. . . . (*Serious Reflections*, xi; emphasis added)

What is this "real story"? A couple of modern scholars have seen in Defoe's own confinement in Newgate Prison the "real history [that] is represented by a confined retreat in an island."[10] These scholars are seeking a "truer," historical or cultural foundation for *Robinson Crusoe*. But why do we need such a foundation for understanding the novel? Why is the fictional *Robinson Crusoe* not a "real story"? Why must the imaginative story relate to the real one by means of "allusion," as Defoe himself says? By the time he writes the preface to his third volume, Defoe has started to make the Enlightenment assumption that fictional is the opposite of true. If it cannot be empirically verified, the fiction is false. What remains is the abstract moral truth displayed through Crusoe's development in the first volume, as Defoe loudly asserts in the preface to *Serious Reflections*:

> Here is invincible patience recommended under the worst of misery; indefatigable application and undaunted resolution under the greatest and most discouraging circumstances; I say, these are recommended, as the only way to work through those miseries, and their success appears sufficient to support the most dead-hearted creature in the world. (xii)

Defoe has come to believe, in Enlightenment fashion, that the moral or religious truths of the novel are separable from the surrounding fictions. Those truths must rest on abstract rationality or on some empirically verifiable, historical fact:

> [A]ll those parts of the story are real facts in my history, whatever borrowed lights they may be represented by. Thus the fright and fancies which succeeded the story of the print of a man's foot, and surprise of the old goat, and the thing rolling on my bed . . . the description of starving, the story of my man Friday, and many more most material passages observed here, *and on which any religious reflections are made, are all historical and true in fact.* (*Serious Reflections* x–xi; emphasis added)

Defoe's inability to appreciate his own realistic novel comes from another source, in addition to the new Enlightenment approach to knowledge. It also looks back to the Puritan unease with imaginative literature. This had been a problem for English readers and writers since the sixteenth century, when Sir Philip Sidney wrote his *Defence of Poesie* (published in 1595) in response to Puritan Stephen Gosson's *The Schoole of Abuse* (1579).[11] But more importantly, Defoe's assumption that true religious meaning *depends on* historical verification looks forward to the era of modern biblical criticism. It looks forward to the assumed conflict between the origins or reliability of a text and its value. The question it brings to the text is an Enlightenment one: what is the literal truth of a narrative if its historical veracity cannot be proven by empirical investigation undertaken by a detached, rational observer? Defoe comes to fear that if *Robinson Crusoe* is known to be fictional, it will be considered meaningless. When *Robinson Crusoe* was first published, however, those fears lay in the future. Crusoe makes his first appearance in the literary world reflecting an earlier understanding of the relation among stories, knowledge, and truth.

Biblical Narrative and Character

Rebellion and Conversion, Trust and Identity in Robinson Crusoe

Some of the most influential scholarship on *Robinson Crusoe* identifies Crusoe's major challenges as overcoming the environment and subjugating the persons with whom he comes in contact, such as his servant, Friday.[12] But Crusoe masters his environment fairly early in the novel, before his character has undergone any significant change. And although Friday serves Crusoe, he proves to be a spiritual leader as well, and he introduces Robinson to a much deeper spirituality. The spiritual challenges are actually more profound than the physical ones for Crusoe, as he tells the tale. His greatest obstacles are to acknowledge his anxiety about death, and later, to develop a capacity for society. He succeeds in both by recognizing the presence of God in his life and by undertaking new pursuits in light of a mature trust in Providence. In fact, the book is not structured around subjugation, but around Crusoe's growing trust in God. Defoe typically brings Crusoe to a point of spiritual crisis, followed by a new incident in the plot that reminds him of a biblical plot or image. When he recognizes and accepts the collision between the biblical story and his own, the crisis pushes him to a greater level of trust in God.

In the early episodes just after the shipwreck, Crusoe neglects his many opportunities to learn from experience. He is beset by fear—the response considered by Defoe's contemporary Dissenters as the direct opposite of trusting in Providence. Crusoe learns little of spiritual value in this part of the book. In the eight months after the shipwreck, he overcomes the basic survival challenges he faces. But achieving a state of relative prosperity by mastering his environment is not the climax of this part of the narrative, despite what Marxist or materialist critics assert. The first climax of the novel does not come until the ninth month, when Crusoe falls deathly ill of a fever and dreams of an angel holding a spear: "Seeing all these things have not brought thee to Repentance, now thou shalt die," says the angel (87). At this point Crusoe's conscience begins to awaken. As a first step, he is led to acknowledge God's existence and providential control over nature. He acknowledges his own misspent life.

This incident provides the first example of the structure of character development in *Robinson Crusoe*. It is immediately followed by a second example. The recognitions prompted by the first incident are the products of Crusoe's "natural" theology. They are the spiritual insights he achieves on the basis of his own conscience. A saving knowledge of God will come later, and it must come from the divine revelation of Scripture.

As Crusoe begins to recover he finds a Bible. In between doses of his medicine, Crusoe "opened the Book casually," reading the first words he finds: "Call on me in the Day of Trouble, and I will deliver, and thou shalt glorify me" (94; Ps 50:15). Crusoe now begins to consider the possibility that his identity is explained within the narratives of Scripture:

> The Words were very apt to my Case, and made some Impression upon my Thoughts at the Time of reading them, tho' not so much as they did afterwards; for as for being deliver'd the Word had no Sound, *as I may say*, to me; the Thing was so remote, so impossible in my Apprehension of Things, that I began to say as the Children of Israel did, when they were promis'd Flesh to eat, *Can God spread a Table in the Wilderness?* (94; Ps 78:19)

At this point we can start to see how Defoe's precritical reading of Scripture works. Bible reading in the Puritan tradition assumes the reader can find a unity of his or her own life with the biblical story and its meanings. The "story" of Psalm 50:15 has three parts: calling on God, being delivered, and glorifying God. The wilderness setting, which Crusoe finds in his reading from Psalm 78, was one of the most popular Puritan images for spiritual uncertainty, opposition, or drought.[13] As he returns to health Crusoe begins to see how God has continually delivered him from his "wilderness." "[B]ut I had not glorify'd him," he realizes (96). During his next Bible reading, Crusoe places himself among the audience that listens to the testimony of Peter and the apostles: "[Christ] is exalted a Prince and a Saviour, to give Repentance, and to give Remission" (96; Acts 5:31). This verse calls forth Crusoe's own prayer for repentance and enables him to understand the "deliverance" of Psalm 50 "in a different Sense from what I had ever done before" (96). That is, he seeks (and finds) deliverance from the guilt of his past life, compared to which physical deliverance from the island would be a figure or analogy. The various passages in Psalms and Acts are quite brief, but their brevity does not diminish the effectiveness of the narrative sequence for someone in the Puritan tradition of Defoe. The continued popularity of *Robinson Crusoe*, especially among Protestant readers from the eighteenth century on, rests on moments like these, where the realism of the spiritual narrative is fused with the realism of the island adventure. These readers saw a biblical Everyman in Crusoe, who recapitulated in his unique island existence, the typical Protestant drama of recognizing the plots of Scripture in one's own life story.[14]

In *Robinson Crusoe*, Crusoe's life frequently collides with biblical types or narratives. These collisions produce striking illuminations of his sinfulness, help him understand his setbacks on the road to conversion, and later, confirm his spiritual maturity. In this novel and in contemporary spiritual autobiographies, the reader of Defoe's day could ultimately come to see that even the disasters of the believer's life had a role in some providential story.

Beginning with his climactic conversion, Crusoe begins to find his world in the stories of Scripture. During the next decade he recognizes that his life is indeed described by Psalm 78:19 and other passages from Scripture. He sees God's table spread before him in the wilderness as he learns to make clothes and pottery, and becomes a baker and goatherd (130). He will also be reminded of God's promised deliverance in Psalm 50:15 during the next crisis point of his life, the discovery of a human footprint on the island.

Equally important, Crusoe begins to reinterpret his life before conversion in terms of biblical narrative. As in Puritan autobiographies, conversion is the most significant plot element of Defoe's story. The other trials of life begin to make sense when viewed from the perspective of conversion. As his identity is re-formed by Christian narrative, Crusoe is able to look back at his youthful opposition to his father as his "original sin" (194). It is important to note that this mode of self-understanding provides Crusoe with a hermeneutic for his life: now that his past and present life make sense in the terms of biblical narratives, he can fully recognize the truth of a fictional story like the parable of the Prodigal Son. In other words, Defoe's narrative does not make the Enlightenment distinction between empirically verifiable/true *versus* fictional/false. Instead, once his character grants the claims of the "history-like" stories of Scripture, his imagination is free to redescribe his own life in terms of biblical narrative. The question of whether a historical prodigal son ever existed is irrelevant.

Biblical narrative provides a structure for *Robinson Crusoe*, but this structure is unobtrusive enough that influential recent scholars have missed or underestimated its importance. They often treat theology merely as way for Crusoe to internalize his own desires or to rationalize his underlying capitalist manner of life.[15] Yet even in passages in which Crusoe's economic concern is prominent, his growing understanding of Providence is usually more fundamental. During his third year on the island, for instance, Crusoe's barley and rice crops are increasing so fast that "I really wanted to build my Barns bigger," he says (123). This would enable him to plant only once a year rather than twice. This plan—which he does not carry out—is almost certainly an allusion to the foolish man who longs for greater barns (Luke 12:18-21). The man in the parable—who never carries out his plan either—is not "rich toward God," which a reader in Defoe's tradition would likely remember and would apply to Crusoe as well. Immediately thereafter, another plan begins to obsess Crusoe: to build an immense canoe and leave the island. The project costs him six months of fruitless labor because in the end he finds it impossible to move the huge craft from the construction site to the water (127). In reflecting on this, he alludes to Luke 14:28, remarking "the Folly of beginning a Work before we count the Cost" (128). Through these allusions, we can see that biblical narratives assume an ever larger, more conscious role in Crusoe's self-understanding as his develops.

By the fourth year of his island existence, Crusoe is taking significant steps in his spiritual pilgrimage. Although his steps are often backward as well as forward, he knows which direction is the correct one. His life frequently answers to Psalm 78, which prompts him to "admir[e] the Hand of God's providence, which had thus spread my Table in the Wilderness" (130). Crusoe is learning to recognize his successes and follies as his own, personal variation on the providential patterns of the psalmists and gospel writers.

The significance of Crusoe's life cannot be reduced to the abstract values that Defoe's later prefaces identify (prudence, temperance, etc.) or to the political and economic ideologies that recent scholars see. Rather, prudence, temperance, and the other qualities Crusoe needs for a good life on the island are developed, over time, within the intersection of his life and the narratives of Scripture.

Crusoe's greatest challenge is to understand the narrative of his life in terms of the stories of the Bible. He treats the Bible as true in the sense that he gradually comes to recognize the authority of its stories for the purpose of reinterpreting his past life and shaping his future life. *Robinson Crusoe*, in contrast with its sequels, gives us a picture of how a fiction becomes history-like when it appropriates the narratives of Scripture to establish the identity of its protagonist.

Fears, Friendship with Friday, and Deliverance

By his fifteenth year on the island, Crusoe appears to be leading a balanced Christian life. At this point, the narrative structure repeats in a new form. Defoe interrupts Crusoe's calm in a way that will force him back to Scripture so he can attain a higher level of trust in God.

> It happen'd one Day about Noon going towards my Boat, I was exceedingly surpriz'd with the Print of a Man's naked Foot on the Shore, . . .: I stood like one Thunderstruck, or as if I had seen an Apparition. (153)

Crusoe is immediately overwhelmed with a fear of cannibals. This "Fear banish'd all my religious Hope; all that former Confidence in God which was founded upon such wonderful Experience as I had had of his Goodness, now vanished" (156).

As in his conversion, Crusoe remembers Psalm 50:15. But Crusoe finds himself unable to call on God or to trust in his deliverance as the Psalm commands. Instead, he thinks of releasing his goats, plowing under his grain, and killing as many cannibals as he can. He begins to look on his dwelling as a "castle," which he fortifies and conceals, as he had done in the fearful days before his conversion. In short, finding the footprint subjects him to "the constant Snare of *the Fear of Man*" (163) and prevents him from "resting upon [God's] Providence" (159). After several wasted years, Crusoe begins to wonder whether he should consider himself the executioner of the cannibals. "How do I know what God himself judges in this particular Case?" he asks (171). He concludes that since God alone is the "Governour of Nations," he will avoid intervening altogether "unless I had a more clear Call from Heaven to do it, in Defence of my own Life" (173).

At this point, Crusoe makes no further advances in his outward manner of life (176). He has ignored the significance of Psalm 50:15 since the discovery of the footprint. His inner life is also at a standstill. Although Crusoe achieves some peace of mind by deciding against attacking the cannibals, his loneliness increases to near insanity over the course of the next nine years. As Crusoe's happiness needed interrupting after his first fifteen years, so his despair in the twenty-fifth year needs interrupting. He goes so far as to consider breaking up a cannibal feast to get one or more slaves. At the cannibals' next visit, one of their victims escapes, running directly toward Crusoe as two of the cannibals pursue him. Crusoe kills one and the fugitive kills the other, leaving the fugitive free. Thus commences the relationship between Crusoe and his "man Friday," which continues until they leave the island three years later. This is the first of several incidents in which Crusoe is able to understand himself as an agent of Providence. Later, he saves the lives of Friday's father and several others, one of whom is the captain of the ship that will restore Crusoe to Europe.

How does Crusoe's relationship with Friday fit into the overall structure of the book? Some modern readers have suggested that Crusoe treats Friday as little more than a slave. Defoe makes it clear, however, that Friday's "conversation"—a term that refers to their relationship, rather than the services he provides—makes their years "perfectly and compleatly happy" (220). Crusoe's first fifteen years on the island had charted his growing ability to see how God had "spread a table for him in the wilderness." The next nine had forced him to come to terms with his fear of cannibals.

The final three years show Crusoe capable of bringing the blessings of Providence to others, especially in the physical and later the spiritual salvation of Friday.

Defoe does not explore Friday's conversion in any detail. Its narrative purpose is to lead Crusoe to deeper growth. In this episode, Crusoe's knowledge of Scripture is broad enough to convey to Friday "the same plain Instruction" that had earlier taught Crusoe "the great Work of sincere Repentance for my Sins, and . . . Obedience to all God's Commands . . ." (221). However, he ultimately comes to admire Friday as a "much better [Christian] than I" (220). For instance, Friday speaks of returning to his own land (along with Crusoe) to teach his people to "know God, pray God, and live new Life" (226). This relationship, like the previous climactic incidents in the book—Crusoe's shipwreck, illness, and discovery of the footprint—has the possibility of pushing Crusoe to a new spiritual level. In each instance Crusoe has to make an individual, imaginative decision to undertake new roles for himself. In his evolving relationship with Friday, he moves beyond the focus on his own life into a spiritual concern for others.

The End of Crusoe's Growth

After Friday's arrival and conversion, Crusoe experiences few inner conflicts. There are no more incidents that cause significant growth in his life. The narratives of Scripture diminish in importance. The end of the novel, like its first sequel, *The Farther Adventures*, reads more like an adventure tale with a Christian character than the tale of a man whose character is being fashioned in mysterious harmony with biblical narratives. The quality of the writing diminishes accordingly. Who can recall with pleasure, for instance, Crusoe's lengthy battle with wolves at the end of the book?

Defoe puts quite as much "religious" matter in volume two, *The Farther Adventures of Robinson Crusoe*, as in the first volume, but now Crusoe has nothing to learn. This is not to say the religious material is uninteresting: Crusoe has significant ecumenical discussions with a Catholic priest who wishes to perform marriages for the men and women who live together on Crusoe's old island; the crew on Crusoe's vessel massacre a village in Madagascar; and Crusoe's constant preaching on the subject leads to his being thrown off the ship at Bengal, where his adventures continue.

The most significant treatment of religion in *Farther Adventures* is the lengthy, disjointed conversion of Will Atkins and his wife, Mary, a native woman. This series of scenes begins with the Catholic priest's insistence that William and Mary profess Christian faith before their marriage. Defoe then turns to the oddity of a Catholic priest participating in a Protestant conversion. Will Atkins' relationship with his father, a reprise of Crusoe's own, comes next. Finally, Defoe concludes with a catechetical dialogue between William and Mary, similar to the conversations in Defoe's earlier work, "The Family Instructor" (1715). Significant religious issues arise in these scenes, but they arise as arguments laid over the top of the narrative. They lack an intrinsic connection to narrative, which *Robinson Crusoe* so amply provides. They sound more like an eighteenth-century salon discussion of religion, rather than a well-crafted collision between scriptural narrative and literary character.

By the third volume, Defoe seems to have forgotten the narrative use of Scripture altogether. The *Serious Reflections* is, in fact, a series of essays (on solitude, honesty, Providence, etc.) and not a tale at all. Scripture has become merely a set of doctrines or illustrative examples. The doctrines, however edifying or meaningful, make few demands on Crusoe. Their edifying material is divorced from the history-like character of the biblical narratives, and the narrator of the later volumes no longer attempts to discover truth through fictional material. There is no fruitful clash between Crusoe's story and the scriptural narratives—the basis for his initial character development.

When Crusoe refers to Scripture at all in the *Serious Reflections* it is merely to confirm what he already knows. Crusoe refers to the Israelites' conquest of Canaan, for instance, to justify military operations against contemporary pagans (*Serious Reflections*, 224). But in *Robinson Crusoe*, Robinson did not use Scripture to justify himself. Instead, the Bible showed him his shortcomings and pointed the need for transformation. Scripture is discussed and applied to life in the final volume, but it is not the primary means for interpreting life. Scripture no longer defines the real world. By the time of the *Serious Reflections*, Defoe has abstracted the fictional narrative of the book from its "meaning." The book's structure—true, nonfiction essays as opposed to false, fictional, imaginative narrative—illustrates the hermeneutical shift that was taking place in the early Enlightenment.

I think the audience for *Robinson Crusoe* has remained large, whereas that of the *Farther Adventures* and *Serious Reflections* is virtually nonexistent, precisely because the history-like conflicts in Crusoe's life are literally inseparable from the first book's moral and religious meaning. Of the three books, *Robinson Crusoe* alone rises to a history-like narrative quality, by which I mean that its representation of reality (moral, spiritual, psychological, economic, etc.) cannot be separated from the novel's particular narrative. An early, influential biography of Defoe by Walter Wilson (1830) shares this view of his achievement. A religious dissenter in the tradition of Defoe, Wilson locates the appeal of the novel in the unity of its realism and religious significance. Defoe's religious lessons are always appropriate, Wilson writes:

> [T]hey are closely interwoven with the story, and are so just and pertinent in themselves, that they cannot be passed over, but the attention is irresistibly riveted to them as an essential part of the narrative.[16]

Wilson's emphasis, one should note, is on the *reader* of the novel. The *reader's* attention is "riveted," he writes: "The reader of *Crusoe* is taught to be a religious, whilst he is an animal being."[17] The reader, in other words, reenacts Robinson's own use of Scripture, which provides an understanding of Crusoe's own identity as he listens attentively to the novel's plots and images.

It is significant that a century after Defoe's novel appeared, a critic locates Defoe's appeal in an earlier way of reading, long out of literary fashion. It is significant that Wilson looks back to a pre-Enlightenment unity between story and knowledge. Despite his common Puritan heritage with Defoe, however, Wilson exhibits no Puritan unease with fiction. He seems to have ignored Defoe's own insistence on the historical nature of Robinson's life. Either Wilson is a bad critic, or (as I think) he understands something deep about the way fiction becomes part of our knowledge—well after the triumph of the Enlightenment.

In the sequels to *Robinson Crusoe*, Defoe begins to hesitate over the validity of Crusoe's fictional narrative, mirroring a larger epistemological change. In the emerging hermeneutics of the

Enlightenment, a historically unverifiable narrative like Crusoe's has a problematic relationship to knowledge. Although the subjective meaning that one detaches from that narrative may have personal validity, it cannot rise to the level of empirical or rational knowledge. Unlike Wilson and many of his readers, Defoe's sequels give in to a separation between the metanarrative truth of the story and the story itself. It is as this point that postmodernism and narrative theology become especially valuable to a reading of this novel. They can give new insight into both Defoe's achievement in *Robinson Crusoe* and his unsuccessful attempts to explain his meaning in the book's sequels.

Postmodernism and Narrative

One of the richest veins of postmodern thought is its critique of the Enlightenment assumption that the truth behind a story—its metanarrative—may be separated from the story itself. I have shown that Crusoe comes to know himself and develop his character through his relation to the stories and images of Scripture. Comparing his own life to the narratives of Scripture changes his beliefs about reality and his personal life. In his life on the island, Crusoe acknowledges no separation between the story and its metanarrative.

On the other hand, postmodern thinkers are also highly critical of "grand narratives," which attempt to embrace all meaningful events under their purview, such as the Bible itself represents in *Robinson Crusoe*.[18] Grand narratives attempt to provide an underlying order to events by universalizing particular plots and characters. In addition to the Christian story of redemption, Jean-François Lyotard instances the grand narratives of the Enlightenment's account of human emancipation through science and the Marxist narrative of overcoming alienation through the proletarian revolution.[19]

"The grand narrative has lost its credibility," writes Lyotard (37). [20] Although he endorses the ability of particular narratives to provide their own "criteria of competence," he is suspicious of grand narratives, for they attempt to provide legitimacy for all smaller narratives (xxiii–xxiv). Unlike a "little narrative," which aspires to a merely pragmatic truth within its own story, a grand narrative aspires to a truth—Lyotard calls it a "metadiscourse"—

that exists outside the story. But in the postmodern age, Lyotard explains, narrative is losing its "great hero, its great dangers, its great voyages, its great goal" (xxiv). The kind of narrative endorsed by Lyotard aspires to no great unifying authority. It is smaller, more popular, and typically at odds with what is considered culturally legitimate: narratives, he writes, "are legitimated by the simple fact that they do what they do" (23).

Lyotard thinks that the primary purpose of grand narratives is to grant legitimacy to the knowledge we claim. These narratives exert control, even totalitarian control, he believes, over all other actors, listeners, and storytellers.[21] Grand narratives are seen as the enemy to freedom. Richard Rorty goes even further in claiming that we can gain freedom only by discarding the stories of others (along with grand narratives) and creating our own story. Rorty's thought sharpens the challenge for using Defoe in the postmodern era: how can we view Crusoe as an authentic, individual character if he finds himself in the grand narrative of Scripture? How can Crusoe be anything more than a placeholder in a story whose beginning and end are already known and whose middle is a series of meaningless episodes to get him from one place to the other?

Rorty identifies "private perfection" with "a self-created, autonomous, human life."[22] Self-created humans are "strong makers" or "strong poets," who are "capable of telling the story of *their own production* in words never used before."[23] Defoe might thus be considered a "strong poet" because, in writing the first novel, he tells a story "in words never used before." But Defoe's novel would be considered a failure by Rorty's second (italicized) criterion: the attempt of Robinson Crusoe to seek his "own production" in the first part of the novel is the story of failure. If Defoe shared Rorty's belief, he would have portrayed Crusoe's character favorably at the outset of the novel, set in Brazil, where Crusoe is most committed to creating an autonomous self. In Brazil, Crusoe makes himself a successful plantation owner in a spasm of self-creation that would make a Horatio Alger character look like a loafer. But Defoe does not present Crusoe as a success. In fact, Crusoe is so driven by greed at this point that he becomes involved in the slave trade, undertakes the journey that results in his shipwreck, and consequently endures an island existence of more than twenty-seven years. Identity does not arise from self-creation in the first English novel.

Fatal inconsistencies arise within postmodern critique of grand narratives when we look at the social role Rorty gives to literature in *Contingency, Irony, and Solidarity*. He celebrates novels and films because they have become "the principal vehicles of moral change and progress" (xvi). He welcomes a literature and literary criticism that will provide new vocabularies, new descriptions, and new contexts for life. These will be valuable, he writes, if they "can tell a story of progress" toward the "good things that have recently happened" (55). Critics must connect us with the "poets" who are the founders of our society, he continues, to help us envision new possibilities for self-creation. The emphasis on change, new life, progress, and self-creation introduces a significantly utopian element in Rorty's thought, as he himself acknowledges: literature will help us to "see strange people as fellow sufferers" and open up "an endless, proliferating realization of Freedom" (xvi). Fiction, he adds, plays a large role in reaching this goal of freedom, for "[i]t is to be achieved not by inquiry but by . . . imaginative ability"— not by theory but by the novel and other narrative media (xvi). Rorty wants literary critics as his moral advisors because "[t]hey have read more books and are thus in a better position not to get trapped in the vocabulary of any single book" (80–81). He realizes that these books recommend antithetical values, but hopes that critics will "perform some sort of synthesis" that can hold them all together in a larger, richer canon (81).

Clearly Rorty does believe in a grand narrative: the journey toward the endless realization of freedom. And yet he has said that he has discarded grand narratives in favor of self-created, original stories. Rorty just as clearly believes in various kinds of "metadiscourse," or foundational truths—in the autonomous, self-creating individual, for instance, quite apart from its presence in any given narrative. Rorty further believes that an imaginative synthesis can hold together books with wildly different values. Although Rorty speaks often of "contingency" and "irony," there is nothing contingent or ironic about his acceptance of these metanarratives. Finally, Rorty holds to a foundational belief, for which he gives no evidence, that the self-created, autonomous individual will wish to create freedom for others rather than, say, a mild despotism or outright tyranny. But why does he believe these things?[24] Or to return to Lyotard's language, how can the postmodern thinker know that his favored "little narratives," of social and political resistance, will produce liberation rather than oppression?[25] Postmodern theory has helped us see the crucial ways in which knowledge is embedded in narrative. But one often gets the feeling that the theorists are trying to have it both ways: they assert foundational truths while dismissing foundationalism; they seek grand results from narrative while dismissing grand narratives.

Crusoe found his identity by listening to the narratives of Scripture. Redeveloping a true art of listening is perhaps the major contribution that Defoe and narrative theologians can supply to the postmodern conversation. Rorty talks about the ability of the strong storyteller to produce his or her identity, but what would be wrong with a "strong listener" who uses his or her imagination to discover himself or herself—with individual differences, to be sure—in the stories of the past? Rorty's strong storyteller is radically individualistic. We read about the past, he says, to secure "tools to use in tinkering with ourselves."[26] Rorty's "self" is kept busy by asserting its autonomy, guarding against the authority of another's description, and dreaming up "new contexts" for itself.[27] But when does this reader pause to listen? When does he or she stop to consider the possibilities, truly outside himself or herself, that will enrich him or her? When does this "self" truly read?

For Lyotard, by contrast, knowledge in the postmodern age does include knowing how to listen.[28] Yet this version of listening turns out to be a kind of utilitarian knowledge. Its ultimate social outcome never goes beyond the pragmatic task of transmitting the rules that establish a social bond. The good listener gains authority only to assume, in turn, the position of narrator. But when does the listener pause to question himself or herself? Is there ever a clash between the stories he or she hears and his or her own self-concept? When does he or she see the need for inner change? When does the listener truly listen?

To go beyond the postmodern understanding of narrative, we must turn to a second critique of Enlightenment epistemology, from narrative theology. This source has the potential to restore the practices of reading and listening in which story and true knowledge are linked.

Learning to Read, Learning to Listen: *Robinson Crusoe* and Narrative Theology

When Defoe's novel appeared, most ordinary people were still reading the Bible in a precritical way.[29] The world described by the narratives of the Bible was considered to be the "primary world," from which everything else derived its significance. Narrative theologians sometimes look back to Erich Auerbach's well-known contrast between the effect of Homeric fiction and that of biblical literature for a statement of this mode of reading.

> The Bible's claim to truth is not only far more urgent than Homer's, it is tyrannical—it excludes all other claims. The world of the Scripture stories is not satisfied with claiming to be a historically true reality—it insists that it is the only real world, is destined for autocracy. All other scenes, issues, and ordinances have no right to appear independently of it, and it is promised that all of them, the history of all mankind, will be given their due place within its frame, will be subordinated to it.[30]

Before the rise of the historical-critical method, there was ultimately only the one, single world of the biblical story, and it was the reader's duty to find his or her personal story in it.[31] Sacred stories are more than classic works of literature, as Auerbach's passage on Homer indicates. Yet they are not merely legitimating authorities that confer authority on the reader, as Lyotard's account would imply. They are more like "dwelling places."[32] They are patterns, in relation to which the mundane stories of one's ordinary life begin to make sense.

This way of reading was taken for granted in the precritical, pre-Enlightenment era. There was a "first naiveté" about the reading of Defoe's day that is reflected in *Robinson Crusoe*.[33] Like other naïve readers, Defoe seems to have assumed that the meaning of a true work should be identical to its historical veracity. When the novel appeared, this naiveté was in the process of being questioned, with profound implications for both fiction and scriptural interpretation. Defoe's naïve assumptions about of the "literal meaning" of Crusoe's experience were questioned on the first appearance of the novel in 1719 because readers doubted its historical veracity. Once its historicity became untenable, he decided the fictional narrative of his story was somehow detachable from its spiritual meaning— its metanarrative. In other words, he passed from the precritical to the critical stage of reading. His anxieties and uncertainties over the truth of his fiction, enacted in the prefaces to volumes two and three of *Robinson Crusoe*, reflect the arrival of the critical era of Enlightenment criticism, as it was practiced on classical and biblical texts.

In the Enlightenment, the empirical, rational inquiries of the historical scholar came to be viewed as the authoritative means of arriving at the literal meaning (or "literal sense") of the biblical text.[34] It almost goes without saying that the authority of this inquiry was quite separate from the traditional interpretations of the church and its supposed authority. To be sure, doctrinal statements about the Trinity or creation could still be made. Personal significance could still be derived from Scripture. But both doctrine and personal significance were, in principle, divorced from historical inquiry by Enlightenment scholars. Many of those scholars often believed in Christian doctrine and took its personal significance quite seriously. Still, they made the true meaning of the Bible entirely dependent on their inquiries into historical factuality of the scriptural narratives. The fragmentation of the biblical text followed naturally. When the meaning of a text came to be dependent on its historical veracity, the modern theologian had no choice but to split the narrative into fragments: the grammatical meaning; the historically verifiable meaning; the personal meaning; and so on.

Hans Frei illustrates this trend with several examples, including one from the deist Anthony Collins just a few years after the publication of *Robinson Crusoe*. In his writings of 1724 and 1727, Collins maintained that because the *literal* sense of Isaiah 7:14 ("Behold a virgin shall conceive") refers to a young woman in the days of King Ahaz, Matthew's claim to find the verse fulfilled in Christ's birth (Matt 1:22-23) was meaningless.[35] No "knowledge" could be arise from its supposed connection to Isaiah.

As the Enlightenment progressed, there was no longer "one story" in the Bible. There was no longer a single narrative structure in which one was challenged to find one's own story. Rather, there were numerous fragments, some of which were probably historically accurate, and others not. Liberal scholars searched for a religious experience that was somehow behind the text.[36] Conservative scholars responded by defending the historical nature of as much of the text as possible, while searching for propositional truths that could be objectively based on verifiable texts. But because both groups identified the historical references of Scripture with their literal meanings, these scholars set aside the narrative meaning of Scripture and sought to base religious knowledge on something else—experience or propositional truths.

In more recent years, narrative theologians have sought to bring together both historical-critical and precritical ways of reading Scripture. They are attempting to create a postcritical, "second naiveté" in the reading of Scripture. Without ignoring the genuine advances of the Enlightenment, they affirm explicitly what Defoe's audience just assumed: that the meaning of a text is not detachable from the stories it tells. "Quite simply, the meaning of the [biblical] texts is the story they tell—'fictive' elements and all!"[37] The "plain" or "literal" sense of Scripture is not to be found in its verifiable historical references, but in its full narrative significance as a whole, read in light of communal and individual life.[38]

For narrative theology, identity emerges in much the same way as it does for Crusoe: through the collisions between experience and the narratives of the Bible.[39] The term *collision* emphasizes the "disorientation and reinterpretation" that spiritual transformation causes. This, of course, is exactly what happens to Crusoe.

As the fourth anniversary of his shipwreck approaches, Crusoe says that his "constant Study, and serious Application of the Word of God" had produced

> different Notions of Things. I look'd upon the World as a Thing remote, which I had nothing to do with . . . and well might I say, as Father *Abraham* to *Dives, Between me and thee is a great Gulph fix'd.* (128; cf. Luke 16:19-31)

The two uses of the word *as* are significant. They imply the possibility of a plurality of perspectives on just what the real world is. This plurality of perspectives links Defoe's non-Enlightenment sensibility with our postmodern times. Crusoe does not identify the literal meaning of his experience with its historical veracity, as a strictly scientific, enlightened thinker would. The world is by no means literally remote from Crusoe, who has spent four years in unceasing, worldly activity. He is saying that the true, literal meaning of his world becomes clear through a reference to a biblical narrative, the fictional story of Abraham and Dives.

The narrative theologian Garrett Green describes the significance of the unassuming word *as* in these terms:

> Kant called "is" the copula of judgment; we can call "as" the copula of imagination. In this quite technical sense, imagination is common to the natural scientist, the poet, and the religious believer . . . With the help of this concept of imagination as the "as" faculty, we can give conceptual precision to Paul Ricoeur's suggestive distinction between a "first" and a "second naiveté."[40]

Defoe may have been a naive reader of Scripture. But perhaps we can recover a "second naiveté" in our reading of Defoe by appreciating Crusoe's pre-shipwreck "world" as the tormenting fires, in which he suffers like the rich Dives in Christ's story. On the island, there is an immediate connection between Crusoe's plans—whether to build barns or canoes—and their true value in God's eyes. The connection is Crusoe's imaginative understanding of Providence. In his island setting, it is obviously foolish to covet more grain or wine or timber than he can use, as Crusoe comes to realize. We may accept or reject Crusoe's perspective, in part or in full. But we are not compromising our individuality by listening, deeply and attentively, to his narrative and taking it into account for our own lives.

Narrative theologians have understood the problem of the grand narrative in a different way from most postmoderns. Bible readers over many centuries and many lands form an ever-changing yet identifiable community. We must locate Crusoe's own reading of the Bible in that communal, mostly Puritan tradition. Crusoe does not discover a new paradigm of reading, as Richard Rorty would like his heroes to do. He does not appropriate stories so that he can assume the position of narrator, as in Lyotard's description. His reading of Scripture is typical of other Puritan readers. This tradition valued every Christian's life as both typical and unique. Every individual's life answered, in a unique way, to the typical plots, images, and characters provided by biblical narratives. What other reader of Psalm 78, for instance, could find in it a way to redescribe a castaway's life on a desert isle?

In each of the crisis points of his life, Crusoe has to make an individual, imaginative decision to undertake new roles for himself. He does not simply "recontextualize [his life] for the hell of it," as Rorty recommends that we do, in a revealing phrase.[41]

Rather, his individual decisions are comprehensible in terms of both his island existence and the Puritan community that formed Defoe's encounter with God.

Listening to biblical narratives is a way of retrieving the past for the sake of both the community and one's individual life.[42] The community offers a particular vocabulary to its members, arising from its history and traditions. Far from beginning as a "blank slate," as some Enlightenment figures taught, the individual therefore comes to his or her past with a host of symbols, plots, and characters. The individual lays hold of these insofar as they help him or her to interpret past events and find a meaningful role in the current life of the community.

Now the more accurate word for *the community*, in this case of the readers of Scripture, is *the church*, and biblical narratives, of course, are found in the canon of Scripture. There are parallels between the Bible and secular fiction, as Rorty describes it, and he has faith when Bible readers are often skeptical and vice versa. Rorty will not trust the "grand narrative" of Scripture, for instance, but has faith in the "canon of literature." Why? He will not acknowledge authority in the traditions of the church, but he accepts literary critics as moral advisors. Why? He would reject the eschatological kingdom of God, but he yearns for a liberal polity. Why? Some postmodern readers make these choices on the basis of purely idiosyncratic choice, others from ideological preference or rhetorical power. But it seems to me that they have simply pushed these issues further down the road. They need to be faced.

For Crusoe, as for current narrative theologians, the authority of biblical narratives is not commanded by a church power. Instead this authority is *recognized*. The difficult journey toward this recognition is revealed through the use of the language of faith by fictional characters or autobiographical subjects. These figures "move toward" faith, or they "move away" from it as the story unfolds. Their movement toward wholeness is halting and fragmented. Sometimes it doubles back on itself.

This movement toward or away from faith is found in the language of Augustine, Dante, and T. S. Eliot, and in autobiography and in fictions like *Robinson Crusoe*. The words of Psalm 50, for instance had initially "made some Impression on my Thoughts," Crusoe said, "tho' not so much as they did afterwards" (94).

Recognizing the authority or even the value of the biblical narrative in one's own life is not like recognizing a military authority or deciding that a logical proposition is true. Those recognitions are immediate; Crusoe's recognition is partial. It clarifies gradually, but often becomes fuzzy again. Readers who are unable or unwilling to enter Defoe's sensibility may see such moments as evidence of Crusoe's hypocrisy or as an indication of his ultimate selfishness. But few recognitions, in fiction or life, are as blinding as those of Oedipus or Archimedes or St. Paul. Most of them involve partial insights, like Crusoe's. Their validity rests on a number of factors: the will of the perceiver and his intellect and memory; an underlying narrative that is rich enough to provide insight into its inevitable collision with individual experience; and a community whose shared ways of reading appeal broadly to many individuals, while remaining recognizable and distinctive to its members. These ways of reading seemed to provide a natural way of gaining knowledge to Defoe when he first wrote *Robinson Crusoe*. We may not call them "natural" in our ironic era, but their validity has a renewed claim as we recognize broader approaches to knowledge in a post-Enlightenment age.

2

THE HYMNS OF ISAAC WATTS
AND POSTMODERN WORSHIP

Like the writers who developed narrative theology in response to the perceived shortcomings of Enlightenment approaches to Scripture, advocates of emerging forms of Christian worship are often critical of how our approach to knowledge has narrowed since the eighteenth century. For instance, they value the experience of religious art and music at least as highly as a well-formed doctrinal proposition.[1] Although their attitude toward established denominations is usually negative, they often look to some form of "community" to validate their experience.[2] Although most of the leaders in this movement are Protestants, they have a decided preference for an "eclectic" approach to theology rather than systematic precision, drawing on sources from the Catholic and Orthodox traditions, as well as Protestantism.

In these criticisms and responses, their approach to the theology and worship of the church is anticipated in the work of the hymn writer Isaac Watts (1674–1748), a younger contemporary of Daniel Defoe. Like Defoe, Watts was a Dissenter whose roots are found in the late Puritan tradition. But unlike Defoe, Watts was conscious of the philosophical changes in the air. He knew that the work of John Locke (1632–1704) in particular represented a significant narrowing of the scope of religious knowledge. Watts responded to the Enlightenment in a variety of ways, but most notably through his congregational hymns, many of which have been sung for nearly three centuries—"When I survey the wondrous cross," "Joy to the world," "O God, our help in ages past," and many others.[3] In Watts' hymns, one sees a thoughtful emphasis on the experience of art—literary art, in this case—and the mysteries it enables one to experience. Watts had eclectic tastes, incorporating the sensibility of the Catholic baroque poet Matthew Casimire Sarbiewski with that of the Puritan heirs of Oliver Cromwell.[4] Like his twenty-first-century descendants in the emergent church, his very choice of genre, the *congregational* hymn, requires the authority of a particular community for its validation.[5]

Watts is perhaps the most influential hymn writer in the English language.[6] Like Defoe, Watts had to work against late Puritan prejudices against his chosen genre. Metrical translations of the Psalms were common and were accepted in Dissenting churches. Yet most English Dissenters, reflecting their Calvinist heritage, discouraged the composition of original texts—hymns—for church use. Some leading Dissenters, such as Richard Baxter (1615–1691), spoke up for hymns, as did a few voices in the established Church of England. Nevertheless, opposition to using original human compositions in worship (as opposed to literal translations of the Psalms) remained strong throughout the seventeenth century.[7] The publication of Watts' *Hymns and Spiritual Songs* (1707), therefore, proposed a major change in the worship practices of his community. When he followed with an *imitation* of the Psalms rather than a literal translation in 1719, the change was even more obvious.[8] Watts' two major contributions to hymnody blurred the contemporary distinction between hymns and psalms. His stated intention in the 1719 *Psalms* was to "accommodate the book of Psalms to [C]hristian worship" (*Works*, 4:118). This meant leading "the psalmist of Israel into the church of Christ" by applying the joys of David, Deborah, and Asaph to "our persons, churches, or nation" (*Works*, 4:123, 116). Just to give one example, what ordinary singer of "Joy to the World" can recognize it as an imitation of Psalm 98? In this hymn—really an imitated psalm— Watts completely transforms a Hebrew poem for Christian worship.[9] Watts' influence spread through Baptist, Methodist, Presbyterian, and Congregationalist communities, including those in America and in Scotland.[10] For nearly fifty years after his death,

Watts remained the leading example and standard for hymnody. Watts also wrote many essays, sermons, and philosophical works. He promoted the revivals of the 1730s by helping to reprint Jonathan Edwards' *Faithful Narrative of the Surprising Work of God* (1737), a popular account of the First Great Awakening in America. But it is Watts' *Hymns* and *Psalms* that have gained him lasting fame. On his two works of hymnody, both published by 1719, his legacy rests.

Watts lived during a time of great revival and great controversy among the Dissenters. In 1719, the Dissenting pastors of London were called on to advise the Presbyterians of Exeter on whether to ordain two candidates who had questioned basic Christian doctrine.[11] When the pastors met at Salter's Hall, a Dissenting meeting-house in London, however, the issue was reframed by the non-Trinitarians. They succeeded in recasting the vote as a question over whether a pastor could be bound by any beliefs (such as the Trinity) that were not specifically stated in the Bible. This version of the question drew off some adherents of Trinitarianism, and the non-Trinitarians prevailed 57 to 53. Watts did not take an active role in that particular debate.[12] Toward the end of his life, however, decades after the publication of his hymns, Watts' prayers indicate his doubts regarding the orthodox view of the Trinity.[13]

The Certainty of Propositional Truth: The Religious Consequences of Locke's Foundation for Knowledge

At the close of the seventeenth century, Locke offered an influential definition of reason that distinguished it from faith and narrowed the modern search for religious truth. Reason is

> the discovery of the Certainty or Probability of such Propositions or Truths, which the Mind arrives at by Deductions made from such *Ideas*, which it has got by the use of its natural Faculties, *viz.* by Sensation or Reflection. Faith, on the other side, is the Assent to any Proposition, not thus made out by the Deductions of Reason; but upon the Credit of the Proposer, as coming from GOD, in some extraordinary way of Communication. This way of discovering Truths to Men we call *Revelation*. (*Essay Concerning Human Understanding*, 689, 4:18)

The philosophical influence of Locke's *Essay* (1689) on the Enlightenment is comparable to the scientific influence of Sir Isaac Newton's discoveries.[14] Locke's definition of reason is at the heart of his philosophical project, and its significance for religion was far reaching. Locke limited reason to the deductive or inductive discovery of "propositions or truths" and insisted on "strict Boundaries between Faith and Reason."[15] Locke continued to write frequently on religion until his death in 1704. At the end of his life, Locke was working on paraphrases of the letters of Paul, to which Isaac Watts responded directly. In *The Reasonableness of Christianity* (1695), Locke stated that Christianity consisted in living "a good life" and accepting the single proposition that "Jesus is the Messiah," which (he believed) all reasonable readers of Scripture could affirm.[16] In all of these works Locke was seeking a tolerant form of Christianity that could be affirmed by all enlightened followers of the faith. He wished to include under the Christian umbrella those who (like himself) had recently moved to the Socinian belief that one could accept Christ as Messiah although rejecting his deity, his death as the satisfaction for sin, and the Trinity.[17]

Locke's approach to knowledge is strongly "evidentialist" and "foundationalist." Knowledge of God, like all other knowledge, must be based on satisfactory evidence. One cannot encounter God directly, in Locke's opinion, either in the sacraments or in other forms of personal, spiritual experience.[18] Locke believed one could gather evidence for Christian belief from three sources: Christ's miracles, the fulfillment of Old Testament prophecies, and the "plain and direct words" of the apostles.[19] Locke considered the biblical evidence for the miracles of Christ trustworthy. He found evidence for Christ's messiahship in the prophecies of Isaiah 9, Micah 5, and Daniel 7 and 9. He concluded that the apostles' direct words proclaiming Jesus as Messiah, together with Jesus' reluctance to make the same claim for himself, were evidence in favor of his messianic status. Locke believed that the basis for this religious knowledge therefore had the same rational foundation that he had given for knowledge in the *Essay:* "[T]he evidence that any Proposition is true (except such as are self-evident) [lies] only in the Proofs a Man has of it," he had written (697, 4:19). Taking his cue from the rapidly increasing authority of early modern science, Locke believed that a secure structure of knowledge could come only from propositions built on a secure foundation, which his definition of reason provided.[20]

Locke believed that one could accept certain Scriptures as true, provided that a rational review of the evidence first warranted their status as authentic revelation.[21] The ultimate arbiter of whether a proposition qualifies as "revelation," then, is reason as he had defined it previously in the *Essay*:

> There can be no evidence that any traditional Revelation is of divine Original, in the Words we receive it, and in the Sense we understand it, so clear, and so certain, as that of the Principles of Reason: And therefore, *Nothing that is contrary to, and inconsistent with the clear and self-evident Dictates of Reason, has a Right to be urged, or assented to, as a Matter of Faith, wherein Reason hath nothing to do.* (695–96, 4:18; emphasis in original)

Locke distinguishes religious ideas that are "according to reason" (such as the existence of God), from those that are "contrary to reason" or "above reason."[22] God's existence is a matter of knowledge, Locke writes, and faith is not required where knowledge is certain. Locke goes on to write that religious ideas that are "contrary to reason," such as a belief in the existence of more than one God, may be held in faith. But this kind of faith is rationally unjustifiable. Locke discounts such a believer as one "in love with his own fancies" rather than with truth, and he rejects any assertions of faith that conflict with reason.

According to Locke, one may have a justifiable faith in propositions that are "above" reason, such as the resurrection of the dead or the rebellion of the fallen angels.[23] These religious notions are "beyond the Discovery of our natural Faculties," he writes, and "we can have no Knowledge at all" of them. Nevertheless, if we determine, on the basis of reason, that such a proposition is a divine revelation, and if the proposition does not conflict with reason, then "it may be a Matter of Faith."

Some religious propositions are true because they are reasonable. Others are justifiable as matters of faith, based on revelation, even though they are not founded on knowledge. In the fourth edition of the *Essay* (1700), Locke added a chapter in which he criticizes religious "enthusiasm" as an unjustifiable "third Ground of Assent," in addition to faith and reason (698, 4:19). In his *Dictionary* (1755), Samuel Johnson would define enthusiasm as "a vain belief or private revelation; a vain confidence of divine favour or communication," which parallels Locke's influential description.[24] Locke views the enthusiast darkly, as someone who "loves not Truth for Truths sake, but for some other bye end" (*Essay*, 697). The enthusiast substitutes "the ungrounded Fancies of [his] own Brain, and assumes them for a Foundation both of Opinion and Conduct." Enthusiasts set up revelation without reason, Locke writes, and identify a proposition as "a Revelation because they firmly believe it, and they believe it, because it is a Revelation" (698, 702). Aided by Swift's satirical portrait in *Tale of a Tub* (1704), *enthusiast* became the term for describing an ignorant and dangerous fanatic, especially as seen by Anglican writers during the Enlightenment.[25]

It should be acknowledged, of course, that religious fanatics, before the seventeenth century and since, have done untold damage. Moreover, Locke gives prudent advice when he warns that personal religious experience should be tested by "Reason and the Scripture, [which are] unerring Rules to know whether it be from GOD or no" (705). It is impossible to read Locke's religious works without being impressed by his seriousness and sincerity. But a guiding assumption of Locke's critique of enthusiasm is that religious knowledge can be reduced to propositions. Even if a religious person succeeds in avoiding the excesses of fanaticism, therefore, Locke's assumption closes off personal religious experience as an avenue for attaining knowledge of God. After any personal experience, it must first submit to Locke's tests (reason and Scripture) and then redescribe the experience in propositional terms. For all practical purposes, the experience itself must be discarded as a merely accidental way of attaining knowledge.

Locke's extraordinary influence on the course of the Enlightenment was apparent from the beginning. Watts called him "the ingenious director of modern philosophy."[26] Beginning in 1689, Locke produced four letters on toleration, which contributed much to eliminate civil penalties for Dissenting religious practices in England and promote religious and political liberty.[27] He succeeded in making Christian belief acceptable to many philosophers by separating religious knowledge from religious faith. But this separation, together with reducing religion to a series of propositions and demeaning the significance of religious experience, produced a pale form of Christian practice, especially within the Church of England. For some, like the gentry of Jane Austen's novels at the end of the eighteenth century, Anglicanism became little more than an accoutrement of English ladies and gentlemen. For others, the effect of banning enthusiasm from Anglican worship was to put worshipers to sleep, as illustrated by the snoring figures in William Hogarth's engraving, "The Sleeping Congregation" (1736). It should not startle anyone that Anglican worship suffered far more from boredom than from enthusiastic zeal in the early eighteenth century. In the years when Hogarth's congregation was dozing, however, the Dissenting congregations in England and America were awakening to the music and preaching of revival.[28]

It is not really surprising that worship has provided wide latitude for exploring beyond the narrowly rational expressions of Christianity, whether in the eighteenth century or the twenty-first. Worship has always offered a natural connection between the intellect and the emotions, and the enthusiasm banned by the philosopher could be restored by the singer.[29] In place of the objective, impersonal authority of reason to validate belief, what happens in worship is validated within particular communities—congregations. Without necessarily descending to the merely private fancies of the enthusiast, then, worship encourages the expression of personal experience. In a healthy congregation, worship encourages the exploration of beautiful art, language, and music as a companion in the search for truth.

Watts and the Philosophy of Locke

Every thoughtful Englishman of the early eighteenth century had to confront Locke's philosophy, political theory, and religious writings. Open disagreement with Locke was difficult. Watts wrote about Locke often, and often he wrote with approval. Watts produced three poems on Locke, and his popular *Improvement of the Mind* (1741), singled out for praise by Samuel Johnson, was something of an evangelical revision of parts of Locke's philosophy.[30] Watts comments on Locke so frequently in his *Philosophical Essays* (1733) that the subtitle of that work ends with *Some Remarks on Mr. Locke's Essay on the Human Understanding*. There, Watts disagrees with Locke's views on identity, the material nature of the soul, and his notion that the mind begins as a blank slate.[31] Of Locke's *Letter on Toleration*, Watts writes approvingly that he was led "into a new region of thought, wherein I found myself surprised and charmed with truth. . . . These leaves triumphed over all the remnant of my prejudices on the side of bigotry, and taught me to allow all men the same freedom to choose their religion, as I claim to choose my own" (*Works*, 5:500).

For Watts, toleration did not mean relativism in doctrinal matters. He is dubious of Locke's theological works, though his tone is charitable. "His writings relating to Christianity, have some excellent thoughts in them," says Watts, "though I fear he has sunk some of the divine themes and glories of that dispensation too much below their original design" (*Works*, 5:501). In a note to his poem "On Mr. Locke's Annotations," Watts sounds the same theme:

> Mr. Locke's annotations on Rom. iii.25 and the Paraphrase on Rom ix.5 [have] inclined some readers to doubt whether he believed the deity and satisfaction of Christ. . . . [H]is notes on 2 Cor v. ult. and some other places give me reason to believe he was no Socinian, though he has darkened the glory of the gospel and debased [C]hristianity, in the book which he calls the Reasonableness of it, and in some of his other works.[32]

Watts' note is really quite surprising. He almost overlooks Locke's possible heresies, such as the Socinian denial of Christ's atonement for sin. Instead, Watts charges that Locke has diminished the "glory" of Christianity. Rather than responding to contemporary arguments over theological propositions, Watts is concerned that Locke's philosophy has diminished the grandeur of the Christian faith. Watts' concerns have been validated by modern religious thought since the Enlightenment, which has tended to limit the acceptable avenues to knowledge of God. Religious thinkers in the traditions influenced by Locke sought for intellectual clarity, based on the same epistemological foundations as were thought to govern modern science.[33] They separated rational statements about theological truth from expressions of God's beauty. Consequently, much modern theology, based on the foundationalist epistemology of Locke and historical criticism, has discounted the significance of the sublimity of God's works, the majesty of his power, and the ineffable mystery of his relationship to mortals—all elements of God's glory.[34] These are irrelevant to the "reasonableness" of Christianity in Locke's epistemology. Not so for Watts.

Watts was concerned with both truth and beauty. He excelled in the medium of poetry, in which he could express God's glory more fully than any proposition or philosophical method could. But, as Johnson wrote in his biographical account of Watts, he did not avoid "combating Locke." Therefore, this chapter will briefly look at his direct responses to Locke's philosophy of knowledge before turning to his hymns.

In *The Improvement of the Mind*, Watts explicitly replies to Locke's narrow epistemological categories of sensation and reflection.[35] Watts combines these two Lockean modes of knowledge under the term *observation* (5:196). Observation, he says, is "the notice that we take of all occurrences in human life, whether they are sensible or intellectual, whether relating to persons or things, to ourselves or others" (5:196). Beyond observation, Watts lists four other "means or methods" to knowledge: "reading, instruction by lectures, conversation, and meditation." In the first three of these, Watts moves beyond the individualistic thrust of Locke's epistemology to include modes of knowledge that are social in nature, a theme that will resurface in his hymnody. Watts' fourth means of knowledge, meditation, highlights the value of personal memory, experience, and even uncertainty in the attainment of knowledge (5:197, 260).

The opening stanza of his poem on "Locke's Annotations" rehearses Locke's distinction between faith and reason. As Watts renders it, reason (as Locke defines it) only feebly confirms what faith directly perceives:

> Thus reason learns by slow degrees,
> What faith reveals; but still complains
> Of intellectual pains,
> And darkness from the too exuberant light.
> The blaze of those bright mysteries
> Pour'd all at once on nature's eyes
> Offend and cloud her feeble sight. (*Works*, 4:469)

The imagery of revelation's "blaze" is a cliché, but Watts' point is clear: reason as defined by Locke is too weak to perceive the mysteries of faith. It finds these mysteries offensive because they cannot be reduced to the propositions that make up knowledge as Locke understands it. In the next stanza, Watts continues to meditate on the central theological mysteries in the Christian faith: the Trinity, incarnation, and atonement:

Reason could scarce sustain to see
Th'Almighty One, th' eternal Three,
Or bear the infant deity;
Scarce could her pride descend to own
Her Maker stooping from his throne,
And drest in glories so unknown.
A ransom'd world, a bleeding God,
And heav'n appeas'd with flowing blood,
Were themes too painful to be understood.

In this stanza Watts begins by referring to the Trinity and incarnation, then moves to three alternative understandings of Christ's atonement: Christ as a *ransom*, a *penal substitution* ("bleeding God"), and a *satisfaction* ("heav'n appeas'd") for the penalty of sin. To understand these three different views of the atonement requires close study of the letters of Paul, which Locke had paraphrased.[36] But Locke was not really interested in pursuing this matter. Why? Because, he writes, Paul's epistles "were writ to those who were in the Faith, and true Christians *already*."[37] Material from Paul's letters therefore cannot be used to teach "the Fundamental Articles . . . necessary to Salvation," says Locke, even when they deal with the incarnation, atonement, or Trinity. Locke remains unwilling to add anything to the single proposition that Jesus is the Messiah. That statement contains "all the Faith required as necessary to Justification." By reducing the scope and method of religious knowledge, Locke simplified all of Christianity. His theological conclusions resolve on a note of bright clarity. Not so with Watts: his meditative poem ends by accepting the uncertainties surrounding the multiple ways of understanding the mystery of the atonement.

Watts' deepest engagement with the Enlightenment is in his hymnody, not in his philosophical works. Through his hymns, he responds in a different medium from philosophical discourse altogether. Perhaps he sensed that the most effective response to Locke demanded a different medium. In choosing to write hymns, however, Watts was not embracing irrationality or placing faith beyond reason. Rather, he was embracing social and aesthetic modes of attaining knowledge—modes rejected by Locke.

It is nearly impossible to overestimate the significance of Watts' hymnody for early evangelicalism through the early nineteenth century.[38] The revivals in the British Isles and America were decisively shaped by the singing of hymns, for which the work of Watts remained highly influential.[39] The aspect of his achievement that has received little attention, however, is the way his hymns broadened the avenues to knowledge.

Hymns and a Broader Approach to Knowledge

Watts' poem on "Locke's Annotations," which I have just discussed, refers to three different explanations of the atoning death of Christ. One will also find the governmental theory of the atonement in Watts, and in his most famous hymn, "When I Survey the Wondrous Cross," one finds yet a fifth, "subjective" view, in which the crucifixion is seen as a moral influence. Because each one may be stated in propositional form, an Enlightenment figure might want to know why Watts does not decide which is correct. Why does he not write his hymns to explain the correct version? Do these aesthetically pleasing works give us any knowledge that we could not gain from a clear, propositional statement of their content?

Watts finds epistemological significance in community, beauty, and eclecticism, all of which go beyond the limits that Locke sought to place on knowledge. The medium of the congregational hymn is a way of testing individual religious experience against the historic practices and experiences of a wider religious community. The aesthetic quality of Watts' verse can make one ask how beauty communicates religious knowledge. Finally, Watts' eclectic theological range can help one rethink the epistemological value of intellectual diversity in the search for knowledge.

"Joys That Cannot Be Express'd": Personal Experience and Community

Watts entered the Enlightenment debate over what counts as knowledge just one generation after Locke. In changing the medium from the treatise to the hymn and the venue from the individual's study to a particular congregation, he may have done little to lay the foundation for universal and timeless knowledge—the task Locke had taken on himself. Instead, the congregational hymn is an expression of individual experience in search of communal approval. This chapter argues that Watts' enduring hymns, sifted by the generations of congregations over many years, have a strong claim to the status of knowledge.

One of Watts' best known hymns, "Come Dearest Lord," provides insight into the role of the community in evaluating claims to religious knowledge:

> Come, dearest Lord, descend and dwell
> By faith and love in every breast;
> Then shall we know, and taste, and feel
> The joys that cannot be express'd.
>
> Come, fill our hearts with inward strength,
> Make our enlarged souls possess,
> And learn the height, and breadth, and length
> Of thine unmeasurable grace.
>
> Now to the God, whose power to do
> More than our thoughts or wishes know,
> Be everlasting honours done
> By all the church thro' Christ his Son.
>
> (*Hymns and Spiritual Songs*, 1:135, in *Works*, 4:289)

According to Watts' epigraph, he wrote this hymn with Ephesians 3:16ff in mind. Through the Holy Spirit, writes Paul, Christ can indwell the believer and make him understand the love "which passeth knowledge" (Eph 3:19). Locke's paraphrase and notes to this passage offer a remarkable comparison with Watts. In Locke's paraphrase, Paul prays for the Ephesians to "understand the exceeding love of God, in *bringing us to the knowledge* of Christ" (*Paraphrase*, 2:644; emphasis added). Locke's paraphrase, in keeping with his philosophy, eliminates any hint that a religious experience, including experiencing the love of Jesus Christ, could *surpass* knowledge.

Watts' hymn refuses to subordinate revelation to reason as Locke had done. It preserves and magnifies the sense of the King James translation: that the love of Christ surpasses what we can express in human language. Watts goes even further than Paul by suggesting alternative modes of apprehension. In the opening stanza, he claims that "tasting" and "feeling," along with knowing, are appropriate ways of apprehending God. What is more, he insists that there are certain "joys" that cannot be expressed—

presumably in rational, propositional language. Both claims challenge Locke's approach to knowledge. The next stanzas use the words *learn* and *know* in similar contexts. The singers ask for an experience of God's grace that transcends what is measurable (stanza two), and they declare to his power to do more than "thoughts" or "wishes" can know (stanza three).

Watts does not challenge the adequacy of the Enlightenment approach to knowledge only through subtle hints in his hymnody. He challenges it openly in his philosophical work, *Logic*:

> [T]here are several objects of which we have not a clear and distinct idea . . . and yet we cannot call the names of these things, words without ideas; such are *the infinity and eternity of God himself, the union of our own soul and body, the union of the divine and human natures in Jesus Christ, the operation of the Holy Spirit on the mind of man*, &c. These ought not to be called words without ideas, for there is sufficient evidence for the reality and certainty of the existence of their objects; though there is some confusion in our clearest conceptions of them; and our ideas of them, though imperfect, are yet sufficient to converse about them, so far as we have need, and to determine so much as is necessary for our own faith and practice.[40]

The italicized words go far beyond the single proposition that "Jesus is the Messiah"—the axiom to which Locke wished to reduce Christianity. Some of these phrases, such as the "operation of the Holy Spirit" are part of the vibrant Dissenting practice that was often dismissed as "enthusiasm." In his *Logic*, Watts gives rational explanations for these elements of Christian practice. In his hymns, he enables a congregation to express them more fully—or to reject his views by simply letting these hymns drop out of use.

In "Come Dearest Lord," the congregational role is not merely assumed. By using the plural pronoun (*our*) and by referring to "the church," Watts clearly has a Christian community in mind. At first, this community was his own, particular congregation. As his influence and popularity increased, it would be more accurate to identify his community with the broader Dissenting movement. Dissent had only recently emerged from persecution with the Toleration Act (1689). Even after that point, Defoe was sentenced to stand in the pillory for writing Dissenting literature, and mobs could be whipped up to burn Dissenting meeting houses.[41] The English Presbyterians, Baptists, Independents, and Congregationalists were bound together in ways that persisted into the eighteenth century: excluded from much of the English mainstream, they created their own educational institutions and engaged in trade rather pursuing careers in the church or the army. The closest thing they had to a "national myth" was the "rumbling, roaring balladry of heroes, prophet, battles, laments and victories" of the tribes of Israel, rather than the consecrated version of the Tudor royal history as found in Shakespeare.[42] When congregations sang Watts' lyrics of the "saints" and referred to the church as a "young Plantation," their language reflected the tribal rhetoric of seventeenth-century Puritanism.[43] Like the Puritans of the older Dissenting tradition, Watts was "conscious of the soul in pilgrimage on the way to Zion."[44] But although some in this tradition were carried away in individualistic enthusiasms, others (as we have seen in the previous chapter) tested their experience by the narratives of Scripture and sought validation in group settings in which hymns were sung and testimonies were given.[45]

The hymns of Watts emerged from the communities of Dissent and (later) more broadly from evangelicalism. Perhaps the fact that churches have continued to sing some of these hymns for three centuries, while rejecting others, could provide some kind of warrant for the validity of their content. As Johnson later wrote in his *Preface to Shakespeare* (1765) apropos of literary judgment, "What mankind have long possessed they have often examined and compared, and if they persist to value the possession, it is because frequent comparisons have confirmed opinion in its favor."[46] In terms of epistemology, the long-standing acceptance of a congregational hymn provides a social mode for reflecting on the "sensations" of individual religious experience. This approach to knowledge would not satisfy the criteria of Locke, but it would be more accurate to see it as a broadening of Locke's categories than a rejection of them. That is to say, it seems to broaden Locke's epistemological categories of sensation and reflection to include the community's validation. The knowledge it produces is neither certain nor absolute, but it does test the "sensations" of the hymn writer against those of a broader community, and it subjects his conclusions to the severe test of time.

Knowing the Shepherd in the Enlightenment: Beauty and Knowledge in Psalm 23

The word *beauty* does not appear in the index Locke made for his *Essay Concerning Human Understanding*, nor does his modern editor include it in the glossary to that work. If one were to read only Locke, one might conclude that beauty was irrelevant to Enlightenment thinking about knowledge. However, some of the first Enlightenment writing on aesthetics comes from the third earl of Shaftesbury, Anthony Ashley Cooper (1671–1713), whose education was supervised by Locke. Shaftesbury reacted against the rationalism of his age in his work titled *Characteristicks* (1711). Shaftesbury's main emphasis, however, like that of his follower Francis Hutcheson (1694–1725), was on ethics, not epistemology. Shaftesbury and Hutcheson sought to find a natural harmony (which they believed was ultimately benevolent) between the human attraction to beauty and ethical behavior. In his *Inquiry into . . . Our Ideas of Beauty and Virtue* (1725), published after Watts' hymns, Hutcheson discusses the aesthetic relationship between virtuous behavior and "the eternal fitness of things."[47] Hutcheson and Shaftesbury raised questions about beauty that Locke had ignored because their primary interest was ethical. By contrast, Watts' hymns probe the epistemological significance of beauty.

It may seem too obvious even to remark that a lasting poetic work must appeal to its readers or singers on an aesthetic level. For a hymn to give pleasure for three hundred years, it must have beauty of some sort. But although English writers since Sir Philip Sidney's *Defence of Poesie* (1595) had reinforced the classical balance between literary "instruction" and "delight," much of the Dissenting tradition (as we have seen in the case of Defoe) emphasized instruction to the exclusion of nearly everything else. The growing popularity of John Milton and John Bunyan in the late seventeenth century, however, gave many Dissenters the experience of undeniable literary beauty from within their tradition, even if they lacked a theory to explain it.

The story of Watts' own attraction to hymn writing seems to draw on the Dissenters' growing interest in aesthetic excellence. According to tradition, the young Watts expressed disapproval of the hymns sung at his family's Southampton chapel.[48] Of one

Puritan hymnodist, Watts' brother wrote, "Honest [William] Barton chimes us asleep." As the story goes, Watts' father then invited Isaac to improve on Barton, which he did by producing first one then many other hymns that the congregation began to use. By 1700 his brother wrote to beg Isaac to publish these hymns, which he did seven years later. As Johnson wrote, "He was one of the first authors that taught the Dissenters to court attention by the graces of language . . . He showed them that zeal and purity might be expressed and enforced by polished diction."[49] It is impossible to separate the literary beauty of Watts' hymns from the religious knowledge they attempt to convey. What I hope to show is that their beauty enables the singer to gain more religious knowledge than logical, rational propositions could attain.

Since the publication of the King James translation (1611), Psalm 23 has posed the greatest challenge for any English poet who would translate or imitate verse from the Bible. Though it was more popular in earlier eras than today, Watts' version of Psalm 23 is still found in many hymnals. It achieved wide usage in America through its wistful musical setting in *Southern Harmony* (1835), perhaps the most popular tunebook ever published.[50] Through its tender imagery, verbal harmonies, and simplicity of its language, Watts' version of Psalm 23 invites the singer to know God as a merciful guide to reassure, correct, accompany, and finally welcome the troubled human traveler.

The first five stanzas of Watts' hymn contain significant reminders of the King James translation, while providing a personal interpretation of Psalm 23. In the opening line, for instance, the verb *supply* spells out the relationship between the Lord-as-shepherd and the believer-as-sheep, which the biblical version omits in its laconic opening ("The Lord is my shepherd."):

> My shepherd will supply my need,
> Jehovah is his name;
> In pastures fresh he makes me feed,
> Beside the living stream.

This stanza silently teaches the singer that the English verb in the opening verse of Psalm 23—"I shall not *want*"—carries an older meaning. This phrase does not mean that one's *desires* will cease or that God will fulfill all of them. Its older meaning is that of *need*: the singer will *need* nothing. The stanza's reassuring words are paralleled by rich internally rhyming vowels: my/supply/beside, and need/he/me/feed/stream.

The third verse of Psalm 23 reads, "he restores my soul; He leads me in the paths of righteousness for His name's sake." In Watts' second stanza, it becomes:

He brings my wandering spirit back
When I forsake his ways;
And leads me, for his mercy's sake
In paths of truth and grace.

The reason why the soul must be restored, unexplained in the Psalm, is made explicit in Watts' hymn: the sheep regularly forsakes the ways of the Shepherd. Watts also directs us to identify mercy as the chief characteristic of this Shepherd, and he steers away from any hint of legalism by substituting *truth and grace* for *righteousness.*

In the third stanza, Watts sacrifices the vivid, biblical *rod and staff*, which comfort the Psalmist, and introduces the metaphor of breath, which is not found in Psalm 23:

When I walk through the shades of death,
Thy presence is my stay;
A word of thy supporting breath
Drives all my fears away.

Thy hand, in spite of all my foes,
Doth still my table spread;
My cup with blessings overflows,
Thine oil anoints my head.

Perhaps Watts felt that his eighteenth-century London congregation would be able to understand the metaphor of breath more easily than one from animal husbandry. It is possible as well that God's "supporting breath" would remind many of Bunyan's allegorical rendering of this verse in *Pilgrim's Progress* (1678), in which an encouraging voice enables Christian to overcome his fears of the ghostly fiends who inhabit the Valley of the Shadow of Death.

It is in the final stanzas, however, that Watts achieves the emotional depth that makes his version memorable. The Psalm concludes with a ringing affirmation: "Surely goodness and mercy shall follow me all the days of my life; and I will dwell in the house of the Lord forever." *Shall* (for second or third person) and *will* (for first person) are older ways of issuing imperatives, not ways of making predictions: thou *shalt* have no other Gods before me; I *will* faithfully execute the office of the President of the United States. The King James psalmist is emphatic and sure about his future. Watts' singer, by contrast, offers a prayer. It is a hopeful prayer, but a somewhat plaintive one nonetheless. It leaves the singer as a vulnerable, childlike traveler who is searching for his home:

> The sure provisions of my God
> Attend me all my days;
> O may thy house be mine abode,
> And all my works be praise!
>
> There would I find a settled rest,
> (While others go and come)
> No more a stranger or a guest,
> But like a child at home.

The unstated auxiliary for *attend* could be the imperative *shall*, as in the Psalm. The line could be affirming emphatically that God's provisions "shall attend me" throughout life. Because the next line is a prayer, however ("O may thy house . . ."), it is more likely that Watts is simply reporting God's continued bounty: the sure provisions of my God *will continue to* attend me all my days. Such ambivalence, between an emphatic affirmation and a mere report of one's experience, would be true to the understanding of many who can recite the Psalm in its King James Version. It is also true to Watts' tone throughout his version. In any case, ambivalence is surely present in Watts' final stanza. The speaker hopes to "find a settled rest" in God's house but remains uncertain of the final outcome. If Watts had been more confident, he would have opened the final stanza by writing something like, "There *will* I find a settled rest."

Watts' version introduces three characters in this short imitation, the stranger, the guest, and the child, none of whom is present in the Bible. To most Christian ears, the psalmist's vow to "dwell in the house of the Lord" conjures an odd image of someone living in a large, ornate temple. The imitation of Watts, by contrast, ends with one who is looking for "a settled rest." When his character has not been walking through the shades of death, he has found temporary shelter as a "stranger or a guest." Watts returns our focus to the character himself, who is "like a child." And his final dwelling recalls the memory of a childhood home, an image that will find an echo in the yearnings of nearly every individual who sings these lines.

In addition to the endorsement of communities of believers who have sung it for hundreds of years, this hymn seeks a sanction for the knowledge it tries to convey by its beauty. Its poetry seeks to persuade the singer by the harmonies of internal rhymes, by the simplicity of common language and common rhythms, and by images that both recall the familiarity of Scripture and create fresh new associations of their own. Its scope is far beyond the propositions that arise from sensation and reflection that can be submitted to empirical or rational proof. It claims even less certainty than the Psalm it imitates. But by aspiring to less certainty, it may create more long-term confidence in the individuals who have sung it. In times of doubt or anxiety, few will have turned to Locke's *Essay Concerning Human Understanding*. Many have recalled a hymn like this one from memory.

An Eclectic Approach to Knowledge: A Dissenter Teaches Sacramental Theology in "When I Survey the Wondrous Cross"

Watts gives voice to various views of the atonement in his hymns, as mentioned earlier. His most famous hymn, "When I survey the wondrous cross," views the crucifixion as a moral influence on the believer. His eclectic approach to theology represents another part of his effort to broaden the approach to religious knowledge. Watts' hymn begins thus:

When I survey the wondrous cross
On which the prince of glory dy'd,
My richest gain I count but loss,
And pour contempt on all my pride.

Watts placed this work in a section of his *Hymns* devoted to the Lord's Supper, a sacrament in many Protestant congregations and a memorial or ordinance in others. This is the ritual, above all, in which believers experience God's son most directly and most regularly. As they do, the epistemological differences between "knowledge," "experience," and "mystery" fall away. The focus of the hymn insistently returns to the human perceiver, for either one gives oneself to the experience or one does not. Although the evidence for Christ's love is by no means divorced from the historical fact of his death, as perhaps a Lockean analysis would note, the hymn's focus is on the present experience of Christ in the believer's life. It urges personal transformation as one is grasped by a true apprehension of the crucifixion. The knowledge that the hymn tries to convey is not that of a proposition or fact. It never seeks to escape from the realm of mystery, wherein the believer encounters the body of Christ, in the atonement and the sacrament.

When Paul instructs the Corinthian church on the Lord's Supper, he preserves the mystery of this encounter:

> But let a man examine himself, and so let him eat of that bread, and drink of that cup. For he that eateth and drinketh unworthily, eateth and drinketh damnation to himself, *not discerning the Lord's body.* (1 Cor 11:28-29 KJV)

The word for *discerning* the body (from διακρίνω) is translated as *recognizing* in another version, whereas a third uses *distinguishing*.[51] In all of these cases, an "unworthy" participant is one who fails to honor the proper relationship between an experience and its epistemological significance, however, mysterious that relationship remains.

By contrast, Locke's paraphrase of this passage diminishes the mystery of the encounter with Christ's bodily death—an encounter that all major English translations render as a mystery—and shifts the meaning away from the crucifixion:

> By this institution therefore of Christ let a man examin[e] him self and according to that let him eat of this bread and drink of this cup. For he who eats and drinks after an unworthy man[n]er without a due respect had to the Lords body *in a discriminat[ing] and purely sacramental use of the bread and wine that represent* it draws punishment on him self by [so] doeing.[52]

In Locke's paraphrase (and in his further explanatory notes), these verses mean that one must understand that the Lord's Supper is for sacramental rather than nutritional purposes. In typical fashion he diverts the reader's attention away from insights that could be derived from an experience toward purely rational ones.[53]

In "When I survey," Watts' language enables him to convey an experiential knowledge of the atonement. The hymn describes

Christ's death in terms of its influence on the person who contemplates it. Its epigraph is "Crucifixion to the world by the Cross of Christ, Gal. vi. 14."[54] The first stanza redirects the believer's "gain" and "pride" to the horizon of the cross. In the second stanza, Christ's sacrifice causes the believer, in turn, to "sacrifice" his or her own vanities:

Forbid it, Lord, that I should boast,
Save in the Death of Christ my God;
All the vain things that charm me most,
I sacrifice them to his blood.

The use of the first person, *I* or *my*, is only absent in the third stanza, and even there the first-person observer is directing another individual—or perhaps the entire congregation—to understand Christ's blood as "sorrow and love":

See from his head, his hands, his feet,
Sorrow and love flow mingled down;
Did e'er such *love and sorrow* meet?
Or thorns compose so rich a crown?

The stanza does not assert a proposition about the atonement. It simply leads the congregation to identify Christ's blood with sorrow and love through the delicate use of chiasmus, the crossing of a pair of words (emphasized above) As a Eucharistic hymn, this stanza prepares the believer to solidify that identification through the experience of the Lord's Supper.

By stanza four, regrettably omitted from most hymnals, the death of Christ is capable of calling forth a life-changing recognition from the believer. Vain and prideful in stanza one, the believer is now "dead" to the world's charms. Another chiasmus illustrates the match between the death of the savior and the metaphorical death of the believer to the allure of the world:

His dying crimson like a robe
Spreads o'er his body on the tree,
Then am I *dead* to *all the globe*,
And *all the globe* is *dead* to me.

By the final stanza, Christ's death has fully transformed the singer's being. Because of the rhetorical control of the preceding stanzas, the passionate outpouring of a believer's very soul to Christ is completely appropriate:

> Were the whole realm of nature mine
> That were a present far too small;
> Love so amazing, so divine
> Demands my soul, my life, my all.

The stanza nearly overflows with liquid consonants (*l, m, n*), which had been linguistic tools for love poetry in previous centuries. The speaker's loving response, rendered with beauty and concision, is a fitting conclusion for the knowledge that an experience of the crucifixion can provide.

As beautiful as this hymn is, however, its view of the crucifixion, taken by itself, is completely inadequate. Watts would have recognized that. It says nothing about Christ paying the penalty for sin, nothing about what Christ's suffering accomplished, and nothing about forgiveness. Watts wrote many more hymns about the crucifixion. Ultimately he addresses all of these issues. For instance, the "governmental" view of the atonement, which emphasizes that Christ was punished in the sinner's place, is found in the following hymn:

> For us his flesh with nails was torn,
> He bore the scourge, he felt the thorn;
> And justice pour'd upon his head
> Its heavy vengeance in our stead. (*Works*, 4:347)

The ransom theory, which stresses Christ's victory over evil, is present in Watts as well:

> Lo, by the sons of hell he dies;
> But, as he hung 'twixt earth and skies,
> He gave their prince a fatal blow,
> And triumph'd o'er the powers below. (*Works*, 4:283)

In other hymns Watts explores the penal substitution and satisfaction theories of the atonement as well (*Works*, 4:283, 299–300). By exploring all five of the major interpretations of the atonement, Watts shows the greatest conceivable intellectual curiosity about this central doctrine. Yet far from seeking a single, definitive explanation of the atonement, Watts gives voice to all of them. Instead of searching for one doctrine, to which all reasonable people should subscribe, Watts shows an extraordinary universality in his work. The result of his work as a whole is to produce for his congregation a full, complex view of the atonement. He neither forces the worshiper to choose a single view nor implies that their differences are inconsequential. His work is thus true to the range of responses that the atonement has inspired among Christians who, over time, have sought to experience its meaning and explain its doctrine.

Together with Watts' other hymns about the atonement, "When I survey" departs from the Enlightenment model of attempting to establish knowledge in propositional form alone. His theology is eclectic, while retaining its Scriptural basis; it is rationally sound, while retaining an openness to new experience. The eclecticism of his hymnody is also bounded by two other principles that he shares with the best postmodern churches: the judgment of the community to validate his experience and the role of beauty in communicating religious knowledge.

"Completing the Sentence" in the Enlightenment and Postmodern Church

Like Watts, most leaders in emerging churches seek an active engagement with their own, contemporary culture. "Culture is met, embraced, and transformed," in the self-definition of one emerging church.[55] Emerging churches have grown up in the postmodern milieu, but they recognize their tension with its culture: Although they shy away from objective certainty, for instance, they affirm the "grand narrative" of Scripture; although they are open to pluralistic expressions of religious faith, their goal is most often a particularly Christian holiness that has historic roots, rather than a vague spirituality.

The most effective response of Watts to the Enlightenment was to compose original hymns and psalms of high literary quality. For many postmodern Christians today, performing new music, or becoming involved in one of the other literary or fine arts, has grown into an essential element of spiritual formation. "[T]he influence of music and art on spirituality is becoming increasingly apparent," writes sociologist Robert Wuthnow:

> Increasingly, churches are advancing other forms of artistic expression as well [as musical ones]: performing skits and dramas, staging

liturgical dance in worship services, sponsoring concerts and poetry readings, hosting theater companies, and organizing book discussion groups.[56]

One emerging church identifies the use of "beauty, art, and creativity" as essential to its "dream" for itself.[57] Near many postmodern worship spaces one is likely to find galleries for painting, sculpture, or ceramics. Bulletin boards announce upcoming plays, concerts, and art shows in the community. In some churches compact discs produced by members of the congregation are for sale. One church I visited has regular meetings for a group of songwriters, and the reading set out for perusal included the bulletin of the local modern art museum.

Postmodern worship has found such a deep response from Protestant evangelicals in part because evangelical intellectual leadership, over the last century and more, stressed the rational power of words almost to the exclusion of every other form of communication.[58] This overemphasis on rational, verbal communication, beginning in the mid-1800s, came largely from the evangelical effort to replicate the Enlightenment project of finding a secure intellectual foundation for theological knowledge. In this case, the inerrant Bible became the source of propositional truths. The hope was that these truths could be set down in clear, rational words—in striking parallel to the rational, empirical project of Locke—and form a universal, timeless basis for theological knowledge.[59]

In contrast, the arts enable believers to express the mystery of spiritual experience and the glory of God beyond the power of words. Artistic expression requires a devotional effort from the participant and holds out the promise of a transcendent experience with the divine.[60] The emphasis is not on arriving at a definitive formulation of particular theological doctrines, but rather on spiritual formation—shaping the individual's relation with God and enabling him or her to express it. Postmodern churches emphasize that the arts open up ways to move beyond and around the Enlightenment categories for religious knowledge, whether those categories are employed by the theologically liberal descendants of Locke or their evangelical opponents.

It is not enough for these members of emerging churches to experience beauty as participants, however. They want to create it. Producing original works of art, or at least being involved in a church whose members are producing art, is part of sharing in the glory and mystery of God. Postmodern church leaders often speak of the significance of participating in the truth as opposed to merely hearing it, interacting with theology instead of merely absorbing it. For worship to be effective, postmoderns must be able to "complete the sentence for themselves."[61] Here, too, the parallel to Watts is strong. Instead of merely translating the Psalms anew, Watts took the nearly unprecedented step of accommodating their devotional sense for Christian worship in his own generation. Singing his hymns allowed the Dissenters of his era a way to pursue their own, original ways of knowing God, beyond those sanctioned by the established intellectual culture of the early Enlightenment. The result was widespread revival in America and Britain. Postmodern fellowships, similarly frustrated with their cultural inheritance, may produce equally unexpected revival, in part by opening up new avenues for knowing God through their art.

The literary art of Watts, however personal, was not primarily an exercise in self-expression. He did not consider his work a "private revelation," to return to the definition of "enthusiasm." Watts submitted his work to his church and the Dissenting community at large, which responded by accepting some hymns, rejecting others, and altering still more.[62] The emerging churches' emphasis on community may succeed in establishing a comparable epistemological function for its art.

Dissenting congregations functioned as the kind of test that Johnson would later consider crucial to good judgment in poetry. They were the "common readers" of Watts, to adapt a fine phrase from Johnson, and they applied intense scrutiny over many years to his work. Johnson's common readers go beyond "the refinements of subtlety and the dogmatism of learning," but not below it.[63] Their seasoned judgment is able to move beyond popular sentiment and intellectual fashion to a more reasoned assessment of quality.[64]

Nearly every recent commentator on the emerging church stresses the hunger for new forms of community.[65] Beyond the search for trust and stability in an age of hypermobility, divorce, and declining social capital, postmodern believers think that truth itself is likely to emerge from the exploration of a group. One emergent church goes so far as to call Christian community "the answer to questions of faith."[66] Believers such as these are unlikely to take up Immanuel Kant's bold Enlightenment challenge to the individual—"dare to know"—unless others are engaged with them in the process. These believers have accepted the postmodern insight that knowledge is conditioned by the interpretive lenses in which one views a situation, and one's particular community is a significant lens indeed. The testimony of one's group, therefore, has an epistemological, emotional, and social appeal. Secular postmodern thinkers often describe the social element of epistemology solely as a matter of power, skeptically asking: "Who decides what knowledge is?"[67] By contrast, believers in emergent churches often see the social element as a way of overcoming modern individualism. A young Christian commentator, for example, identifies his generation as *tribal*, a word that (as we have seen) has been used for the Dissenting congregations that first sang Watts' hymns.[68] Beyond the social intimacy that community gives, these congregations have a deep insight into social element of knowledge itself. The test of religious knowledge does not rest just with the individual alone, no matter how rigorous his or her philosophical method may be, but also with communities.

Congregations, whether in the early Enlightenment or in the postmodern era, have always had at least as much at stake in the expressions they accept into their community as philosophers have. Although their methodology is less easily described than Locke's, I see no reason to consider their assessments, over time, any less rigorous than that of the academy. The test of postmodern worship, like that of Watts' hymns, is ongoing. For Watts, it consisted in his ability to produce hymns that worshipers chose to sing or dropped from their repertoire: without intellectual assent and emotional participation, Watts' hymns would simply die—and most of them did. A similar laboratory has been created in today's emerging churches, in which new works of theologically informed art are being tested through the response of many communities over time.

If a community opens up the approaches to knowledge of God through expressions of beauty, it will almost certainly experience a great variety of theological opinion. What the emergent church celebrates as eclecticism, of course, skeptical outsiders may view as confusion—and no doubt some confusion exists. There is probably a measure of old-fashioned "enthusiasm," as well, which refuses to have its insights tested. But theological diversity in the day of Watts was a source of strength to early evangelicalism. It can be a strength of the emergent church as well.

Watts took the best from his Puritan tradition and the new intellectual inquiries of his day. His knowledge was both broad and formidable, stretching from ancient languages, theology, and philosophy, to history and the new natural sciences pioneered by Newton, Robert Boyle, and John Ray.[69] His breadth of interests is reflected in hymns that range from his joy in the created world to the fulfillment of Hebrew prophecy, from consolation in death to the pure contemplation of God's power.[70]

Because of his theological acumen and literary skill, Watts was able to produce hymns that bridged the denominational gaps that had split Protestantism. The history of the early Anglo Americans revivals, from the 1730s on, is one of remarkable interdenominational cooperation, which came in part from the eclecticism of Watts' hymns.[71] Watts said his *Psalms* were for "sincere christians, whose judgments may differ in the lesser matters of religion" (*Works*, 4:118). For the physicist Michael Faraday (1791–1867), Watts was a model for open-mindedness, tolerance, and receptivity to experience.[72]

The eclecticism of the emergent church is illustrated in the subtitle of an influential statement of an emergent church leader, Brian McLaren's *A Generous Orthodoxy: Why I Am a Missional, Evangelical, Post/Protestant, Liberal/Conservative, Mystical/Poetic, Biblical, Charismatic/Contemplative, Fundamentalist/Calvinist, Anabaptist/Anglican, Methodist, catholic, Green, Incarnational, Depressed-yet-Hopeful, Emergent, Unfinished CHRISTIAN*. The theological diversity represented by McLaren and other emergent leaders is most compelling on such issues as worship itself, spiritual formation, and their understanding of what a "church" is. In his sociological analysis of U.S. spirituality, Wuthnow argues that the high value on theological eclecticism derives from an increased emphasis on the arts, as opposed to doctrinal statements. Past eras put more emphasis on theological instruction from clergy:

> At present, however, serious pursuit of spiritual growth has come largely to mean engaging in devotional activities that encourage a reflective orientation to life, drawing on resources in one's religious upbringing that give a kind of ambiance to one's spiritual reflections, adhering to a religious tradition that is *held with a certain degree of*

openness toward other traditions, engaging in some deeds of kindness toward others, and especially cherishing experiences in which one feels close to God.[73]

The insistence of the emergent church on eclecticism comes from both its emphasis on community and from the array of experiences its members bring. Because they see the search for truth as a communal enterprise, emergent books and Web sites instinctively refer to sources in Catholicism and the desert fathers, in Orthodox traditions and Third World Christian practices. Their "community of Christians" extends back to the past and outward to the non-Western world. The diversity and interdenominational cooperation among emergent churches is therefore energized by a wide range of interests, parallel to that of Watts, and bounded by a recognition of their responsibility to the historic Christian movement.

The postmodern church is attracted to artistic beauty, a wider religious community, and eclecticism for many of the same reasons that attracted Watts. As the movement seeks to stay healthy, it could profit from much in the practice of Watts. His deep commitment to his craft of writing teaches some hard lessons about balancing artistic desires against the needs of one's community. For all his youthful criticism of his church, Watts' Dissenting society was a learned one, and through it, his earliest education prepared him for his life work.[74] When he began writing hymns in earnest, Watts had studied more than twenty Psalters. He had read deeply in church history and biblical commentary. He was concerned about "the dull indifference, the negligent and thoughtless air, that sits upon the faces of the whole assembly, while the psalm is on their lips."[75] His life work was a creative response to that problem. In his hymns, Watts disciplined his poetic abilities (which are on full display in his lyric poems, *Horae Lyricae*) to the needs of his congregation. He self-consciously trimmed his metaphors and sacrificed his most sonorous lines of verse.[76] Not every artistic expression in the emergent church will need to make sacrifices like these, but negotiating the tensions between the desires of the artist and the needs of the church will remain a delicate matter.

For all of his criticism of Enlightenment epistemology and his dissatisfaction with the older hymns of his tradition, Watts also has something to teach the emergent church about the love for the culture that gave one birth. Occasionally emergent churches use the terms *Western* and *evangelical* almost as terms of abuse. McLaren admits that his treatment of evangelicals does not "even pretend to be objective or fair" in *A Generous Orthodoxy*.[77] I have attended an emergent church that sang a hymn lamenting the entanglement of Christian practice with "Western culture." We read the words of the hymn with the help of leading digital technology, sitting in mostly individual seats, and worshiping in perfect religious liberty. In other words, we criticized the West as we took for granted Western advances in science, Western assumptions about individualism, and Western achievements in politics. By contrast, Watts' criticism of Locke is so mild that we find him making excuses for, Locke's Socinianism and overlaying his theological reservations with praise for Locke's political achievements.[78] His criticism of his Dissenting tradition is so muted that we know it only by hearsay. The Anglo American revivals influenced by Watts had untold sociopolitical implications, but he focused on doing his chosen work well, and he did it in a profoundly generous spirit.

By shunning the foundationalist approach that has held sway since the Enlightenment, the emergent churches will also have to develop new and effective approaches to the questions of theological orthodoxy that are bound to arise. After he had written his *Hymns* (1707) and *Psalms* (1719), Watts had to face the controversies over the Trinity that came to a head at Salter's Hall. The victors in that controversy scrupled to add any doctrinal requirements beyond "the Protestant principle that the Bible is the only and perfect rule of faith."[79] After the meeting, Dissenting pastors were free to form their own beliefs concerning the Trinity and other Christian doctrines apart from the historic creeds of the church. This was ultimately a victory for the Socinian and other non-Trinitarian movements. Many Baptist and Presbyterian churches drifted to Unitarianism, and in his later years Watts himself prayed that God would reveal "whether he be one pure and simple being or whether thou art a threefold deity."[80] On the other hand, many Congregational churches retained a vibrant, orthodox faith in part because they continued to sing the hymns of Watts.[81] Ironically, as the study became the site of theological doubt for Watts himself, the meeting house became a site of confidence for the congregations who sang his hymns. Emergent church leaders often express impatience with past theological controversies, but theological controversies will persist, and new ones will erupt.[82] Like Watts, they will have to think about what is truly central to the witness of the church.

The forms of Christianity that used Enlightenment means to search for permanent, rational foundations for faith, whether on Locke's rational basis or on the basis of an inerrant Bible, have less and less appeal in the postmodern world. No one can guarantee the flourishing of the emergent church in the postmodern world. But neither could anyone have predicted the success of the First Great Awakening in America or the corresponding revivals in Britain. Perhaps like Watts, the postmodern church will find in the arts a way of bridging theological divides without sacrificing intellectual integrity, and a way of embracing a pluralistic approach to theological truth without giving way to a formless spirituality. The postmodern church can learn from Watts how to exercise theological rigor without obscurity and how to apply artistic craft without self-absorption. Perhaps it can remain open to the broad traditions of faith, while remaining rooted in particular communities. Without any guarantee of permanent success, Watts' achievement may help a postmodern generation of believers to complete the sentence for itself.

3

JONATHAN SWIFT'S INFORMATION MACHINE AND THE CRITIQUE OF TECHNOLOGY

When the Internet first became popular, I started having a recurring nightmare that we would someday arrive at the point where all knowledge was instantly accessible, but no one would know what it meant. A few years into the Internet revolution, Google adopted the first part of this dream in its stated mission "to organize the world's information and make it universally accessible and useful."[1] The unstated promise of much information technology, epitomized in Google's mission, is that society will be better off when we can download all imaginable information from our individual computers. The assumption is that the knowledge of the world should be quite literally at our fingertips.

Not everyone is convinced of the social or personal desirability of this promise. Many prominent critics of technology today share some version of my nightmare. In one form or another, the more optimistic of these critics argue that knowledge only becomes wisdom when its users pursue some humane purpose for that knowledge. They insist that increased knowledge must increase its user's connection with the human or natural worlds. More pessimistic cybercritics doubt that any such connections can be reestablished at this late date.

Nearly three hundred years ago, Jonathan Swift (1667–1745) observed a similar explosion in knowledge and its accessibility

67

early in the Enlightenment. He urges his readers to question the promises of ever-increasing knowledge and ever-faster data retrieval. His satire on the technology of his own day, notably in *Gulliver's Travels* (1726), embraces both optimistic and pessimistic elements, similar to critiques of technology today. From Swift to our own day, these writers warn that treating knowledge as a commodity will result in dehumanization.

In this chapter, the connection between the eighteenth-century figure and more recent commentators is more complex than in the previous ones. Wendell Berry, whose critiques most resemble Swift's, is hardly a postmodern figure. The leading postmodern writers that I will treat, François Lyotard and Jacques Derrida, come at the challenges of technology in strikingly different ways. In addition, this chapter will depart from the rest of the book's typical organization by incorporating recent critiques throughout its treatment of the topic, rather than leaving them largely to the last section.

Enlightenment Technology, Enlightenment Optimism, and Jonathan Swift's Satirical Response

Spurred by the undeniable advances of science, large numbers of Enlightenment writers began to consider the consequences of rapidly expanding knowledge. For the most part, they foresaw only benefits—material, political, and even moral—from this increase. Knowledge, accumulated by methods that could be imitated by any properly trained mind, would be widely available and were imagined to be completely beneficial. The Marquis de Condorcet, a *lumière* of the late eighteenth century, can barely contain his optimism for the progress of learning:

> [A]s the number of known facts increases, the human mind learns how to classify them and to subsume them under more general facts, and at the same time, the instruments and methods employed in their observation and their exact measurement acquire a new precision. . . . [S]o truths that were discovered only by great effort, that could at first only be understood by men capable of profound thought, are soon developed and proved by methods that are not beyond the reach of common intelligence.[2]

Condorcet's optimism begins from "a hope that is almost a certainty . . . of the absolute perfection of the human race." This hope, coupled with his observation of the Enlightenment's intellectual and material progress, leads him to predict vastly more abundant food, cheaper manufactured goods, improved working conditions, the elimination of disease (and possibly death), the gradual disappearance of prejudice, and the perfection of laws and public institutions—all as the result of education. Many of Condorcet's material predictions have come true over the last two centuries. At the same time, however, the Enlightenment faith in human perfectibility, based on the expansion of knowledge, has been largely destroyed. Enlightened intellectuals have often been complicit in political tyranny, from the French Revolution through Marxist-Leninist movements, and modern science has produced weapons capable of the complete destruction of humanity.[3] Condorcet himself completed his work in hiding from the Reign of Terror. He escaped the guillotine only because he died in prison, possibly by suicide. Still, Condorcet maintained his faith that all enlightened men would come to share the principles of the French Revolution and that enlightened nations would agree on the principles of politics and morality, leading to the eradication of war.

Information technology raises different questions from those examined in the first two chapters. There epistemological questions were asked: how do we know? This chapter will ask social questions about how knowledge arises and what its purposes should be. Condorcet's language represents a shift typical of the Enlightenment: instead of assuming that knowledge arises from the learner's relationships to a teacher or the external world, Condorcet sees knowledge as the cumulative assembling of facts. Its results are inextricably tied to greater outputs and material well-being. By putting increasingly lifelike machines between the teacher and student in the search for knowledge, information technology makes this shift all the more palpable. In one of the seminal books of the postmodern era, Lyotard marked this change by explaining that knowledge is increasingly viewed as a product: "The old principle that the acquisition of knowledge is indissociable from the training (*Bildung*) of minds, or even of individuals is becoming obsolete and will become ever more so."[4] He predicted that knowledge would increasingly be viewed as a commodity that is produced to be sold.

The ideology of knowledge as a commodity, as something that can be measured like corn and sold by the bushel, was not first questioned by postmoderns or cybercritics. It was strongly satirized by Swift, who anticipated many of the contours of our present disagreements over technology.[5]

A good way to understand Swift's critique of the Enlightenment's bloated promise of unending human progress is to begin with his examination of language, particularly the mechanization of language. The goal of reducing language to a mechanical process, already current in Swift's time, has striking parallels to the treatment of language in today's information technology. Swift saw it as a crucial step on the road to treating knowledge, and ultimately human beings, as commodities.

The main character of *Gulliver's Travels* assumes that knowledge is a product that can be manufactured and distributed. Gulliver's view is ultimately a dehumanizing one, of course, and it leads to the dehumanization of others. As Swift's persona for a gullible believer in progress (among many other things), Gulliver never actually understands how this debasement happens. When he experiences it near the end of the book, however, it drives him mad. Gulliver's madness is the resounding conclusion to Swift's sharp satire on technology in *Gulliver's Travels* and his previous works. It results from the mechanization of language, the treatment of knowledge as a commodity, the dehumanization of others, and ultimately the dehumanization of the self.

In the course of the four voyages that make up *Gulliver's Travels*, Gulliver frequently mentions his obsession with knowledge. Despite the two terrifying voyages that begin the book, Gulliver undertakes a third. What does Gulliver hope to discover in the course of this journey, as he embarks on a ship named the "Hopewell"? His answer is straightforward: his "Thirst . . . of seeing the World."[6] Swift's eighteenth-century readers would have understood Gulliver's third voyage as part of a search for knowledge.

Gulliver's Travels draws from many literary genres, but probably the most obvious is travel literature. One of the most popular genres in the Enlightenment, travel literature is characterized by the large amount of new information it promises, as mediated through an observant authorial eye.[7] Travelers were in a particularly good position to accumulate "sensation or reflection," which John Locke identified as the two rational sources of truth. It is fair to ask, then, what kind of knowledge Gulliver accumulates and conveys in his travels. How does this knowledge change him morally, psychologically, and intellectually? These are basic questions about knowledge, of course, parallel to asking how knowledge changes any learner at any time. Likewise, in asking how Gulliver conveys this knowledge, we are raising the same question that may be addressed to any teacher, whether he or she is a conventional teacher, a Web master, or a technologist. In short, *Gulliver's Travels* asks how we learn and how we teach.

In his third voyage, Gulliver is set adrift by pirates and then rescued by the inhabitants of Laputa, an island that hovers above the country of Balnibarbi. The king and his court live aloft, on the island, where they have made a reputation for their expertise in mathematics and music. After a time Gulliver returns to earth, where he visits Lagado, the capital city of Balnibarbi, and has various other adventures before making his way back to England.

Swift's descriptions of the societies of Laputa and Lagado have strong parallels to the emerging scientific culture of the Enlightenment. The Laputians' abstract, fearful speculations parallel the predictions of some astronomers in Swift's day that the sun might swallow the earth or a comet might burn it up.[8] Some time before Gulliver's arrival, Balnibarbians had spent five months up in Laputa and then returned to establish an "Academy of Projectors" in Lagado, which aimed to put "all Arts, Sciences, Languages, and Mechanicks upon a new Foot" (176). The Grand Academy of Lagado is a satirical version of the Royal Society of London for the Improvement of Natural Knowledge, the English institution most conspicuously associated with the scientific Enlightenment.[9] As hard as it is to believe, many of the experiments of Swift's fictional Grand Academy are satirical exaggerations of actual reports in the Royal Society's *Transactions*. These experiments include mixing colors with the help of a talented blind man; curing colic by thrusting a bellows into the anus and pushing the bile toward the mouth; using spiders to spin silk; and conserving summer sunbeams by trapping them in cucumbers and releasing them during inclement weather.[10]

Gulliver finds some of the laboratories unpleasant, but he never questions the Academy's underlying attitude toward knowledge. He never probes its utopian goal of contriving new rules for building so that "a Palace may be built in a Week, of Materials so durable as to last for ever without repairing" (177). He never questions its new methods of agriculture, which promise that "All the Fruits of the Earth shall come to Maturity at whatever Season we think fit to chuse" (177). Gulliver seems to accept without question the reasons given by the scientists for their failure to deliver on their technological projects: lack of funds and the opposition of backward common people.

The issue that most strongly parallels current debates over information technology is the Laputians' treatment of knowledge as a commodity. The Laputians believe they have reduced language to a mechanical process, which in turn influences their attitude toward knowledge. By beginning with the mechanization of language, I hope to show how Swift anticipates some of the best current critiques of technology and warns against its dehumanizing aspects.

The Mechanization of Language in Gulliver's Travels and Today

In the division of "speculative learning" at the Grand Academy of Lagado, Gulliver is privileged to visit a professor who presides over the operation of an information machine. Swift directs his satire to Gulliver's unquestioning belief in technological progress. Gulliver looks in awe upon this "frame" (as he describes it) that promises to "improv[e] speculative Knowledge by practical and mechanical Operations" (182). With meticulous care Gulliver describes the work of the inventor and his forty assistants:

> [B]y his Contrivance the most ignorant Person at a reasonable Charge, and with a little bodily Labour, may write Books in Philosophy, Poetry, Politicks, Law, Mathematicks and Theology without the least Assistance from Genius or Study. He then led me to the Frame, about the Sides whereof all his pupils stood in Ranks. It was Twenty Foot square, placed in the middle of the Room. The Superficies was composed of several Bits of Wood, about the Bigness of a Dye, but some larger than others. They were all linked together by slender Wires. These Bits of Wood were covered on every Square with Paper pasted on them; and on these Papers were written all the Words of their Language. . . . The Professor then desired me to observe, for he was going to set his Engine at work. The Pupils at his Command took each of them hold of an Iron Handle, whereof there were Forty fixed round the edges of the Frame; and giving them a sudden Turn, the whole disposition of the words was entirely

changed. He then commanded Six and Thirty of the Lads to read the several Lines softly as they appeared upon the Frame; and where they found three or four Words together that might make Part of a Sentence, they dictated to the four remaining boys who were Scribes. (182–84)

The machine, identified as "a primitive computer" by the editors of the popular *Norton Anthology of English Literature*, breaks the elements of language into its component bits.[11] Its inventor assumes that reassembling these elements in arbitrary ways will produce new knowledge. The words—now regarded merely as bits of information—are randomly combined, then selected by the professor and the "Six and Thirty" lads who search for meaningful fragments. The professor in charge of the project promises that his machine will "give the World a compleat Body of all Arts and Sciences." All he needs to accomplish this goal is for the "Publick [to] raise a Fund for making and employing five Hundred such Frames in Lagado, and oblige the Managers to contribute in common their several Collections." In other words, the professor needs a grant backed by political authority to carry out his scheme. Gulliver is so taken with this knowledge machine that he sketches it for his *Travels*. He promises that its illustrious inventor will have sole credit for it in England and will reap all of the material advantages that belong to him as its "right Owner." He never asks, however, whether this machine provides a suitable model for true human learning.

Gulliver then enters the "School of Languages," run by three professors of the Grand Academy. This part of the satire takes the reader beyond the mechanization of language. In this episode, Swift satirizes the Enlightenment dream of producing a language of utter rationality, in which the relation between words and their referents is no longer contaminated by human error. To accomplish this goal, the three professors propose to abolish all words.[12] "Since Words are only Names for Things," Gulliver reports, the sages have decided to carry on their backs everything they need to communicate about:

I have often beheld two of those Sages almost sinking under the Weight of their Packs, like Pedlars among us; who when they met in the Streets, would lay down their Loads, open their Sacks, and hold Conversation for an Hour together.

The three projectors urge the abandonment of words and speech for the sake of brevity, physical health, and universal communication. By eliminating speech, they believe they will diminish the corrosion of their lungs, resulting in longer life. By using things rather than language, ambassadors and foreign princes can anticipate eliminating linguistic confusion and restore a "universal language." Like all historical attempts to give language the universality and precision of mathematics, however, the Laputian plan has failed. It has been defeated by the "Women, in conjunction with the Vulgar and Illiterate," who threatened a rebellion unless they were "allowed the Liberty to speak with their Tongues, after the manner of their Forefathers." Gulliver is disappointed and angry, denouncing the protesters as "irreconcileable Enemies to Science."

Although Swift subjects this project (and Gulliver himself) to withering satire, a universal, clear language has appealed to the imagination since at least the story of the Tower of Babel (Gen 11:1-9). In that story, like the episode in *Gulliver's Travels*, universal communication teams up with improved technology (brick-making, in that case) to promise a civilization without limits.[13] In the Enlightenment, when technical advances in print culture led to an explosion of books, the goal of finding a universal language was promoted in different ways by Gottfried Leibniz, Condorcet, and other figures.[14] The Enlightenment saw several efforts to develop a universal language, a single tongue in which words corresponded directly to things. In the late seventeenth century, Leibniz proposed combining a universal writing system that would be guided by a rational set of rules, so that controversies could be settled through calculation.[15] A century later, Condorcet expressed the hope that a universal language would make knowledge of the truth easy and error almost impossible. It would give every science the certainty of geometry.[16] Likewise, a figure actually known to Swift, John Wilkins (1614–1672), proposed a universal language in 1668.[17]

Wilkins, a founder of the Royal Society and later bishop of Chester, promised that his language would promote commerce, improve natural knowledge, spread religion, and clear away religious differences.[18] He invents an entirely new "character"—that is, a system of alphabetic signs and symbols—which distinguishes his efforts from previous attempts to find a universal language. These earlier attempts merely adopted the alphabets of "some particular Language," he charges, "without reference to the nature of things."[19] By contrast, Wilkins proposes to overcome the arbitrary or conventional relationship between word and concept in actual languages. He assumes that before thoughts are formulated into words, "men do generally agree in . . . the same internal Notion or Apprehension of things."[20] By developing a "universal character" that can refer directly to images and natural things, he believes he has made contact with an immediate, prelinguistic form of communication. His rewriting of the first words of the "Lord's Prayer," however, illustrates the overwhelming difficulties of such a language. Wilkins substitutes *Our Parent* for *Our Father*, because *father* signifies *male parent*, which is not "the strictest sense" of Christ's meaning. He even rejects his own, written symbol for metaphor, which would signify that God is a metaphorical parent: "[S]uch a Metaphor [for God as parent] is generally received in other Languages, therefore there will be no necessity of using this mark." In the first phrase of his universal language, then, Wilkins relies on large cultural assumptions about conventional usage in the actual languages of the world. His substitution of *parent* for *father*, moreover, enforces a particular interpretation of the Lord's Prayer. In short, Wilkins speaks with his own, individual voice—like every other human being who has ever used spoken language—despite his effort to find a universal voice. Consequently, his effort to find a universal, direct relation between the printed or spoken word and its conceptual meaning was doomed from the start.

Linguists today would understand why. They recognize that language is a system of conventionally recognized differences among written or spoken words.[21] For instance, the differences between walking, trotting, jogging, streaking, racing, sprinting, and so on are based on human conventions, peculiar to particular English-speaking cultures, not on universal reality. Real human languages cannot aspire to a direct, universal relationship between printed or spoken words ("signifiers") and their meaning. The goal of Wilkins, like that of Swift's Lagadians and some modern cyberneticists, is to make language into a mere tool, where the relationship between word and thing is utterly transparent, with no need of a mediating human intelligence to interpret—and possibly misinterpret—meaning. Because transparency would eliminate the need for human interpreters, it would often seem to eliminate the need for humans as well. If language is merely a tool, a machine can handle it. Or to put it another way, human beings may be viewed as language machines. Man inputs information and outputs decisions—often inaccurately and inefficiently, as Wilkins and his descendants lament. Still, some Enlightenment figures continued to wish to diminish or eliminate the human role in language. A few years after *Gulliver's Travels* the French author Julien Offray de la Mettrie published *Man a Machine* (1748), which takes great pains to equate human language with that of animals: "A geometrician has learned to perform the most difficult demonstrations and calculations, as a monkey has learned to take his little hat off and on, and to mount his tame dog. All has been accomplished through signs. . . ."[22] Like the modern cyberneticist Norbert Wiener, who rejects unscientific words like *life*, *purpose*, and *soul*, de la Mettrie considers *soul* an "empty word, . . . which an enlightened man should use only to signify that part in us that thinks."[23] The human body is a large watch, concludes de la Mettrie, and the soul is an enlightened machine.[24]

The ugliness of the language of technical proficiency—*input*, *output*, *user-friendly*—is not accidental. Its users see language purely as a matter of functionality, and they consequently ignore beauty. Beauty is irrelevant in Lagado. It would be unrecognized if it appeared. Even physical attraction is ignored by the intellectuals of Laputa. Swift satirizes this consequence of the linguistic failures of the Laputians as well. The women of Laputa take lovers who will actually pay them some attention, even brutal or lower-class lovers, and they are eager to leave the floating island altogether (165–66).

The physical ugliness of the professors at Lagado and the disgusting qualities of their experiments result naturally from their intellectual projects. The man Gulliver meets in the first laboratory "was of a meager aspect." On meeting the second, Gulliver is "almost overcome with a horrible stink" from his project of reconstituting food from human excrement. In this experiment, political projectors detect traitors by examining what they eat, what hand they use to wipe their posterior, and the color, odor, taste, and consistency of their excrement.

Swift, of course, expects us to laugh at all of this. He expects that his readers will instantly understand that the Laputians' trust in technology springs in part from their mechanistic view of language, and that it results in a contempt for human relationships. Swift counts on readers who have a different view of language— who can use their ordinary intelligence and ordinary humanity to evaluate, judge, and interact with his language.

Computer languages and recent machine translation technology, whether actual or speculative, often attempt to eliminate the need for human intelligence and to replace the "natural languages" actually used by humans with a machine substitute.[25] In a proposed system of "post-symbolic communication," for instance, the "malleable, synthetic sensorium of Virtual Reality" promises to make language obsolete.[26] Postsymbolic enthusiast Jaron Lanier believes that, with increased use, we can actually inhabit virtual reality, a term he claims to have invented.[27] As we begin to inhabit virtual reality, the need for written and spoken language—"a stream of little discrete symbols" that he finds "very limited . . . very narrow"—will drop away:

> [W]hen you're able to improvise reality as you can in Virtual Reality and [when] that's shared with other people, you don't really need to describe the world anymore because you can simply make any contingency. You don't really need to describe an action because you can create any action. . . . Let's suppose that you could have a time machine go back to the earliest creatures who developed language, our ancestors at some point, and gave them Virtual Reality clothing. Would they have ever developed language? I suspect not because as soon as you can change the world in any way, that is a mode of expression of utter power and eloquence; it makes description seem a little bit limited.

Lanier's postsymbolic communication proposes an immediate and perfect relationship between reality and thought, rather than the mediated and inexact relationship that natural languages provide. The only problem, as he admits later in the interview, is that he is not really sure what communication without language would mean: "I don't really know what direct reality communication would be like." Lanier is proposing to realize the Lagadian project by employing virtual rather than material objects.[28] If only Swift's sages had replaced their sacks with computers, he seems to suggest, they could have succeeded.

Swift helps us to see that these projects, whether inspired by the flourishing of print culture in the early Enlightenment or information technology in our day, call for more than a refutation. They call for a belly laugh. His irony and humor show us that the attempt to mechanize language is ridiculous.

Machines, on the other hand, do not laugh, and their capacity for irony is distinctly limited. Enlightenment language projects and current machine translation efforts aim at clear communication, not humorous or ironic language. By contrast, natural human language is fraught with irony, sometimes intended, often accidental. Swift accepts and exploits this irony. It is part of our humanity as embodied creatures. Only mature human beings can pay attention to each other's language and seek to understand the many nuances of what is spoken or left unsaid. By contrast, the intellectual leaders of Lagado and Laputa care so little about true communication that they must employ "flappers" to follow them with balloons filled with peas or pebbles, hitting them softly on the mouth whenever their speech wavers from reality. By rejecting natural language and the ironies that attend it, Swift's characters have not achieved pure communication. They have begun to masquerade as machines. And when masqueraders do not know they are playacting, their actions are ridiculous.

Knowledge as a Commodity: Teachers and Students or Information Processors?

Human relationships are noticeably weak in Lagado and Laputa. Gulliver frequently complains that he receives too little attention during the third voyage. He is "but ill entertained" in the School of Projectors, "too much neglected" on Laputa, and attracts "not the least Notice" of the king. Because Laputian intellectuals are so involved in their abstract speculation, Gulliver converses only with "Women, Tradesmen, Flappers, and Court-Pages" during his two months aloft (173).

But Gulliver has little cause for complaint. He undertook the third voyage in search of knowledge, and he shares the Laputians' views about knowledge in the most significant respects. The only project of the Grand Academy that he rejects is its single sensible plan, to reward political ability, virtue, and service. He generally reports the experiments at the Grand Academy in the flat, objective tone of an eighteenth-century traveler and is "highly pleased" with some of its craziest schemes. His inhospitable treatment is entirely consistent with the projectors' view of knowledge and the anthropology it entails. The Laputians view human beings as information processors, to use the anthropology of cyberneticist Norbert Wiener, and Gulliver has no more reason to complain of the consequences of that view than a computer would.[29]

Gulliver's experience gives him no insight into the cultural shortcomings of Laputa—or the Enlightenment. He seems unaware that the students of the Grand Academy carry out merely mechanical functions as they are ordered about by their professors, as opposed to learning an intellectual discipline from them. He does not seem to realize that, by continually appealing to him for money, the professors are reducing him to little more than a piece of silver. As is typical of his satire, Swift depends on our ability to recognize Gulliver's faulty perception to call attention to his satire of the Enlightenment: by treating knowledge as a commodity, its human purposes are being lost. Enlightenment Europe is in danger of becoming Laputa, a land where knowledge has become "*la puta*," the prostitute, in Spanish.

Today's ever-rising flood of information poses similar challenges to human relationships, especially in the context of education. Technophiles embrace the new era with greater or lesser degrees of enthusiasm. Not all of them endorse cyberneticist Wiener's identification of man as a system of data retrieval, and most are too savvy to consider our technological tools as merely neutral instruments. Still, a naive admiration for the increased quantity and accessibility of information is common. This admiration can cause one to ignore the difference between mere information and knowledge. It can tempt schools and universities to treat knowledge as something to be packaged, to regard the teacher as the packager, and to view the student as consumer.

For Swift's inventor of the information machine, knowledge is "out there" as a commodity to be captured. The information may be stored in a human mind or a book.[30] That his intellectual project involves other human beings—namely students—is irrelevant. Knowledge is viewed as an object to be created, traded, and manipulated. But Swift's satirical purpose is to refocus our attention on the humane use of knowledge. He makes us realize that a book without individual human mind behind it—without the personal knowledge needed to communicate with another human mind—is useless. It contains nothing. Its words have the same value as hieroglyphics before the discovery of the Rosetta stone.

Because knowledge is a commodity in Laputa, there is no shape to the knowledge produced at the Grand Academy. There is no structure that unites the efforts of the intellectuals within its walls. Consequently, Gulliver loses the ability to distinguish triviality from significance in his stay among the intellectuals. Like the professors at the Grand Academy, he distances himself from every intimacy that the pursuit of knowledge might present: there is no personal relationship at the Grand Academy between the learner and what he learns, no intimacy between professor and student, and no relationship between the knowledge produced by the Academy and the larger society.

Corresponding cultural pressures in our own day are evident even among scholars in the humanities. Computer technology has magnified the temptation to identify knowledge with measurable bytes of information and to diminish the human relationship between teacher and student. James O'Donnell, a leading Augustine scholar, technophile, and Provost at Georgetown University, describes the professor-student relationship in the modern university as one of nudging, pushing and "sometimes pull[ing] students through the . . . tasks of processing information."[31] He claims to see "personal contact" between teacher and student as the most effective form of intellectual motivation, but he describes university as "a suite of software . . . chosen for its power, speed, functionality, ease of use, even for its user-friendliness." O'Donnell favors mechanical language—"software," "processing information," "functionality"—to describe teaching. Even the phrase "personal contact" has a functional, superficial ring. He frankly doubts that we can justify the study of the humanities by claiming that it makes people "better, more virtuous, more wise." He reserves his enthusiasm for the "tools and energy and the possibility of enacting a more powerful sense of connectedness to all those with whom we share the planet."

For those who are more skeptical of the promises of the information age, descriptions of education like O'Donnell's will raise many of the same issues found in *Gulliver's Travels*. In contrast to the technophile's assumption that knowledge is out there in cyberspace, waiting to be accessed and processed, the cyberskeptic tends to stress the personal, intimate connection between significant knowledge and a particular human mind and heart.[32] Technology enthusiasts often embrace "connectedness"—a pale, mechanical alternative to "community." But the skeptic might ask whether we can have a language for the virtues that bind the good society together without a renewed belief in humanities, where language is central—literature, philosophy, political science, and theology, among others.

Beyond his degradation of teacher-student relationships, the inventor of the information machine at the Grand Academy of Lagado promises a complete body of knowledge. This completeness gives the machine a more suggestive, symbolic meaning. In the modern Western mind, the image of a complete body of knowledge is associated with the encyclopedia, a project first carried out during the French Enlightenment.[33] More powerfully, the image of the "complete library" provides a temporal and spatial extension of the archetype of universal knowledge.

An instance of this archetype in our age is the image of the virtual library, where information is complete, instantly accessible, and indestructible—apparently without any material buildings or books. The virtual library will require altogether new intellectual and social structures than those of the libraries of the past, writes O'Donnell.[34] It will give us a "fuller representation of the world" through conflicting voices, constant flux, and transformation of readers into publishers. Near the end of his chapter on the demise of the old and rise of the new, O'Donnell reaches this astonishing implication: "If the idea of a stable, reassuring set of texts and truths on which to nourish the young fades, then it will not be at all clear what it is we need to do to or with our young people to acculturate them to the ways of their elders."[35] I believe his conclusion is something like this: the technophile does not know what education will do, but it will do it quickly.

Now it would be easy, at this point, to parallel the approximately $50,000 annual fee for an education at O'Donnell's Georgetown with the fees sought by the academicians at Lagado. What is more alarming than the price of this vision, however, is that it moves further down the road from the mechanization of language to the treatment of knowledge as a commodity. In place of the character-forming role of older texts (which O'Donnell mistakenly identifies as "reassuring"), O'Donnell embraces a kind of education that may be measured by its power, speed, and functionality.

Perhaps the most powerful modern critique of the archetype of the universal library may be found in the 1941 short story by Jorge Luis Borges, "The Library of Babel." Here, Borges looks at the end of the process that had just begun with Lagado's information machine. In his story, the library's "indefinite, perhaps infinite" hexagonal galleries contain a complete set of all imaginable combinations of the twenty-five orthographic symbols of the alphabet. Initially, the news of the library's completion produced "unbounded joy," for "[t]here was no personal problem, no world problem, whose eloquent solution did not exist. . . . The universe was justified" and the actions of every person vindicated. After four hundred years of searching out life's fundamental mysteries, however, the characters in the story finally give up the hope of discovering anything useful at all. The narrator in the story, like Gulliver, nevertheless retains his hope in the "enlightened, solitary, infinite, perfectly unmoving" library. But Borges, like Swift, counts on his reader to recognize that attempting a perfect technology of knowledge is a nightmarish project.

Swift's satire, like the story of Borges, raises a number of questions about the claims that information technology makes for itself. How will we judge whether electronic representations of the world are really "fuller," as O'Donnell predicts, rather than simply a greater collection of trivial ones? In Swift's Lagado, the "several volumes in large folio already collected" contain nothing but "broken sentences"—though the inventor promises future achievements if enough money keeps coming his way. How will we judge if our new electronic networks really produce just and good communities as opposed to mere "connectedness"? Finally, O'Donnell hopes for greater dialogue within the new electronic network, but how will we know if the technology of electronic media really produces better dialogue, as opposed to more worthless chatter?

Swift's book, like the story of Borges, depends on readers who can recognize the fantasy and the nightmare simultaneously. Through their mastery of multiple tones and narrative perspectives, these authors create multiple voices—not the single "authoritative discourse" that O'Donnell associates with books. Surely a literate culture, worthy of the name, nurtures readers who can hear different voices in a single text. Its success has little to do with technology. It depends rather on connecting the transmission of knowledge with a profound understanding of what it means to be human.

Technophiles are so awed by the resources of accessibility and the entertainment-value of information technology, that they have often stopped asking the difficult questions about what education is for. They know that tuition dollars are attracted by promises of wireless accessibility, faster Internet resources, and more convenient educational delivery systems. But what should they be teaching? The response of one critic of technology, Wendell Berry, is as simple as it is hard to attain: education must prepare young people for life and that involves preserving and passing along the "thoughts and words and works and ways and standards and hopes without which we are not human."[36] But many universities are no clearer than O'Donnell about what their institution should do. "The essential elements of a liberal arts education lie scattered everywhere at Harvard, waiting to be picked up," writes a recent graduate, "But little guidance is given on how to proceed with that task."[37] In a telling inversion of the library archetype, he compares the Harvard curriculum to "a great library ravaged by a hurricane" and laments that the triumph of postmodern theory has made the humanities irrelevant:

> In the field of English there is little pretense that literature is valuable in itself and should be part of every educated person's life, rather than serving as grist for endless academic debates in which every mention of truth is placed in sneering quotation marks.

The entire article chronicles a combination of intellectual laziness and obsessive careerism, where the curricular vacuum is replaced by intense competition for honors, offices, internships, and grades.

The loss of curricular coherence in U.S. higher education reaches back into the late nineteenth century, when religion was no longer capable of providing intellectual unity among the disciplines.[38] As religious claims retreated, one modern scientific discipline after another offered itself for religion's vacant spot, with evolutionary biology as the current favorite to synthesize knowledge: "Because a wide range of disciplines from geology to sociology, adopted evolutionary approaches, many intellectuals believed that these disciplines could be synthesized into an overarching evolutionary philosophy that would offer a comprehensive view of life."[39] The hopes for a comprehensive view, however, have not been fulfilled, as the experience of the young Harvard graduate makes clear. Between 1964 and 1993, concludes a study of fifty leading U.S. institutions, schools gave way to a "wholesale dissolution of curricular structure."[40] Significant general education requirements were either abolished or replaced by vague distribution requirements like Harvard's, degrading curricular coherence. What used to be a curriculum is now a menu of equally valuable options. These components are interchangeable parts, like the components that make up industrially produced commodities from mousetraps to microwaves.

Treating knowledge as a commodity has made the elements of the curriculum resemble the parts of a machine: science is usually taught in isolation from the humanities; writing instruction is often divorced from any particular content; students may select nearly any history course they wish, and choose several helpings from an incoherent menu of literature, philosophy, and the arts. But what effect will this have on our sense of what it means to be human? To begin answering this question, we must return to the effect of technology on Gulliver.

Colonizing the Self, Colonizing Others: Technological Dehumanization and the Recovery of the Person

The fictional Lemuel Gulliver is more of a technologist than a true scientist. He acts like a scientist when he sends three giant wasp stings from Brobdingnag to Gresham College, the home of the Royal Society. He speaks like a natural scientist when he reports on the "splacknuck," an exotic creature that he encounters in Brobdingnag, and in the spirit of science, he produces maps for each country that he visits. But Gulliver's development, in both his aspirations and his ultimate madness, is driven by his technological projects to improve human civilization through the use of applied science.

The term *project* in Swift's writing usually has a bad connotation. Samuel Johnson's 1755 *Dictionary* defines *projector* as "One who forms wild impracticable schemes." For Swift, the projector is someone who is trying to accomplish a task without recognizing the incompleteness of his knowledge or the limitations of his strength. In other words, the projector fails to recognize a fundamental mismatch between knowledge and humanity. Sometimes this is merely comical, as when Gulliver returns from his first voyage with the project of propagating miniature sheep from Blefuscu, which he fully expects will prove "much to the Advantage of the woolen Manufacture, by the fineness of the Fleeces" (78, 80). Never mind that these sheep are only a couple of inches in height. At other times, the projects have a more serious social dimension. The technological projectors of Lagado propose to plow the fields of their food-starved land by planting nuts and vegetables at six-inch intervals, and then driving cattle into the fields to root up the ground.[41] The costly experiment fails and the misery of the inhabitants continues, but Gulliver has no doubt the technique can be improved. Similar agricultural innovations have similar effects. Although the projectors promise to bring forth the fruits of the earth "at whatever Season we think fit to chuse, and increase an Hundred Fold more than they do at present, . . . none of these Projects are yet brought to Perfection." The result is the disruption of family and community relationships in the countryside around Lagado. Not surprisingly, its landscape resembles Ireland of the 1720s, which had begun to exercise Swift's political energies: "[T]he whole Country lies miserably waste, the Houses in Ruins, and the People without Food or Cloaths." Soon to be razed is the one effective community that supports numerous farmers, produces a wide variety of agricultural goods, and boasts a noble house, "built according to the best Rules of ancient Architecture." Its landlord is the "old and willful" Lord Munodi, who tells Gulliver that he must soon give way to "modern Usage."

When Gulliver turns from technology to the moral realm, he comes to believe that the publication of his *Travels* will put "a full Stop . . . to all Abuses and Corruptions, at least in this little Island." He quickly descends into utter misanthropy and madness, preferring to communicate with his horses rather than his family (6, 289–90).

By treating language as a mechanical instrument and knowledge as a commodity, Gulliver himself falls prey to the bloated promises of technology. By attempting more than is fit for a man, he ends up denying the humanity that he actually possesses.

Gulliver's most inhuman technological proposal comes in his voyage to Brobdingnag, where he introduces the sixty-foot tall king to the benefits of gunpowder:

> I told him of an Invention discovered between three and four hundred Years ago, to make a certain Powder; into an heap of which the smallest Spark of Fire falling, would kindle the whole in a Moment, although it were as big as a Mountain . . . That we often put this Powder into large hollow Balls of Iron, and discharged them by an Engine into some City we were besieging; which would rip up the pavement, tear the Houses to Pieces, burst and throw splinters on every Side, dashing out the Brains of all who came near. That I knew the Ingredients very well. . . .[42]

Where Gulliver accepts without question the promises of the technology of the early Enlightenment, the king is more than skeptical. At the end of Gulliver's 300-word tribute to gunpowder,

> The King was struck with Horror at the Description I had given of those terrible Engines, and the proposal I had made. . . . As for himself, he protested, that although few Things delighted him so much as new Discoveries in Art or in Nature; yet he would rather lose Half his kingdom than be privy to such a Secret; which he commanded me, as I valued my life, never to mention any more.

The king of Brobdingnag represents a more ancient form of knowledge, and he shocks Gulliver with his backwardness: "A strange Effect of narrow Principles and short Views!" he remarks, on the king's refusal of gunpowder. The king's library is small, paralleling the small number of ancient books compared to modern.[43] Brobdingnagian culture, like that of classical antiquity, is most interested in "Morality, History, Poetry, and Mathematicks"— subjects that Gulliver dismisses—and cannot be drawn to the abstract thought of the European Enlightenment. Gulliver does not go mad until after he returns from his fourth voyage, but he is already in the process of losing his humanity by his trip to Brobdingnag. By allowing technical knowledge to become untethered from moral and historical knowledge, he is permitting his humanity to slip away.

By the second voyage, then, Gulliver is well along in the process of giving control to the supposedly superior insights of technology, rather than making the complicated human judgments about the value of a new practice or invention. In his *Tale of a Tub* (1704), Swift had looked at this dynamic in even greater detail. One of the ways that he satirizes the inhumanity of the ideological fanatic is by pointing out that "the first Proselyte he makes" to his new system of belief "is Himself."[44] The fanatic allows a system of belief to control every aspect of his soul, and soon his imagination, understanding, and common sense are "kickt out of Doors." It may help to call this dynamic a form of voluntary "self-colonization," for by relinquishing control to a superior power, it relates strongly to Swift's critique of English policy toward the Irish in the 1720s.

That Swift connected the satire of *Gulliver's Travels* with colonialism becomes clear just a few paragraphs from the end of the book. There, Gulliver confesses to "another Reason which made me less forward to enlarge his Majesty's Dominions by my Discoveries":

> A Crew of Pyrates . . . see an harmless People, are entertained with Kindness, they give the country a new Name, they take formal Possession of it for the King . . . Ships are sent with the first Opportunity; the Natives driven out or destroyed, their Princes tortured to discover their Gold. . . . And this execrable Crew of Butchers employed in so pious an Expedition, is a *modern Colony* sent to convert and civilize an idolatrous and barbarous People.[45]

The willingness of a superior power to use up the resources of a distant people under its jurisdiction for its own benefit, without regard to the common humanity of both, is the definition of a debased colonialism. In the voyage to Laputa, technology is used for such purposes. From their lofty position in the clouds, the rulers of Laputa use their knowledge of gravity and magnetism to maintain political control. The king can order the floating island to hover over a disobedient town to deprive it of sun and rain. In more obstinate cases, the island itself can drop on the inhabitants' heads, destroying both homes and persons below. Gulliver does not remark on the inhumanity of this policy. He simply reports that the king's ministers have recently avoided it because it would "render them odious to the People" and damage the king's property on the island (171).

In the five final paragraphs of the third chapter of this voyage, however, Swift makes the temptation to use technology for political oppression clearer. There, he gives an allegorical version of Irish resistance to England's attempted introduction of a debased brass coin, patented by an iron manufacturer named William Wood.[46] In this episode, Swift takes the technological temptation one step further: the use of applied science to oppress colonized people. The Laputian king threatens to crush the second most populous city of his domains (corresponding to Dublin), which was in rebellion for unspecified "Oppressions" (309). The inhabitants threaten to draw down the floating island with a magnet of their own, forcing the king to accede to the wishes of the town. Beginning in 1724, the year he wrote the *Voyage to Laputa*, Swift composed a total of seven public letters attacking Wood's halfpence. Ireland had effectively lost its self-governing authority in 1720, and Wood's halfpence further inflamed national sensitivity over Irish rights and liberties. Under the name of M. B. Drapier, Swift's fourth letter stopped just short of accusing the crown of demeaning Ireland from its rightful status as a kingdom to a mere colony. This resulted in a reward for Swift's arrest. No one turned him in, however, and Swift became a national hero. Swift, along with the Archbishop of Dublin and others, succeeded in persuading the Prime Minister to withdraw Wood's patent in 1725.

Wood's halfpence had represented a technological solution to the real problem of a lack of coinage in Ireland. But its low copper content failed to win the confidence of Irish leaders and seemed to threaten economic ruin by another round of Gresham's law: the debased coins would lead to the hoarding of more valuable specie, eliminating any trustworthy medium of exchange altogether.[47] During the controversy, the value of Wood's coins benefited from the unquestionable reputation of Sir Isaac Newton, Warden of the Mint, who assayed the worth of some of the coins—selected by Wood himself—and reported them to be equal in value to the copper money coined for England.[48] The language of Newton's assay, as one would expect, is scientific and mathematical. Later that summer, the Privy Council's support for Wood's halfpence made its case in largely technical language as well, in this instance using of economic analysis.[49] Swift's Drapier follows in the same style as Newton and the Privy Council, but he distorts the mathematical and scientific descriptions to predict economic disaster and tyranny from the coins. In the conclusion to the "Fourth Letter," for instance, Drapier responds to a rumor that Prime Minister Robert Walpole had vowed "make us swallow his Coin in Fireballs" by masking his fury with pseudotechnical language:

> As to Swallowing these Half-pence in Fire-balls, it is a Story equally improbable. For, to execute this Operation, the whole Stock of Mr.

Wood's Coin and Metal must be melted down, and molded into hollow Balls with Wild-fire, no bigger than a reasonable Throat can be able to swallow. Now, the Metal he hath prepared, and already coined, will amount to at least fifty Millions of Half-pence to be Swallowed by a Million and a Half of People; so that allowing Two Half-pence to each Ball, there will be about Seventeen Balls of Wild-fire a-piece, to be swallowed by every Person in the Kingdom: And to administer this Dose, there cannot be conveniently fewer than Fifty thousand Operators, allowing one Operator to every Thirty [persons].[50]

Swift was a master at the use of calm, technical language to mask a dehumanizing project. His most famous work of this kind, "A Modest Proposal," appeared at the end of the 1720s. There, Swift assumes the mask of an enlightened, Presbyterian-leaning Irishman, who advises the breeding of Irish babies for sale and consumption. On its simplest level, he is offering a new agricultural technology, based on contemporary mathematics and economics, to solve Ireland's economic problems. His proposal—cannibalism—is only a satirical exaggeration of what the English are actually doing: treating the Irish people as commodities.

Swift's later Irish writings of the 1720s draw attention to a major deficiency in the people's English overlords: they have lost their own humanity and are using technology to oppress the Irish. Throughout the decade, Swift explored various ways in which technology, divorced from a broad knowledge of the humanities, would end up debasing humanity. Whether its object is Wood's half-pence, Gulliver, or the Laputians, Swift's satire continually exposes this evil, as magnified through the power and mechanical language of technology. His final satirical object, the Modest Proposer, has so diminished an understanding of humanity that he puts cannibalism forward as an enlightened project.

However dark his writing becomes, Swift's satires lead readers away from the misanthropy of Gulliver and toward a greater willingness to sympathize with other persons. Unlike the mechanical language of the information machine, his satires depend on knowledgeable readers who can recognize the many tones of his ironic prose and assess its underlying meaning. Reading Swift is a good way of recovering, preserving, and extending our humanity in a technological age.

Learning to Teach Again: From the Grand Academy
to Plato's Academy

In recent years, a number of writers have addressed concerns similar to Swift, not just about technology as a whole, but the particular challenges that information technology for the creation, transmission, and preservation of knowledge.

The most potent symbol of the mechanization of language in our own age is, of course, the computer. There is no shortage of cheerleaders for the promises of computer technology to extend our knowledge and to amass and sort information.[51] Among the prominent critics of technology, Berry announced his intention to avoid buying a computer in 1987, partly because he did not believe that he "or anybody else could write better or more easily with a computer than with a pencil."[52] Berry's concerns parallel those of Swift when he warns that words require the tactful treatment of human intelligence. Words are "verbal tokens or signs of things that finally must be carried back to the things they stand for to be verified. This carrying back is not specialist work but an act generally human. . . ."[53] Like Swift, Berry is worried about substituting a mechanical connection for the human relationship between words and the knowledge they are intended to convey. All of the stylistic elements that we expect from the good use of language—authorial perspective, irony, double meanings, tone, a range of connotation—presuppose a human author and a human reader. These are the ways human beings negotiate the mysteries of describing reality, while acknowledging the shortcomings of their language. From a machine language, one can expect neither humility nor style nor the range of meanings that characterize human language.

As Berry's critique continues, he worries about the image for education that our current practices imply:

> If we represent knowledge as a tree, we know that things that are divided are yet connected. We know that to observe the divisions and ignore the connections is to destroy the tree. The history of modern education may be the history of the loss of this image, and of its replacement by the pattern of the industrial machine.[54]

Our current language for the academic curriculum—*distribution* requirements that are taken in various *departments* or *divisions*—is fraught with bureaucratic or business connotations. There is no resonance between these words and the organic metaphors for knowledge, such as "branch" or "tree," or the quasi-metaphorical, human verbs for education, such as mentoring, nurturing, or cultivating. Like Swift, Berry and others see that our reliance on information technology is both a cause and effect of treating knowledge as a commodity. Computer-generated information causes us to organize knowledge in ways that can be reduced to formulae. Our reliance on computers therefore tempts us to neglect the connections among different kinds of knowledge.[55] Our reliance on technology is also an effect of viewing knowledge as a commodity. Skeptics of technology resort to the language of commerce to indicate their concern over this issue and have even satirized the tendency to view the "student as customer."[56]

The tendency to treat knowledge as a commodity has deep causes, but I believe it ultimately stems from the loss of a "narrative" that ties the forms of knowledge together.[57] The loss of narrative was discussed in the first chapter on *Robinson Crusoe*. But it bears notice that recent observers link the grand narratives' loss of authority to our ever greater infatuation with the power to assemble information.[58] In this situation, the professor is "no more competent than memory bank networks in transmitting established knowledge." In other words, the dehumanized students in Swift's Grand Academy, early in the Enlightenment, have become the dehumanized professors of the postmodern era.

In Swift's satires, the final steps of dehumanization involve subjecting oneself to a superior outside force—"self-colonization," I have called it—and then extending that sway over others. By voluntarily exchanging organic metaphors for education (tree, growth, nurture) for mechanical images ("suite of software"), we have taken the penultimate step in this process. The ultimate step will be to eliminate personal contact among students and professors altogether and award credit hours through a virtual, online university.

Swift's Grand Academy raises questions about language, knowledge, and humanity that have occupied Western philosophy since antiquity. Under the pressure of technological and philosophical changes, they resurfaced in the Enlightenment and in postmodern times. Long before Swift confronted the challenges of print culture, however, Socrates questioned the benefits of an even earlier revolutionary technology, writing. His critique has become a major source of postmodern analysis.

In Plato's *Phaedrus*, Socrates asks whether writing has truly benefited human memory and wisdom. Socrates admits that writing aids our recollection, but "those who acquire it will cease to exercise their memory and become forgetful; they will rely on writing to bring things to their remembrance by external signs instead of on their own internal resources . . . As for wisdom, your pupils will have the reputation for it without the reality . . ." (275a). Like Swift, Socrates is interested in the internal resources of individuals. He wants to know how they develop true knowledge and wisdom, not merely whether they can "access" information through writing. His skepticism of the new technology of writing parallels Swift's skepticism of the technology of the book. Together, they parallel elements of the cyberskeptics' critique of current information technology.

Earlier in the *Phaedrus*, Socrates had described the highest form of love between two individuals as the joint pursuit of wisdom, inspired by a vision of beauty (256a, 251). In the conclusion of the dialogue, he recommends "the art of dialectic" over writing. He opens his discussion of the dialectic by describing it as "the legitimate brother of written speech":

> SOCRATES: I mean the kind [of communication] that is written on the soul of the hearer together with understanding; that knows how to defend itself, and can distinguish between those it should address and those in whose presence it should be silent.
>
> PHAEDRUS: You mean the living and animate speech of a man with knowledge, of which written speech might fairly be called a kind of shadow.
>
> SOCRATES: Exactly.[59]

In an influential postmodern reading of this passage, Derrida finds it remarkable "that the so-called living discourse should suddenly be described by a 'metaphor' borrowed from the order of the very thing one is trying to exclude from it," namely, writing.[60] He finds the writing metaphor ("written on the soul") remarkable because it seems to upset the "pattern that will dominate all of Western philosophy"—namely the pattern (as he discerns it) of exalting the spoken word over writing. In Derrida's interpretation,

Socrates pits writing against speaking by associating writing with the moribund, the ignorant, and the external. Speaking, by contrast, is associated with what is natural and intelligible. Derrida believes he has deconstructed Socrates' argument by his subtle analysis of the way Socrates' metaphor admits writing into the "living discourse" of speech, despite Socrates' critique of writing.

Through this maneuver, Derrida believes he has deconstructed Socrates' contrast between writing and speech. But surely Plato, that most artful man, arranged the language of Socrates with an awareness of its metaphors and ironies.[61] Socrates calls the communication that is written on the soul the *legitimate brother* of writing, after all, and he recommends writing as a suitable pastime, though not higher than the dialectical vocation of a philosopher (276d). If Plato had meant to condemn writing altogether, I think it highly doubtful that Socrates would have recommended anything as its "brother," legitimate or otherwise.

Socrates passes beyond mere speech and writing to promote the "dialectic" as the highest form of discourse. Dialectic is a form of communication that submits to questions, unlike mere speechifying. It is capable of distinguishing dream from reality, right from wrong. It requires a human auditor who talks back to the speaker on the basis of the listener's own understanding. It requires someone capable of perceiving the significance of nuance, tone, irony, and silence.[62] Socrates uses an agricultural metaphor to explain his meaning:

> [F]iner still is the serious treatment of these subjects which you find when a man employs the art of dialectic, and, fastening upon a suitable soul, plants and sows in it truths accompanied by knowledge. Such truths can defend themselves as well as the man who planted them; they are not sterile, but contain a seed from which fresh truths spring up in other minds; in this way they secure immortality for it, and confer upon the man who possesses it the highest happiness which it is possible for a human being to enjoy.[63]

In the *Phaedrus*, Socrates rejects the bloated promise that the new technology of writing will enable one to capture knowledge apart from the art of dialectic. He does not reject writing, however. He rejects the dehumanizing efforts to divorce persuasive language from knowledge, beauty from knowledge, and love from knowledge. When language is treated as a mere instrument, as it is in Swift's Grand Academy, knowledge is divorced from all three. Today's technological temptation to regard language instrumentally is a revival, in a more powerful form, of the temptations that Socrates and Swift warned against. But resisting that temptation does not require the elimination of computers any more than Swift's resistance of the information machine required him to eliminate books, or Plato to eliminate writing.

I began this chapter with a nightmare vision of an instantly accessible, virtual library that no one could profitably use because our knowledge of meaningful connections had evaporated. My waking vision is nearly the opposite: in some ways, the contents of all libraries and databases are irrelevant. Because their proper use depends on individual human beings who perceive the importance of their information, all books and bytes could vanish with no immediate consequence at all. The educational moment depends on teachers who know how to connect their subject, meaningfully and humanely, to their students; for that, neither libraries nor computers are necessary.

In the first two chapters, I argued that we needed a broad enough view of knowledge to embrace the understanding we could attain through narrative and beauty, and to recognize the role of communities in validating that knowledge. In this chapter I have tried to establish that the transmission of knowledge must remain a fundamentally human process rather than a mechanical one. A major temptation of technology in each new era is its offer to reduce language to an impersonal system and knowledge to a commodity. The critiques of Swift and today's cyberskeptics help us see that neither language nor the learning process can be mechanized. The transmission of knowledge depends on human beings, who read and write imperfectly, and who speak and listen inadequately. They reflect on their failures and try again. Without that reflection, we are like Lagadian lads who try to overcome the deficiencies of knowledge by merely spinning the tiles of an information machine. With it, we may understand what it means to learn and to teach in the postmodern age.

4

CHRISTOPHER SMART'S POETRY AND THE DIALOGUE BETWEEN SCIENCE AND THEOLOGY

With this chapter the debate over knowledge moves into the mid-eighteenth century, when the challenge and promise of the Enlightenment had more fully entered the consciousness of thoughtful Europeans. These are the decades that saw the publication of that monument of the French Enlightenment, the *Encyclopédie* (1751–1772), which aimed to assemble knowledge in one set of volumes. John Leland's *View of the Principal Deistical Writers* (1754–1756) described a set of Enlightenment religious tenets—belief in one God who must be worshiped and obeyed, absent Christian doctrines like the Incarnation and Trinity.[1] Voltaire's poem on the Lisbon earthquake (1756), followed by *Candide* (1759), demolished the standard explanations for how a benevolent God could allow evil to flourish. But most brilliant were the triumphs of natural science during this period: theories to account for electricity proliferated; in 1758, as predicted, the comet named for Edmund Halley returned to view; and eight years later the race to determine the longitude at sea would come to a successful conclusion. Many of these advances made use of the physics or the mathematics of Sir Isaac Newton, whom Joseph Addison had called "the Miracle of the present Age."[2] Science was coming to be the recognized arbiter of knowledge.

Christopher Smart (1722–1771) is a pivotal figure for the story I am trying to tell in this book. He is much more aware of the broad significance of the Enlightenment as an intellectual and cultural movement than the previous figures I have discussed. During his most creative period, from 1750 to 1763, his poetry responds to the Enlightenment challenge to the knowledge of God, society, and nature—the three topics that link the figures in this book. His most profound response is to that most prestigious of Enlightenment modes of knowledge, natural science.

This chapter examines his encyclopedic poem, *Jubilate Agno*, a long fragment written between 1758 and 1763, and "A Song to David" (1763), both of which entered into the contemporary debates over knowledge.

During the years he wrote *Jubilate Agno*, Smart was confined to several madhouses for debt and an annoying propensity to public prayer. Smart's confinement was controversial at the time and remains so today. "His infirmities were not noxious to society," Samuel Johnson told James Boswell. "He insisted on people praying with him; and I'd as lief pray with Kit Smart as any one else."[3] Smart's best modern biographer says that the nature of his illness is "impossible to diagnose at this distance in time."[4] But even if the most significant treatments of science in *Jubilate Agno* are the work of an eminently sane imagination, it is undeniable that the work is more suggestive than definitive. His poetry does not provide a final answer to the relation of religion and science, either for an Enlightenment or post-Enlightenment age.

As the chapter proceeds, the reader may notice that some of Smart's failed efforts at finding usable connections between scientific and religious knowledge parallels the failures of the other figures in this book. Daniel Defoe did not really understand the epistemological significance of the narrative he produced in *Robinson Crusoe*. Isaac Watts' hymns did not keep him from doubting the Trinity at the end of his life. And the truths of Jonathan Swift's satires never intended to provide us with a method of discriminating the good effects of technology from the bad ones.

With the poetry of Smart, I hope the reader will see that this book is not simply trying to say, "If only we had listened to Defoe, Watts, Swift, and the rest, we could have avoided the problems of the Enlightenment." The demand for historical verification may have constricted Defoe's fiction, but it certainly has its place. The critique of enthusiasm may have unduly narrowed religious truth, but it pointed out the danger of fanaticism.

This chapter illustrates the complexity of the story I am trying to tell about the Enlightenment and postmodernism. Not every critique of the Enlightenment, whether by eighteenth-century or postmodern writers, is valid. I will argue, for instance, that some leading postmodern figures, including Jean-François Lyotard, have made serious errors in treating science merely as a particular discourse with no special connection to reality. This is a mistake, and it can lead to much greater foolishness than can be found in the most obscure lines of Smart.

One cannot simply answer the Enlightenment by adopting postmodernism. Instead, one must engage in a serious dialogue with the particular advances of the Enlightenment and look for the best minds of our own day as partners. For this chapter, with its focus on science and religion, I will argue that one should seek out those scientist-theologians who have actual experience as modern scientists.[5] Like Smart, such writers often examine the presuppositions, methods, and models of science and theology, creating a dialogue about knowledge. I will show that, like Smart, they do not try to assimilate one field to the other, as eighteenth-century natural theologians did, nor do they completely separate the two, in the manner of some recent commentators. I will try to describe this "dialogue," in the poetry of Smart and the recent work of John Polkinghorne in particular, both of whom presuppose wonder at the cosmos then move to experiment and experience in an effort to express their knowledge of the cosmos. Central to this dialogue for both Polkinghorne and Smart is the Christian symbol of the *logos*, which they use to explore God's active role in the universe, the codelike quality of much knowledge, and the way that knowledge flows to human beings.

Four Responses to Newtonian Science

As Addison's early praise suggests, Newtonian physics was the body of knowledge that gathered the single greatest prestige in the eighteenth century. By giving a rigorous, mathematical explanation of the laws of planetary motion according to the force of gravity in the *Principia* (1687), Newton unlocked many of the secrets of the universe. His *Opticks* (1704) established the highest experimental standards and revolutionized the understanding of light and color. Knighted in 1705, Newton was President of the Royal Society from 1703 until his death in 1727. In Newton's epitaph at Westminster Abbey, Alexander Pope wittily imagines Newton as a creative partner to God:

> Nature and Nature's Laws lay hid in Night,
> God said, let Newton be, and all was Light.

But how did the new knowledge discovered by Newton fit—if it did—with the rest of what a thoughtful person in the eighteenth century knew? In this book I have been telling a story of the fragmentation of knowledge in the eighteenth century. Although several of the figures in this book were caught unawares by that trend, by mid-century it was obvious. As the influence of Newtonian mechanics grew, it threatened to split scientific from religious knowledge because there seemed to be little need for a God who sustained the daily realities of the universe.[6]

The choices before most eighteenth-century thinkers, as they contemplated the new science, parallel the ones that are available to this day: conflict, integration, independence, and dialogue.[7] Some saw Enlightenment science in conflict with religion and promoted one over the other. The eighteenth-century followers of the atheist Baron d'Holbach (1723–1789), for instance, believed there was only one valid path to knowledge, that of material reality alone. The Christian followers of John Hutchinson (1674–1737) also believed in a single path to knowledge and tried to force scientific evidence into the cosmology found in Genesis.[8] Others tried the "integration" approach. Deistic thinkers integrated the elements of Christianity that could fit into the emerging scientific tradition of Newton and the philosophic tradition of John Locke, and eliminated the rest. Other writers, such as William Derham, updated the long tradition of "natural theology." They emphasized the gratitude that should result from a scientific understanding of the universe and tried to integrate the advances of science into a Christianity that consisted almost exclusively of praise. Still others came to see science and religion as asking completely independent questions with independent methods of gaining knowledge. Oliver Goldsmith's popular *History of the Earth, and Animated Nature* (1774) considers science an amusing leisure activity and completely separates the scientific realm from religious and moral questions.[9]

None of these three approaches—conflict, integration, or independence—adequately describes the work of Smart. Instead, Smart's poetry tends in a fourth direction, toward "dialogue" between the languages of science and theology. This approach seeks for common ground between the presuppositions, methods, and conceptual models of science and theology, without trying to integrate the two into a single unity. Like those who are drawn to the dialogue approach today, Smart's poetry investigates some common presuppositions of science and Christian theology, such as the assumptions that nature is ordered and that an appropriate response to that order is wonder. As for method, Smart's major nature poetry emphasizes the significance of experience itself, and his verse is strongest when his experience is most direct and personal. Smart has interesting things to say on the presuppositions and methods of science and theology, but his most original and creative ideas are in his poetic analogies between these modes of knowledge.

The mechanical image of the universe finds no more purchase in Smart's work than the mechanization of language found in Swift's. And as Swift focused on the relationships that arise between learners through the medium of language, Smart sought relationships between the human observer, the natural world, and God within the structure of language itself—the alphabet, the names for God, and above all, the symbol of the *logos*, or "word," as it was available in the Christian tradition. I will try to show how Smart uses these images to express the continual flow of information from God to the cosmos and its human inhabitants. At the end of the chapter, I will argue that the analogy between scientific information and the *logos* anticipates some of the most fruitful dialogue between science and theology in our day.

Although Newton's followers popularized a mechanical picture of nature, the great scientist himself did not believe in a nature devoid of spirit. As a recent biography notes, "A purely mechanical theory for the world's profusion of elements and textures . . . lay too far beyond his reach."[10] Nor would a greater scientific reach have made a purely mechanical theory acceptable to him. "[M]ere mechanical causes could [not] give birth to so many regular motions" in the heavens, Newton wrote. "This most beautiful system of the sun, planets, and comets, could only proceed from the counsel and dominion of an intelligent and powerful Being."[11] Moreover, within his discussion of mechanics, Newton also postulated certain unobservable concepts such as absolute space and absolute time.[12] These two metaphysical concepts posit a frame of reference from which all other observers can mark their motion and the progression of time. Newton's explanation of these two concepts had profound consequences. In the *Opticks*, Newton identifies absolute space with "the *sensorium* of God." In other words he posited "absolute space" as something like a "bodily organ for divine sensation."[13] This understanding of God, in turn, presupposes an Aristotelian notion of space as a receptacle. Space is contained by an Unmoving God at rest, with absolute space as its center.[14] "[God] is omnipresent not virtually only but substantially," he explains,

> for virtue cannot subsist without substance. In him are all things contained and moved; *yet neither affects the other*: God suffers nothing from the motion of bodies; bodies find no resistance from the omnipresence of God.[15]

Despite the implications of this passage, Newton believed that God interacted with the universe. For instance, he believed that God was needed to correct the eccentric orbits of heavenly spheres from time to time. Newton's view of absolute space, however, seriously diminished God's relationship with the cosmos. Rather than sustaining an ongoing relationship, God merely intervened occasionally.[16] Against his wishes, then, Newton's physics contributed to the materialistic view that the universe is merely matter in motion.

In the decades leading up to Smart's day, the most influential interpreters of Newton in England were deists and natural theologians. Their tendency to make Newtonian physics into a comprehensive material and mechanical system may be seen in the famous Boyle lectures, for example, established by the chemist Robert Boyle in the late seventeenth century.

> The early Boyle lectures, which did much to promote understanding and acceptance of the philosophy [of Newton] both as a system of nature and as a bulwark of religion, achieved this aim partly through emphasizing the value of natural religion at the expense of scriptural revelation; but this approach was liable to represent revelation as almost superfluous; and, as the new science demystified the complexities of nature, the universe could come to appear so well-

regulated a mechanical system that there was no need to bring in God to account for its workings, but only for its creation. Newtonian philosophy could therefore be criticized for encouraging deism, and anti-trinitarianism, with which one recent critic has described it as "indissolubly connected."[17]

Other Boyle lectures, such as those by Derham, tried to integrate the advances of science into a framework of natural theology. Delivered in 1711–1712 and published under the title *Physico-Theology*, Derham marvels that the universe is adapted to human and animal life, and he often remarks that the design of the universe should produce gratitude to its designer.[18] He concludes the book with thankfulness and praise for the Creator, and he considers the universe as a finished system, complete in itself. Thankful though he is, Derham has nothing to say about an ongoing relation between God and the cosmos.[19] He calls for Sabbath worship at the end of his book, but says nothing about the work of Jesus Christ, which is the focus of Christian worship.

The shortcomings of deism and natural theology for a Christian poet like Smart are obvious. In his long work *Jubilate Agno*, Smart denies that the universe can be adequately understood as matter in motion, as implied by the early Boyle lecturers.[20] He insists on the importance of relationships among the elements of creation, to which their mechanical imagery fails to do justice. Above all, he emphasized the ongoing significance of the incarnate Christ as the sustaining word of creation, which had dropped from the view of contemporary deists and natural theologians.

On the other hand, the crucial starting place for Smart's poetry is the same as Derham's natural theology: praise. Smart was affected by a number of streams of thought that his poetry does not ultimately endorse. To take another relevant example, Smart, like the "Hutchinsonians," was skeptical of the implications of Newton's physics.[21] Unlike them, however, he neither believed that science and theology were in conflict, nor did he aspire to find a philosophy that would displace Newton altogether. Instead, Smart's poetry tried to find analogies between theological and scientific knowledge that would find common ground between them. Whereas the Hutchinsonians found in Newton's rejection of the Trinity reason to reject his science entirely, Smart was motivated to investigate a more active relationship between the godhead and creation.[22] To these two aspects of Smart's poetry,

his gratitude and his search for analogies between theology and
science, I now turn.

"For the Method of Philosophizing Is in a Posture
of Adoration"

The feature in Smart's poetry, above all, that marks his efforts to
find a language that can accommodate science and faith is praise.
Praise, in its full sense of delight, adoration, and awe runs through
his early Seatonian Prize poems (1750–1756), which draw on the
natural theology tradition, down through the encyclopedic *Jubilate
Agno* (written 1758–1763), and onto his "Song to David" (1763),
an extended lyric on the Hebrew king and poet.[23]

In the earlier Seatonian poems, Smart does not stray far
beyond the natural theology tradition of Derham. These poems
emphasize the poet's wonder at nature and his grateful response.
All of his Seatonian verse makes use of "sublime" imagery, which
eighteenth-century thinkers identified with the powerful, awe-
inspiring, and even dangerous aspects of nature and acts of God.[24]
Although the earlier poems are more conventional than his later
works, they mark the maturing of Smart's intellectual and aesthetic development.[25] Even in the first Seatonian poem, "On the
Eternity of the Supreme Being" (1750), Smart moves beyond
the God of the deists, who does little beyond providing a support
for physics, and imagines a much more active Creator.[26] Smart
also indicates his future direction in the fourth Seatonian poem,
"On the Power of the Supreme Being" (1753), in which he refers
to current scientific issues and shows a willingness to question the
scientific explanations of the day.[27]

In his more ambitious, mature works, *Jubilate Agno* and "A
Song to David," Smart moves beyond the natural theologians'
typical response of gratitude and beyond their goal of seeking to
integrate science into theology. By the end of the 1750s, when
Smart begins work on *Jubilate Agno*, nearly all of his poetry can be
said to have a religious framework.[28] He seeks for analogies that
will illuminate a range of relationships between the patterns of
nature and the human perceiver without being false to scientific
or religious experience. As I will show later, these responses link
Smart with some of the most creative thinkers of our own day in
the dialogue between science and theology.

Smart's interest in science, although not remarkable by comparison with his eighteenth-century contemporaries, is striking to a modern reader.[29] In *Jubilate Agno*, he ranges over Newton's principles of motion, optics, magnetism, the problem of discovering the longitude at sea, fossils, the natural history of exotic birds, mammals, fish, flowers, and gems. Smart's knowledge of science, was "wide rather than deep," as his editor comments, but this failing is perhaps an occupational hazard for anyone who wishes to respond to Enlightenment epistemology.[30]

More serious failings of Smart's work include his use of outdated science and some of his criticisms of Newton. In the face of readily available scientific knowledge, he denied that light had velocity. He attributed the rise and fall of the barometer to the outmoded scholastic notion of cosmic "sympathies" rather than air pressure and believed that the moon appears larger at the horizon "because she actually is so."[31] Smart's willingness to make incautious criticisms of Newton probably stem from the revelation of the scientist's anti-Trinitarian beliefs. These beliefs came to light in 1754, when two previously unknown letters of the great scientist were published.[32]

Sometimes Smart went beyond what was responsible—claiming that he had shown the falsity of Newton's principle of inertia, for instance. But Smart never attempted a serious critique of Newtonian physics. Rather, Smart's critiques reflect his effort to think through the starting point for nearly every serious observer of the natural world: wonder. Smart probes the attitude toward nature that Newton himself displayed, rather than the proud confidence of later Newtonians or Newton's critics. In any event, Smart was no obscurantist, despite his errors. His first conversation with Johnson ended with a discussion of "fluxions," Newton's term for differential calculus.[33] He was genuinely interested in the wide range of scientific issues that preoccupied mid-century England, but he was bothered by the metaphysical basis that was forming to support the new science. God was being reduced to a mere concept, whose sole role was to provide transcendent support for a mechanical view of the universe. This he could not accept, and his poetry demonstrates a search to enrich the dialogue between science and theology.

The second part of *Jubilate Agno*, known as Fragment B, is structured around Smart's poetic mission of discovering a language that can bridge the widening gap between science and religion. For Smart, this means starting with the language of praise: "For the method of philosophizing is in a posture of Adoration" (B268). "Philosophizing" embraces an earlier English meaning of the term *philosophy* that includes *science* as we use that term today. Philosophy also suggests broader sources of knowledge and wisdom.[34] Newton had used the Latin version of *philosophy* in the title of his 1687 landmark, *Philosophiæ Naturalis Principia Mathematica* (*Mathematical Principles of Natural Philosophy*). What is most striking about Smart's line is that it embraces poetry (by its form) and science (by its content) within a single "posture." What does he mean by that posture, and why is "adoration" a particularly appropriate one for the observer of nature? To answer these questions, a fuller explanation of *Jubilate Agno*'s treatment of science is needed.

Jubilate Agno and Science

Smart's lines about science come primarily in a concentrated portion of *Jubilate Agno*, from lines 160 to 295 in Fragment B. Even though this part of the poem is a fragment, like *Jubilate Agno* itself, there are markers that indicate its deep significance to Smart's larger purposes—purposes that he never fully accomplished when he stopped working on the poem in 1763. Before looking at Smart's critique of Newton here, it is important to understand Smart's setting for this portion of the poem.

Smart begins Fragment B in the persona of a prophet: By virtue of his confinement to the madhouse, he is in "captivity" like Ezekiel; by virtue of British successes in the Seven Years War, he looks forward to peace like Isaiah.[35] Smart views himself, however, as a modern *Christian* prophet. He intends to "preach the very GOSPEL of CHRIST" to his own time and people (B9). Smart says that Christ, the "King's Fisher" in the lines below, has redirected his energies (formerly directed toward poetic "beauty") to the "pearls" of an evangelical vocation:

> Let Hushim rejoice with the King's Fisher, who is of royal beauty, tho' plebieian size.
> *For in my nature I quested for beauty, but God, God hath sent me to sea for pearls.* (B30)

It is well known that Smart had been deeply influenced by the recent explanation of Hebrew verse in Robert Lowth's *Lectures on the Sacred Poetry of the Hebrews* (1753).[36] In these lectures, delivered shortly after his election as Professor of Poetry at Oxford (1741) and published in 1753, Lowth established the modern understanding of parallelism in Hebrew poetry, an insight that influenced the structure of Smart's verse in *Jubilate Agno*.[37] Smart was also influenced by Lowth's treatment of the powerful or "sublime" effects of Hebrew metaphors. In his seventh lecture, Lowth notes that even ordinary, "rustic images" can attain these heights. Smart's *Jubilate Agno* often uses powerful imagery to express awe at common elements of nature. This leads to Lowth's third major influence on *Jubilate Agno*: his stress on the "expressive" style of Hebrew prophetic poetry. As opposed to representative descriptions, which attempt to portray an object with exactitude, expressive poetry aims at giving the effect of an object on the observer, a technique that helps account for some of the eccentricities of Smart's poem.[38]

Early in Fragment B of *Jubilate Agno*, these elements of Lowth's thought merge with Smart's scientific interests and evangelical calling. Smart prays that *Jubilate Agno*—his "Magnificat"—would become a poem useful to Christ:

> Let Jubal rejoice with Cæcilia, the woman and the slow-worm praise the name of the Lord.
> *For I pray the Lord Jesus to translate my MAGNIFICAT into verse and represent it.* (B43)

The form of *Jubilate Agno* generally consists of lines beginning with *Let* or *For*. It is modeled on Lowth's theory of "alternate choirs" that sang the Psalms antiphonally.[39] In this set of two lines, or "distich," Smart refers to Jubal, a descendant of Cain who is "the father of those who play the lyre and pipe" in Genesis 4:21. "Cæcilia" refers to the patron saint of music, St. Cecilia and to "the slow-worm." The "Cæcilians" are "a curious family of Amphibia," according to the *Oxford English Dictionary*, "having the form of serpents, but the naked skin and complete metamorphosis of Batrachians." The "Let" line, then, is filled with images of change and transformation: a descendant of Cain who blesses all civilization as the first musician; a musician who becomes a saint; and an amphibian who undergoes metamorphosis. The second line, beginning with "For," brings Smart and his poem into the picture. He puts *Jubilate Agno* in the lineage of Mary's Magnificat (Luke 1:46-55), a poem that rejoices in the privilege of being the vessel of salvation. Like the Magnificat, which affirms that God "has scattered the proud in the thoughts of their hearts" (Luke 1:51b), *Jubilato Agno* often goes against established cultural forces. For Smart, this includes questioning certain aspects of Enlightenment science, especially its "method of philosophizing" (B268). For the poem to succeed, Smart (or his poem, at any rate) must be changed. He ends by praying for the Lord to "translate" his unusual nonmetrical work into poetry. The second line of the distich then, ends with a personal instance of aesthetic transformation, paralleling the physical transformations of the first line.

After putting his poem in line with the Magnificat, Smart asks God to make him an apostle, a "fisherman" in the imagery of the gospels: "Let Gilead rejoice with the Gentle [a fish bait]—the Lord make me a fisher of men" (B110). In other words, Smart asks God to confirm his evangelical calling. Smart continues to define his calling by writing twelve distiches that link his poetic project with the twelve apostles (B123–B134). For instance:

> Let Matthew rejoice with Uranoscopus, whose eyes are lifted up to God
> *For I am inquisitive in the Lord, and defend the philosophy of the scripture against vain deceit.* (B130)

Pliny's *Natural History* describes the gall of the "uranascopos," or "star gazer" fish, as useful for improving vision by healing scars around the eyes.[40] This allusion, together with the "for" line, suggests that Smart's listeners will learn a "philosophy" that will counteract the "vain deceit" of the age. Smart goes on to bless "the name of the Lord Jesus for a miraculous draught of men" (B158), an allusion to Luke 5:1-11, in which Jesus turns the disciples' miraculous catch of fish into a promise that they will henceforth "be catching men."

In both of these examples, the two-line distich illustrates a typical pattern in the poem: first, a biblical name is associated with a person or element of natural history. In the both sets, the element is from the animal kingdom ("Cæcilia," "Uranoscopus"), though elsewhere he draws on astronomy, geography, geology, botany, agriculture, and history. For the most significant portion of Fragment B, the *Let* portion consists of a series of fish, together with a long series of New Testament names, beginning with the four apostles who were fishermen.[41] In the *For* portion of the verse, Smart introduces a connection between the fish (or fisherman) and a situation from Smart's own time. In both sets, the connection comes from his personal experience: in the first, he prays God to "re-present" his "Magnificat" into a new form of verse; in the second, he aligns himself with St. Paul's warning against those who would deceive others with "vain deceit" (Col 2:8). In other lines, the eighteenth-century connections come from ecclesiastical, geographical, psychological, scientific, or other issues.

From Lowth's lectures on Hebrew poetry, Smart developed a new structure for *Jubilate Agno*, using parallel lines to reinforce or contrast a meaning or to pursue a more subtle and obscure relationship. As is evident from the lines I have just explained, these relationships can be obscure indeed. Smart was driven to a certain degree of obscurity by the nature of his project—namely his search for a dialogue among many different fields of knowledge, including science and theology. To accomplish this, Smart not only looked back to the parallel structure of Hebrew poetry, but also to its obscure, expressive imagery. Hebrew prophecy, as Lowth had explained, does not seek precise descriptions in giving the divine perspective on historical and natural subjects. Prophetic poetry "avoids too great a degree of exactness," he wrote, "and too formal a display of the minuter circumstances; rather employing a vague and general style of description, expressive only of the nature and magnitude of the subject; for prophecy, in its very nature, implies some degree of obscurity . . ."[42] Together with other contemporary books on the sublime, such as Edmund Burke's *Philosophical Enquiry into . . . the Sublime and Beautiful*, Lowth taught that prophetic poetry seeks images that will excite the passions of its hearers, rather than to delineate objects with clarity.[43] As against the confident and certain language that was increasingly employed by the popularizers of Newtonian mechanics, sublime verse accommodates even obscurity when that is necessary for the proper expression of the divine. As Smart says, in vindication of his own obscure poetry:

> *For my talent is to give an impression upon words by punching, that when the reader casts his eye upon 'em, he takes up the image from the mould which I have made.* (B404)

Smart does not give the reader an exact representation of the world. He gives an "impression," which produces an "image" for the reader to take up. Smart is saying that it is not enough for an observer to delineate the outside world objectively. Because the observer has become involved with the objects he observes, it is appropriate and even necessary to express the effect of those objects as well.

Before moving on to Smart's critique of Newton, I want to summarize his position to this point. Smart has maintained that a "posture of adoration"—praise—is the one appropriate for "philosophizing," whether scientific, poetic, or theological. He has answered a prophetic call to bring a "philosophy of the scripture" back into England through his verse. He has adapted the parallel form, expressive imagery, and sublime scope of Hebrew poetry for this purpose. All of this is in the background of Smart's dialogue with Newton and his science, which extends from line B159 through the end of Fragment B.

In criticizing Newton's influence, Smart by no means rejects science as the Hutchinsonians did. His criticism of Newton is selective. One of his most direct criticisms of the physicist reads:

> For Newton is nevertheless more of error than of truth, but I am of the WORD of GOD. (B195)

Word in *Jubilate Agno* has three meanings: first, it means the Bible; second, it means the logos by which God created the universe and continues to sustain it (Gen 1:1-3; John 1:1-3); finally, it means the incarnate Word of God in the person of Jesus Christ.[44] In this rich set of connotations, the term *logos* unites the rational order of the universe and its ongoing relational elements in the Trinity. As against Newton's insistence that only God the Father is included in the term *God*, Smart affirms the logos as it had been understood in orthodox biblical interpretation and the Trinity more broadly.[45] At creation, John 1:1-3, affirms the presence of "the word" with God at creation and Genesis 1:2 describes the "Spirit of God" moving on the face of the waters. For all of his scientific insight, then, Newton's failure to accept the full significance of the logos makes him "more of error than of truth." In Smart's view, his anti-Trinitarianism would ultimately impoverish his ability to attain adequate knowledge of the universe.

Smart's second, direct critique of Newton occurs some-what later in the poem: "*For Newton's notion of colours is* αλογοσ *unphilosophical*" (B648). By "*alogos* unphilosophical," Smart cannot mean that Newton's *Opticks* is irrational, as "unphilosophical" might imply. Nor is Smart simply appealing to the authority of Scripture in these passages and opposing biblical authority to that of Newton, as the contemporary Hutchinsonians did. Instead, Smart is filling out his earlier thought from the line we have just examined: Newton's philosophy—his science, his theology, and his metaphysics taken together—ignores "the logos" in its full meaning.

Newton's God relates to the universe as the Creator who began it and intervenes in discrete moments to keep it going. But there is no life-giving relationship of God to the creation, either through the personal incarnation of God in Christ or an ongoing role in nature. Newton's God is distinguished almost entirely by his dominion: "It is the dominion of a spiritual being which constitutes a God," Newton wrote, "and from his true dominion it follows that the true God is a living, intelligent, and powerful being."[46] He relates to creation from his place of absolute rest and absolute time, his *sensorium*. In God "are all things contained and moved," he writes. But one consequence of Newton's thought is that God cannot have an ongoing relationship with the cosmos as a true par-ticipant. As Thomas F. Torrance puts it:

> If God Himself is the infinite Container of all things He can no more become incarnate than a box can become one of the several objects that it contains. Thus Newton found himself in sharp conflict with Nicene theology and its famous *homoousion*, and even set himself to defend Arius against Athanasius. Here, then, we have a revival of the old Hellenic dualism . . . [now] built into the structure of western thought under the sanction of absolute space and time. Thus against all his religious intention Newton paved the way for the rationalist deism that developed in English thought.[47]

Smart had observed the rise of the watchmaker God of deism in the decades after Newton's death and seen Newtonianism corrode the relationship of the Creator to the creation. He had no inkling, of course, that later scientific discoveries themselves would under-mine the clockwork universe. His critique was a theological and aesthetic one. He insisted that a true account of nature must be able to accommodate a vital relationship between nature and the divine, one that embraces both our reason and our experience of wonder. Smart provides a rich analogy for understanding this relationship in the symbol of the logos as I shall explain.

Smart's other direct criticism of Newton also picks up on the need for God's continued involvement with creation:

> Let Barsabas rejoice with Cammarus [a kind of lobster]—Newton is ignorant for if a man consult not the WORD how should he understand the WORK?—*For there is infinite provision to keep up the life in all the parts of Creation.* (B220)

Smart once again insists on the significance of the incarnate Word, Jesus Christ, not just for theology, but for a dynamic understanding of the cosmos. The life in "all the parts of Creation" requires "infinite provision," not the one-time activity of a watchmaker God. Barsabas was part of the delegation sent by the Council of Jerusalem to straighten out the church at Antioch on the meaning of God's "word" regarding the Gentiles (Acts 15–16:35). For the "work" of God to proceed, in Acts, the church needed to consult "the word," and Smart is saying that the same is needed in the England. Newton's work, however, implies that the continuous work of the Creator is unnecessary. Where the universe of Newtonian mechanics functions largely independently of God, *Jubilate Agno* expresses a dynamic universe, filled with relations between the cosmos and the divine.

Here is how the relationships work in this part of the poem. Each distich has a *Let* portion, followed by a *For* portion as we have seen. Smart uses the distich to associate biblical names, sea creatures, contemporary science, and prayer with each other. Through this association, he means to express the vital relationships among nature, humanity, and God.

In the *Let* portion, the biblical names (such as Barsabas) come mainly from the Book of Acts. They are drawn almost entirely from ordinary Christians who appear in Acts 9:36–21:16 and have some role in taking the gospel of Christ to the Gentiles—Dorcas, Tychichus, and other little-known figures.[48] Smart probably focuses on this portion of Acts because it names ordinary characters with access to the power of the Holy Spirit, which came with a "sound from Heaven, as of a rushing wind" (Acts 2:2). The *Let* portions of the lines go on to associate those names with fish and other sea creatures (such as the "Cammarus"), which recalls and extends the well-known biblical analogy between fisherman and evangelist.[49]

Up to line B220, most of the accompanying *For* lines reflect scientific interests in the 1750s and 1760s, ultimately focusing on the science and technology of air: "For the AIR-PUMP weakens and dispirits but cannot wholly exhaust" (B218). Why air? Because of contemporary scientific interest in air and because its association with the Holy Spirit enabled Smart to suggest important spiritual analogies.[50] After his critique of Newton in line B220, Smart begins exploring the spiritual significance of air. At this point, the *For* lines shift to an exploration of air as a medium for sound—speech, clapping, echoes, and above all prayer: "For ECHO is greatest in churches and where she can assist in prayer" (B237). The lines conclude, then, in the posture of prayer, which Smart has already identified with the proper "method of philosophizing."

In this section of *Jubilate Agno* Smart has drawn analogies between the evangelistic works of biblical figures from Acts and scientific efforts to understand the nature of air. The *Let* portions focus on biblical figures and their evangelism, whereas the *For* portions reflect on contemporary science and its broader implications. Smart is aspiring to be an evangelist to his own culture by explaining the spiritual implications of its growing understanding of nature: "For the AIR is purified by prayer which is made aloud and with all our might" (B225). Smart's message is that we cannot ultimately separate our scientific understanding, of air or other significant natural phenomena, from its wider relationships to humanity and the divine. In so doing, Smart takes large risks—his "sympathetic" explanation of the workings of the barometer, for instance, was already outdated by the time he wrote his poem[51]— because he is searching for relationships between the natural and spiritual world that may be meaningful to his contemporaries.

Throughout *Jubilate Agno*, the language used by Smart is lively and active. When Smart adopts the terms of physics, such as matter and motion, he connects them to the vital principle of the universe:

For MATTER is the dust of the Earth, every atom of which is the life . . .
For MOTION is as the quantity of life direct, and that which hath not motion, is resistance. (B160–61)

I cannot believe that Smart considered his language for terms like *matter* and *motion* scientifically more precise than Newton's. For Smart to put his views of matter and motion on the same scientific plane as Newton's *Principia* would be madness indeed. What Smart affirms throughout Fragment B of *Jubilate Agno* is the irreducible element of relationships—living, changing, and dynamic relationships—within the universe. He stresses the human role in the creation of knowledge, including both scientific and theological knowledge. He insists that the language in which we express our knowledge—including our analogies—is not just a transparent glass that can be discarded once we obtain that knowledge. On the other hand, Smart realizes his own fallenness and the weakness of his own language. Like an astute scientific observer, he realizes that ordinary words, concepts, and analogies are often inadequate for the expression of new insights. As Torrance writes:

> [I]n the advance of natural science . . . we must be prepared to do violence to our ordinary forms of thought and speech if we are to apprehend what is genuinely new. We have to devise new languages and step up to higher levels of thought in order to push knowledge beyond the limits of ordinary experience, yet all this remains within the limit of nature, for we ourselves belong to nature and are unable to rise above it.[52]

If human beings seek, on their own, for a language that will attempt to describe God, Torrance continues, they will be drawn to mythology. That is plainly unacceptable to the scientist who is a Christian, as it was to the Hebrew poets on whom Smart models his poem. The alternative is to seek an orientation from beyond oneself "in the coming of the Word of God," as Torrance writes. "Word," here has a Trinitarian significance, similar to is significance in Smart's poem. It helps explain why Smart was drawn to a strong Trinitarian theology and to the sublime imagery of biblical verse, as Lowth had explained it:

> The sacred writers have, therefore, recourse to description, amplification, and imagery, by which they give substance and solidity to what is in itself a subtile and unsubstantial phantom [the omnipresence and infinite wisdom of God]. . . . They conduct us through all the dimensions of space, length, breadth, and height. . . . [When the intellect] has compassed the boundaries of creation, it imperceptibly glides into the void of infinity—whose vast and formless extent, when displayed to the mind of man in the forcible manner so hap-

pily attained by the Hebrew writers, impresses it with the sublimest and most awful sensations, and fills it with a mixture of admiration and terror.[53]

At its best, Smart's language, like good science, pushes beyond the known to the unknown by discovering new relationships and new order. In the earlier portions of Fragment B, as we have seen, he often uses the powerful language of the sublime. At other times, he uses comic and playful language, as in the famous description of his "Cat Jeoffry," which closes this fragment. Jeoffrey "leaps up to catch the musk, which is the blessing of God upon his prayer" (B699):

For his ears are so acute that they sting again.
For from this proceeds the passing quickness of his attention.
For by stroaking of him I have found out electricity . . .
For God has blessed him in the variety of his movements.

(B758–60, 763)

Smart is not saying that he has achieved a scientific understanding of electricity by stroking his cat. Yet he is affirming that his personal experience with his pet has introduced him to this much-discussed scientific concept. And in the final line, Smart affirms an ongoing connection, blessing, that is essential to those who seek a dialogue between science and theology, between God's creation and the vital workings of nature.

Smart's *Jubilate Agno* attempts to express the fullness of creation. He seeks a language that will express the relation of God and his Word to every rose, rock, and daily event of his life—including his experiences of suffering in the madhouse: "FOR I pray the Lord JESUS that cured the LUNATIC to be merciful to all my brethren and sisters in these houses" (B123). Smart's great achievement is in his effort to reestablish an epistemological connection between various kinds of knowledge—personal, historical, religious, and scientific. He was not always successful. In the next part of *Jubilate Agno*, "Fragment C," Smart allows his personal fantasies—cabbalistic, Masonic, Pythagorean, and numerological—to derail the broader scope of the poem. Still, by perceiving the epistemological problems raised by science and by crafting a language of adoration as a way to bridge the divide, Smart's poem links to some of the most promising avenues suggested by the scientist-theologians of our own day.

Alphabets and the Analogy of Information

A curious feature of Smart's nature poetry is his frequent use of the alphabet, or sometimes just particular letters, to structure his verse. Seven letters of the Greek alphabet provide the foundation for the seven-day creation in his highly structured lyric, "A Song to David" (1763). In the fragmentary *Jubilate Agno* (1758–1763), Smart had used the letters of the English alphabet as well. The poetic use of the alphabet is by no means original with Smart, of course. He was familiar with the Hebrew alphabetical acrostic of Psalm 119 and more esoteric uses of the alphabet in Masonic and cabbalistic lore.

Together with the numerals of mathematics and the symbolic languages of science, the alphabet is essential to Western philosophical assumptions about how information is organized.[54] Physicist Robert K. Logan, a collaborator of media theorist Marshal McLuhan, writes that, together with monotheism and codified law, the alphabet encouraged the development of Western science by providing the framework for a "unifying principle [that] ruled the universe." Coding knowledge in alphabetic form provided a medium for new ideas to emerge. Like other communications media, the alphabet is neither passive nor neutral, but plays its own, active role in establishing modes of perception and social interaction.[55] As the "Great Chain of Being" lost credibility during Smart's era, a new analogy was needed to express the connections among various kinds of knowledge.[56] As I have explained, Smart was not drawn to the mechanical images used by deists and natural theologians. Instead, he used letters and the alphabet to develop one of his greatest imaginative achievements: language as an analogy for God's active involvement with creation.[57]

The topics of *Jubilate Agno* range from precious stones and flowers to insects, fish, and mammals, and from the planets and contemporary science to current political events. Smart couples biblical characters and contemporary personages with natural objects and creatures. All of this leads Smart's modern editor to speculate that he aimed at a complete "system of universal correspondences."[58] The alphabet provides an image for embracing those correspondences, as Smart himself indicates with this line on the letter "A": *For A is the beginning of learning and the door of heaven* (B513).

In Fragment B of *Jubilate Agno*, Smart goes through the entire English alphabet twice (B513–61). In his first abecedarium, the letters draw attention to the attributes of God and his relation to humanity. In the second, Smart generally emphasizes the correspondence between acts and words.[59] The correspondences between the code of language and the creation are more comprehensible, however, in Smart's fifteen verses on the single Hebrew letter, *lamed*, (B477–91). This letter puns on the sound of the English letter *l* and the Hebrew name for God, *El*.[60] In this passage, Smart finds the name of God, and therefore his presence, throughout creation:

> *For the letter ל which signifies GOD by himself is on the fibre of some leaf in every Tree.*
> *For ל is the grain of the human heart and on the network of the skin . . .*
> *For ל is upon every hair both of man and beast.*
> *For ל is in the grain of wood . . .*
> *. . . For ל is on the scales of all fish.*
> *For ל is on the petals of all flowers.* (B477–78, 480–81, 483–84)

In these lines, Smart is searching for God's beauty and active presence in all parts of the cosmos. He is not proposing a spiritual language that would displace natural science. But by drawing an analogy between the language for God's name and his ongoing relation to the cosmos, Smart implicitly rejects the clockmaker view of God. Instead, Smart expresses God's integral relation to nature in a common bit of information, the *lamed*, which connects all of the phenomena he surveys. There is something about the constitution of language, Smart seems to say, that enables us truly to understand nature as a whole. Language, the information that we both receive and express, unites us—heart, hair, and skin—with forest, fish, and flower. The passage suggests that all of creation relates to God in his role as a communicator. Instead of the clockmaker's mechanical analogy for God's relation to the universe, Smart constructs an analogy of language to signify the active information that God conveys to his creation.

Smart's verse goes on to find the Hebrew letter *lamed* in inanimate nature and in the biological phenomena he has already described. This letter, "which signifies GOD," is "in the veins of all stones" and "upon the Sapphire Vault" (B479, 490):

For ל is in the constituent particles of air.
For ל is on the mite of the earth.
For ל is in the water yea in every drop.
For ל is in the incomprehensible ingredients of fire.
For ל is in the stars the sun and in the Moon. (B486–90)

I have shown that Enlightenment arguments from design typically urged gratitude to God, but resulted in a static relation between Creator and creation. The passage from Smart, by contrast, exploits the active, ongoing theological significance of "the Word," to put the *lamed* in its fullest context. The passage does not, of course, attribute causality to the lamed: this alphabetic reminder of God simply "is" here, there, and everywhere, actively connecting the Creator with human hearts and water drops, flowers and fire. Physicists often call a theory that successfully unites such disparate elements "elegant." Smart describes the lamed in similar terms. He calls it "the line of beauty" (B548). His poem, of course, seeks to imitate that beauty.

The beginning of *Jubilate Agno* had signaled the central role of language in the poem:

Rejoice in God, O ye Tongues; give the glory to the Lord, and the Lamb.
Nations, and languages, and every Creature, in which is the breath of Life.
Let man and beast appear before him, and magnify his name together. (A1–3)

The first line paraphrases the opening verse of Psalm 66. But Smart changes a key word, *lands*, to *tongues*.[61] The poem's heightened emphasis on words is confirmed when the second line refers to "languages," whereas the third line reinforces his goal of uniting all creation in praise.

Letters and alphabetic systems, then, provide Smart with an analogy for the correspondences between creation, human knowledge of creation, and human response to that knowledge.

Smart further explores the analogy of language in his next major poem after *Jubilate Agno*, the 1763 lyric "A Song to David." In this poem, he chooses seven letters of the Greek alphabet, beginning with alpha and ending with omega, to represent the structure of creation. He introduces this middle section of the poem by referring to the seven pillars of wisdom in Proverbs 9:1 and God's drawing on the face of the deep in Proverbs 8:27:

> The pillars of the Lord are sev'n.
> Which stand from earth to topmost heav'n;
> His wisdom drew the plan;
> His WORD accomplish'd the design,
> From brightest gem to deepest mine,
> From CHRIST enthron'd to man. ("A Song to David," stanza 30)

When Smart uses the seven Greek letters to organize his examination of creation in the next seven stanzas (31–37), he directs the reader to the outworking of God's active word in his creation, from gems to humanity.[62] He chooses seven letters, corresponding to the seven days of creation, that have strong ties to names for God. Smart's achievement is to develop a set of correspondences between language, creation, and the universe:

> Alpha, the cause of causes, first
> In station, fountain, whence the burst
> Of light, and blaze of day;
> Whence bold attempt, and brave advance,
> Have motion, life, and ordinance
> And heav'n itself its stay. (181–86)

As in *Jubilate Agno*, Smart wants to convey the fullness of creation by finding its analogy in the active information of the divine logos. The alpha here is not just a cause that does its work and vanishes. It provides motion and life; it is the source of "bold attempt, and brave advance."

This seven-section section ends with a stanza on the sabbath and the letter omega. Like the alpha, omega is firmly associated with Christ through several biblical references in the book of Revelation. In Smart's verse, omega provides blessing for the world and a goal for the universe. After this section ends, Smart addresses David as the "scholar of the Lord":

> Such is thy science, whence reward
> And infinite degree;[63]

Although it is noteworthy that Smart embraces the artistic, theological, and natural knowledge of David under the term *science*, he does not treat the knowledge that comes from poetry as if it is the same as scientific or theological knowledge. Smart seeks for analogies between scientific and theological explorations through the medium of language. This medium provides him a vital source of models by contrast with other, mechanistic models during the Enlightenment. His analogies resonate with more recent attempts to account for the natural order.

Modern Science and Theology: Integration, Conflict, and Independence

Many thoughtful scientists across the philosophical spectrum express awe for the beauty or order of nature, yet not all of them have a view of knowledge that can connect this reaction with their scientific investigations. But should it not? Should not a satisfying approach to knowledge be able to embrace the awe that so many scientists feel and express? Many scientists, from the Enlightenment to today, also see the need to express their understanding of nature in images and models. Some of these models attempt to express the living quality of information. Should current discussions of science not follow the consequences of those models? Like the work of some of today's most thoughtful scientist-theologians, Smart's analogy from language provides a fruitful model for a dialogue between science and theology. Before turning to the dialogue model, however, I want to reconsider the three alternative approaches: integration, conflict, and independence.

As I have shown in my analysis of Derham's *Physico-Theology*, the strength of the "integration" approach is that it seeks for a unity among the various forms of knowledge. Its adherents are often drawn to an argument from design—God as designer of the clockwork universe, for its eighteenth-century followers, or (more recently) the Divine Mind that fine-tuned the universe to such a miraculously precise degree that it could support life. This approach continues to have able exponents and much intellectual appeal. Its continued shortcoming, however, is that it tends to assimilate theology to science (or vice versa). It risks reducing the full role of each kind of knowledge. Current proponents of this view, for instance, marvel at the finely tuned physics of the big bang (the expansion of the universe, the strong nuclear force, the production of carbon, etc.) and call for a new appreciation of

God's initial design. The need for a robust Christian theology, however, with a significant, ongoing role of the divine with the created order is rather small.[64]

Perhaps the most eloquent spokesman for the conflict between science and religion is Richard Dawkins, Oxford's Professor of the Public Understanding of Science. An evolutionary biologist, Dawkins admits to being contemptuous of organized religion and hostile to such cultural power as it retains. Recent attempts to find convergence between religion and science, he says, are a "shallow, empty, hollow, spin-doctored sham."[65] The only good reason for believing anything, he says, is "evidence," which (he says) comes exclusively from direct experiences of observation.[66] Evidence, in turn, is strictly separated from "tradition, authority, and revelation," which he calls three *bad* reasons for believing. Dawkins tries to resolve the conflict between different modes of knowledge by excluding any mode that fails to operate according to observable evidence. It is perhaps needless to say that theological knowledge, in his view, fails to measure up.

Yet even so hardened an atheist as Dawkins shares "a feeling of awe at the majesty of the universe," along with other scientists that he identifies as atheists or modern deists—Carl Sagan, Stephen Hawking, Albert Einstein, and Paul Davies.[67] He goes on to dismiss any serious connection between science and religion. But Dawkins fails to account for what he has just described: the observable evidence of awe among a number of major scientists. Surely it is worth probing the relationship between the capacity for wonder and scientific knowledge. Surely it is not just accidental that so many excellent scientists, of various religious persuasions or no religion at all, attest to the ongoing experience of wonder in their professional lives. By narrowing his view of knowledge to what can be attested by observable evidence, Dawkins lacks the language to explain even the well-attested reaction of the scientist's awe of nature.

Dawkins' "conflict" approach produces a more obviously contradictory result when he confronts the ethics of Darwinism. He says that we must accept Darwinist science but oppose Darwinist ethics, for that would justify the most selfish acts in the name of survival or propagation.[68] Since his 1976 book, *The Selfish Gene*, Dawkins has been urging us to resist the tyranny of our genes, while at the same time he recognizes that science cannot decide what is ethical: "[A]t the same time as I support Darwinism as a scientist, I am a passionate anti-Darwinian when it comes to politics and how we should conduct our human affairs." Oxford theologian Alister McGrath calls this an "important—indeed a remarkable—distinction between humanity and every other living product of genetic mutation and natural selection."[69] A critique of Dawkins by physicist-theologian Stephen Barr goes even further:

> We come down to this: our reason enables us to rebel against the implications of Darwinism. But why rebel? Where does the moral standard come from that says we should? Of course, the question is moot. For the fact of the matter is that rebellion against nature is impossible if atheistic Darwinism is true. We are a part of nature and cannot be anything but that.[70]

The "conflict" approach falls short because its most thoughtful practitioners, like Dawkins, must inevitably confront issues that they cannot explain with the limited language of science. Dawkins' receptivity to awe and his ethical seriousness point beyond the constrictions of his own model of conflict between science and other modes of knowledge.[71]

The "independence" approach to science and religion seeks to keep the two apart. In the writings of biologist Stephen Jay Gould and theologians Langdon Gilkey and Karl Barth, science and religion occupy separate realms of knowledge altogether— non overlapping magisteria, to use Gould's term.[72] Science covers the empirical facts of the universe and the theories that explain them, whereas religion uses a different language to approach the questions of meaning and morals. Religion asks "why" questions, whereas science restricts itself to questions of "how."[73] The two do not overlap. This approach has the laudable goal of respecting the integrity of different modes of knowledge, while maintaining civility. It acknowledges that one cannot simply define knowledge so that either science or theology alone prevails, as the conflict model does.

For all of the strengths of this approach, however, it has led to serious errors in recent thought. Beginning with the Lyotard's influential *Postmodern Condition*, there has been a growing tendency to consider the language of science as simply one kind of discourse, a language game that can claim no special insight into the nature of reality. By identifying scientific discourse as a "language game" (as Ludwig Wittgenstein used that phrase), postmodern thinkers are losing the ability to distinguish new age quackery from true science. What Wittgenstein means by a language game, writes Lyotard,

> is that each of the various categories of utterance can be defined in terms of rules specifying their properties and the uses to which they can be put—in exactly the same way as the game of chess is defined by a set of rules determining the properties of each of the pieces, in other words, the proper way to move them.[74]

But when did the language of chess ever give us new knowledge of the world beyond the game of chess? I do not mean, "When did thoughtful chess players draw useful *analogies* between their game and other aspects of life?" When they do that, the players move outside of the game of chess and apply insights into domains not governed by the rules of their game. Chess then becomes an analogy for a useful dialogue about reality. But if one accepts Lyotard's notion, that scientific language functions "*exactly* the same way as the game of chess," one gives up the notion that scientific knowledge gives us broad insights into nature. Science is confined to its own "game," which is independent of the other knowledge games, whether they concern chess or child psychology, poetry or political science. Quoting the philosopher Gaston Bachelard, Lyotard writes that scientific proof is "[n]ot: I can prove something because reality is the way I say it is. But: *as long as I can produce proof*, it is permissible to think that *reality is the way I say it is*."[75] Lyotard's formulation may seem to introduce a refreshing humility, for he is acknowledging his uncertainty about the shape of ultimate reality. In truth, however, he is exalting the subjective "I" over everything, as the italicized words indicate. For Lyotard, the final goal of the language game is to not to understand nature better or arrive at a deeper understanding of truth. "The problem [before the scientist] is not to learn what the opponent ('nature') is, but to identify the game it plays."[76]

Like Smart, Lyotard acknowledges the importance of language. But unlike Smart, Lyotard and some of his followers write as if they have reduced the world to a construct of language. "[T]he physical world could be analysed perfectly adequately by means of language and presuppositions quite different from those employed in the modern scientific community," writes Michael Mulkay. *"There is, therefore nothing in the physical world which uniquely determines the conclusion of that community.* . . . [T]here is no alternative but to regard the products of science as social constructions like all other cultural products."[77] This extreme form of postmodernism finds it unnecessary to seek experimental confirmation "in the physical world" of the truth of one's language.

By abandoning a commitment to describe the physical world faithfully, practitioners of this theory have, at times, lost their capacity to distinguish sense from nonsense. To expose such foolishness, the physicist Alan Sokal submitted a parody of postmodern writing that was accepted as a serious essay by a leading postmodern journal.[78] In this article he leaps from valid scientific statements to absurd conclusions, denying the existence of an external world and maintaining that physical reality is merely "a social and linguistic construct." The moral significance of his hoax was equally revealing: he gave unstinting flattery to the theoretical school to which the editors and publishers of the journal belonged. They accepted it for publication and then reacted with outrage (rather than embarrassment) when they learned the truth.[79]

It would be unfair to indict all those who pursue this approach to science and theology with this criticism. However, the "independence" model does encourage a fragmentation among the different forms of knowledge that, among the most thoughtful commentators, can be anguishing. In 1954 the great physicist Erwin Schrödinger gave eloquent voice to the torment that this separation can bring:

> I am very astonished that the scientific picture of the real world around me is very deficient. It gives a lot of factual information, puts all our experience in a magnificently consistent order, but it is ghastly silent about all and sundry that is really near to our heart, that really matters to us. . . . [I]n brief, we do not belong to this material world that science constructs for us . . . [T]he scientific world-view contains of itself no ethical values, no aesthetical values, not a word about our own ultimate scope or destination, and no God if you please. . . . Whence come I? and whither go I? That is the great unfathomable question, the same for every one of us. Science has no answer to it.[80]

If the postmoderns' failure to see the limits of their theory is comic, Schrödinger's recognition of those limits is tragic. There is great integrity to Schrödinger's cry. But there may be a response to it. We may be unable to assimilate all forms of knowledge into a single method, but we can still find connections among them. Smart found comic connections between cats and electricity, and modern thinkers probe the epistemological connections between the uncertainty of quantum mechanics and free will. Scientists testify to the sublime experience of awe, an inexplicable yet undeniable response to the power of observed nature. Perhaps one may begin the current dialogue there, from a "posture" similar to that of Smart's.

The Dialogue between Science and Theology: Information Please

The approach to science and theology that most accurately characterizes Smart's poetry is that of dialogue, which seeks common ground between the presuppositions, methods, and models of science and theology.[81] The scientist-theologians who best exemplify this approach, in my view, are Ian Barbour and John Polkinghorne.[82] Like the "posture of adoration" that Smart presupposes in his poetry, joy in the rational order of the universe underlies the work of Polkinghorne.[83] Barbour often ends his lectures with magnificent images from space projected onto a screen. Polkinghorne insists on an analogy between the methods of experimentation in science and theology as well. Doctrines such as the Trinity and Incarnation, writes Polkinghorne, arose from critical reflection on experience, not from biblical evidence alone or metaphysical speculation.[84] This pattern of experience and reflection is critical to good theological methodology, he says, and to science. Although he admits the shortcomings of the analogy, Polkinghorne argues that the New Testament records are "as indispensable to Christian theology as are experimental notebooks to science." There are clearly shortcomings in many of Smart's poetic efforts as well. But at his best, such as his poetry on the logos, Smart's analogies arise from reflection on experiences that suggest new relationships between the natural and the divine.

It is above all in the models used by Smart, Barbour, and Polkinghorne that the dialogue between science and theology is the most interesting. I particularly want to focus on the broad significance of "information" in the dialogue between the two fields.

Barbour usefully defines information as

> *an ordered pattern* that is one among many possible sequences or states
> of a system (of alphabetical letters, auditory sounds, binary digits,
> DNA bases, or any other combinable elements). Information is *com-
> municated* when another system (reader, listener, computer, living
> cell, etc.) responds selectively—that is, when information is coded,
> transmitted, and decoded. The meaning of the message is dependent
> on a wider *context of interpretation*. It must be viewed dynamically and
> relationally rather than in purely static terms, as if the message were
> contained in the pattern itself.[85]

Like an understanding of the *lamed* in Smart's poem, the transfer
of information depends on a context, a recipient, and a relationship. Barbour seems especially interested in the parallels between
the biblical concept of "the Word" and information exchanged
within the genetic code.[86] In a developing embryo, he goes on
to explain, information flows interactively, both to and from the
genes in the context of an actually functioning system. Like a
working human language and unlike a mechanical process, genetic
sequencing is influenced by environmental factors. Understanding
the information flow in the DNA molecule is thus closer to learning a language than to understanding a set of objective facts or
the workings of a machine. The language analogy has its limits
of course: unlike human language, genes are not self-conscious
or playful. Still, it captures the active, relational quality of natural
knowledge that Smart emphasizes as well.

Moving from biology to physics, Polkinghorne has explored
the analogy between God's providence and the workings of
"active information" on the quantum level. "Active information"
represents "the influence that brings about the formation of a
structured pattern of future dynamical behaviour."[87] Analogous to
the "guiding wave" explanation of quantum theory, as explained
by David Bohm, active information influences motion and direc-
tional preferences without any transfer of energy: "[I]t is active
in a non-energetic way." Polkinghorne proposes this as a way of
understanding God's providential way of interacting with creation.
By directing the cosmos through the active input of information,
rather than through causal, energetic interventions, God is no longer seen as merely a prime cause or an occasional intervener.[88]

When they begin from "the posture of adoration," the working poet and the physicist acknowledge the remarkable similarity of their assumptions: that the universe is orderly and awe-inspiring; that human beings can imagine this order with a high degree of truth; and that human languages, scientific and poetic, can express these truths reasonably and faithfully. By highlighting language itself as analogy for our understanding of creation, Smart explored an analogy that is still bearing fruit in the effort to connect scientific and theological knowledge, without reducing one mode of knowledge to the other. He seems to have anticipated this invitation from Polkinghorne:

> [W]e need to explore with profound seriousness all avenues of our meeting with reality as they open up for us. The impersonal is not to be preferred to the personal, the objective to the subjective, the quantifiable to the symbolic, the repeatable to the unique. All are part of the one world of our experience.[89]

I have noted the shortcomings of Smart's verse as well as its achievements. Though much of *Jubilate Agno* is now understood to be the work of a sane mind, it is often manic. Its analogy of language, like the information analogies of Polkinghorne and Barbour, is suggestive rather than definitive. Like the other figures in this book, Smart, Barbour, and Polkinghorne offer ways to broaden our knowledge without guaranteeing certainty.

In this and the previous chapter, the major front in the battle over knowledge, both in the eighteenth-century and more recent times, has been over the nature of language. In the next chapter, that front will broaden, from language to other human ways of organizing and acknowledging the most important objects of knowledge. In their rejection of the hyperrational approach to knowledge, the French revolutionaries pioneered new modes of language, new festivals, and a new calendar for advancing their goals. They believed their advance beyond the Enlightenment was sublime. Whatever their actual achievement, they certainly succeeded in inspiring awe and terror.

5

FESTIVAL AND DISCIPLINE
IN REVOLUTIONARY FRANCE
AND POSTMODERN TIMES

"Without God, all is permitted." This chilling refrain runs through Fyodor Dostoevsky's 1880 novel *The Brothers Karamazov*. It serves as the author's warning of the willingness of the Enlightenment to eradicate freedom and inflict cruelty in the name of a higher rational goal. As I noted in chapter 4, the evolutionist Richard Dawkins comes close to acknowledging a secular version of this logic. He admits his scientific mode of knowledge is powerless to counteract the biological imperative of ruthless evolutionary competition. Yet Dostoevsky's understanding reaches to a much deeper level than Dawkins'. The tragedy portrayed in his novel is that, in the absence of religious faith, men will make themselves worse than beasts. In the name of enlightened virtue and social regeneration, they will invent reasons for killing that fail to rise even to the Darwinian standard of death for the sake of survival of the fittest.

This chapter and the next, both devoted to the French Revolution, will discuss eighteenth-century and more recent thinkers on the limits to the Enlightenment social critique. This chapter will focus on efforts to exceed the power of Enlightenment reason with regard to social transformation. The next will look at Edmund Burke's alternative, which searches for a more organic knowledge of society and a more limited role for the power of reason.

Enlightenment figures produced powerful critiques of contemporary religion, politics, and social life. But in the French Revolution, where this critique went furthest, Enlightenment thinkers failed to provide a sustainable alternative. The church was satirized, and the clergy either swore loyalty to a new, revolutionary constitution or lost their posts. Monarchy was denounced, and the king and queen were executed. But satire, denunciation, and executions did not supply new social bonds to replace the ones they destroyed. Dislodging the established religion did not satisfy the human need to worship.

Among the French thinkers who saw most clearly the limits to this approach were Maximilien Robespierre (1758–1794), Gilbert Romme (1750–1795), and Philippe Fabre d'Églantine (1750–1794). All of them fell victim to the revolutionary violence that accompanied their social vision. These men were among the most visionary leaders of revolutionary France. They realized that the Enlightenment critique of the past was insufficient to create the "new man" that their rhetoric called for. A new order was needed to construct "the citizen," who would displace the "the gentleman" and the habits, rituals, and customs that had sustained that ideal over centuries.[1] For humanity to be regenerated in France, these thinkers saw that it was not enough to institute rational, enlightened laws. For the new man to achieve the virtues he needed, Robespierre came to realize, the French Republic would ultimately have to extinguish the past by means of terror.[2] Even beyond the terror, however, he saw that the citizen of the new republic would have to acquire new rituals and new holidays to replace old religious festivals. Time itself would have to demonstrate the irreversibility of the revolution.[3] With these goals in mind, Romme and Fabre served as the principle architects of the revolutionary calendar that was approved in late 1793. Robespierre agreed with their goals, and in the weeks before his own arrest and execution he feverishly promoted a new religious holiday, "The Festival of the Supreme Being" (June 8, 1794).

We live in an age with passionately competing views of the just society and the good life for individuals. There is a spectrum of views among those who would like to reform social and individual life, some favoring moderate reform and others favoring radical transformation. As their commitments to postmodernism and political ideologies intensify, the parallels to the eighteenth-century often intensify as well, although political realities in the United States and other Western democracies decisively modify their expression. I will explore these parallels in this chapter. I will try to show that the critique of the past, when it is done by those with postmodern presuppositions and strong ideological commitments, is frequently accompanied by efforts to discipline their opponents. Along with this discipline, they often promote calendrical reforms—months of celebration and new holidays—that offer new social rhythms to displace the old and to supply emotional resources for the new citizens they seek to create. These celebrations and holidays raise questions regarding discipline, punishment—and knowledge—in an acute form.

This chapter will more than list the dangers of ideological extremism. It will show how these efforts, in revolutionary France and the postmodern West, illustrate the overarching theme of this book: the need for approaches to knowledge that overcome the fragmentation of the Enlightenment. These social movements demonstrate the need to find connections between political knowledge and its expression in our social and religious rituals. This is an understandable and perhaps even a natural response to modernity. As these movements have become more extreme, however, they have introduced a worrisome measure of authoritarianism.

Revolutionary France set the pattern that one can observe in today's postmodern or hypermodern ideological groups, especially on university campuses[4]: The most visionary leaders became convinced of the inadequacy of a merely rational critique of the past; they saw the need for a new humanity, which required codes of control and correction; they instituted calendrical reforms by which they hoped to establish new social rhythms; and they ultimately overstepped their power in their efforts to discriminate the regenerate persons from the reprobate. In France, the result was the violence of the reign of terror. In United States, the result is often the despotism of the schoolmaster, to adopt the language of Alexis de Tocqueville.[5]

Beyond the Enlightenment Critique: Constructing a Revolutionary Humanity

In the years before the outbreak of the French Revolution in 1789, critiques of the French political and religious traditions were found everywhere in France. From "The Marriage of Figaro" by Beaumarchais and the contemporary paintings of Jacques-Louis David, to the pornographic satires on Marie Antoinette, the aristocratic foundations of the old regime were increasingly degraded during the decade of the 1780s. A few weeks before the assembling of the Estates-General (May 1789), the abbé Sieyès published an extremely influential political pamphlet, "What Is the Third Estate," in which he attacked the historic privileges enjoyed by the nobility and the clergy. Following the political theory of Jean-Jacques Rousseau, Sieyès argued that the nation's identity derived from the "general will" of the people, whereas other forms of authority—French constitutional traditions, monarchy, and the historic privileges of the nobility—were illegitimate.[6] For Sieyès, the authority of his language came from its enlightenment. Its appeal to rationality deeply influenced the early political discourse of the Revolution.[7]

Among the critics of the French religious tradition, none had more influence on the French Revolution than Voltaire (1694–1778). The tone of his religious articles in the *Philosophical Dictionary* (1764) implies that only a fool could dissent from Voltaire's enlightened religious skepticism.[8] Like Sieyès, he was only one among many writers who attempted to expose the irrationality of the old regime. His memorable if untranslatable cry—*écrasez l'infame!*—rallied support for crushing the institutional church along with other artifacts of the old regime in France. Voltaire's religious significance was underscored by the transportation of his remains to the Panthéon on July 11, 1791. This festival, rife with religious symbolism, pointedly excluded the clergy while the body of the prophet of enlightenment was laid to rest in a secular temple.[9] But if his burial suggested an alternative ritual and transference of emotional loyalties from Christian saints to pre-Revolutionary heroes, Voltaire himself recommended rationality in religion. He specifically criticized religious irrationality. The religion of his fictional "El Dorado" in *Candide* (1759), for instance, is that of a mild, enlightened deism, and his poem on the Lisbon earthquake (1756) savages the irrationality of trying to explain the deaths of over 30,000 souls in terms of divine providence.

As the religious symbolism of Voltaire's burial illustrates, the revolutionary appeal to reason was neither pure nor stable.

Leaders such as Marquis de Condorcet, who attempted to maintain the authority of the Revolution on reason alone, were rapidly outpaced by events.[10] When tensions between the Revolutionary government and the clergy finally came to a head in the fall of 1792, to choose another example of this instability, the Hébertists and their allies in the new republican government attempted to replace the role of the Church with a "cult of Reason." Secular authorities were now charged with recording births, baptisms, and deaths. Divorce was legalized and the clergy (regarded as civil servants since 1790) were urged to marry. This new cult culminated in "Festivals of Reason" that were celebrated throughout France in the fall and winter of 1793, most notably in Paris, where the bishop renounced his faith and the Church of Notre-Dame was renamed the Temple of Reason. At the climax of these celebrations, an actress enacted the triumph over prejudice.[11] Neither the object of worship nor its liturgical content was clear, however. No prayers were offered, and the "triumph" personified by the actress represented various abstractions (depending on the site of the festival), including Liberty, Reason, Nature, or Victory. What tied these festivals together, in the view of most historians, was simply their hostility to Christianity, rather than any program of their own.

In an important speech on November 21 (1 Frimaire), Robespierre denounced the "de-Christianization campaign" that accompanied the cult of Reason. Robespierre considered the cult little more than the atheism, and he associated it with the old regime:

> I've said that I'm not speaking as an individual or a systematic philosopher, but as a representative of the people. Atheism is *aristocratic*; the people are drawn to the idea of a great being who watches over oppressed innocence and punishes flourishing crime.[12]

Robespierre realized that the new citizen, whose creation had begun in the Enlightenment culture of pre-Revolutionary France, needed more to sustain him than an attack on the old regime, supported by a rational religion. The citizens of the new Republic had to develop new virtues or rather they had to revive the virtues of republican Rome, as depicted in the contemporary revolutionary paintings of David, such as self-sacrifice, simplicity, and strength under adversity.[13] In the process of destroying the despotic old regime, they would obliterate the distinction between the private and the public realm, and subordinate family loyalty to the needs of the nation. But far from relying on pure reason, let alone atheism, Robespierre said that the new republicans would require the powers of the heavens to defend the natural sensibility that is engraved on the human heart.[14]

What Robespierre saw so clearly was that the Revolution must aspire to a complete regeneration of man, as envisioned in the new figure of the revolutionary "citizen": "It is no longer a question of forming gentlemen (*messieurs*)," he declared in his speech of 18 Floréal, "but of citizens."[15] In this speech, Robespierre promoted a new Cult of the Supreme Being, which would replace the Cult of Reason. He pointed out the deficiencies of individual reason and called for a cult that would elevate the soul.[16] The formation process he envisioned would not just involve a new set of virtues, intellectually understood, but new rituals, manners, and festivals. The process would therefore require a high degree of control, followed by a process of sorting the friends of the Revolution from its enemies.

Early in the speech, Robespierre illustrated the link between control and the new humanity with a popular metaphor for scientific advancement—the lightning rod:

> The world has changed and must change yet more. What do we have in common with what has come before? . . . Man has conquered lightning and deflected it from heaven . . . Assess the distance between the astronomical observations of the Asian mages with the discoveries of Newton. . . . All has changed in the physical order; all must change in the moral and political order.[17]

For Robespierre, the lightning rod, invented by the much-admired Benjamin Franklin, was a symbol of the ability to harness the most powerful and irrational of forces.[18] What the scientist had accomplished through technology, Robespierre intended to do through politics and new social customs.

Robespierre's greatest attempt to exert social control came about in June 1794, with the Festival of the Supreme Being (June 8), followed two days later by the "law of 22 Prairial," which inaugurated the "Great Terror" that lasted for about six weeks. Although there are many excellent treatments of the Terror, little attention has been paid to the deep social understanding of its leaders—Robespierre, Fabre, and Romme.[19] They realized that it was not enough to separate the new citizens from the "ladies and gentlemen" of the old regime through the political and judicial apparatus of the Terror. They understood that the new revolutionary citizens, once created, had to be properly nurtured through new social rhythms and celebrations.

Sorting Friends from Enemies: The Festival of the Supreme Being and the Revolutionary Calendar

A year after the fall of the Bastille, the French people celebrated the "Festival of the Federation," in Paris and the provincial towns, in what seemed to be spontaneous bursts of enthusiasm, even to those who had their doubts about the Revolution.[20] William Wordsworth witnessed this festival of July 14, 1790, at Calais, where he had landed the day before. Wordsworth was later disenchanted with the Revolution, but he initially found "benevolence and blessedness / Spread like a fragrance everywhere," and his southward journey took him past "triumphal arcs" of flowers and "dances of liberty."[21] By contrast, Burke, commenting on the more famous Paris commemoration, thought it more "detestable" than October days of 1789, when the Paris mob invaded Versailles, killed their guards, and forced the king and queen to return to the Tuileries as virtual prisoners. He explicitly linked its elements to the philosophy of the revolution:

> Those who have made the exhibition of the 14th of July, are capable of every evil. . . . They are modern philosophers, which when you say of them, you express every thing that is ignoble, savage, and hard-hearted.[22]

However joyful and spontaneous this first significant revolutionary festival appeared to most people, Burke's 1791 comments may be the first in an enduring debate over the link between revolutionary festivals and violence.[23] After a celebration of the Festival of the Death of the King later in the 1790s, Burke's observations go even deeper. Profoundly aware that the revolutionaries grasp the nonrational sources of politics, Burke points out the close connection between control and violence in the festivals' role of establishing new manners:

The commonwealth which acts uniformly upon those principles [of putting monarchs to death]; and which after abolishing every festival of religion, chooses the most flagrant act of a murderous Regicide treason for a feast of eternal commemoration, and which forces all her people to observe it—this I call *Regicide by establishment* . . . Manners are of more importance than laws. Upon them, in a great measure, the laws depend. The law touches us but here and there, and now and then. Manners are what vex or sooth, corrupt or purify, exalt or debase, barbarize or refine us, by a constant, steady, uniform, insensible operation, like that of the air we breathe in. They give their whole form and colour to our lives. . . . Nothing in the Revolution, no not to a phrase or a gesture, not to the fashion of a hat or a shoe was left to accident. All has been the result of design.[24]

Burke had long been criticized by rationalists like Thomas Paine for theatrical rhetoric like this.[25] Ironically, however, Burke's counterrevolutionary sensibility is actually closer to the revolutionaries' than Paine's. Like them, he realizes that what we know about politics and its underlying social supports cannot be fully captured by rational thought. Our knowledge of liberty, equality, and fraternity—or diversity and tolerance in our own day—is so firmly integrated into our manners, seasonal observances, dress, gestures, and holidays, that it cannot be adequately communicated through logical, empirical rationality.

The 1794 Festival of the Supreme Being may serve as the most illuminating illustration of Burke's observations on the controlled nature of the revolutionary festivals. It was engineered by Robespierre and others in large part as a replacement to the Festival of Reason the year before. After 1790, the highly planned revolutionary festivals proclaimed liberty but contained almost no spontaneity.[26] Indeed, as the Revolution lost popular support, the more spontaneous elements often came from burlesques at the expense of Robespierre and other symbols of radicalism. In the Festival of the Supreme Being, celebrated on 20 Prairial Year II (June 8, 1794), every detail was rigorously set out, down to the arrangements of little girls' hair and the procession from an obelisk (where Fanaticism was ritualistically destroyed) to the Temple of the Eternal.

In his speech of 18 Floréal a month earlier, Robespierre had promoted the Cult of the Supreme Being as a way of binding France together in unity.[27] As France moved into the final weeks of the Great Terror, it was becoming clearer how the Festival of the Supreme Being established this unity in Paris and throughout France. Like the previous revolutionary festivals, exclusion was as important as inclusion. As the first Festival of the Federation had made a point of sorting out citizens from aristocrats, so this festival distinguished the regenerated citizens from the atheists.[28] In addition to its religious message, it aimed to unify France through its myth of utopian plenty. The starvation that was now threatening parts of France was excluded from view. Instead, plentiful cornucopias and agricultural products were put on display. Pregnant women were ordered to assemble early in the morning for the celebration, symbolizing the revolution's fecundity. The artistic program for the festival's most sacred space, a mountain around which the unified citizenry should take their rest, was painstakingly devised by Jacques-Louis David. The Festival of the Supreme Being even formalized its sorting mechanism by specifying punishment for those who sabotaged it: one could be declared a public enemy simply by failing to enjoy the festival.

The revolutionary effort to reorder time began in 1790 with the introduction of new festivals. But these holidays were merely a beginning. Enlightened French opinion had long hated the calendar of the old regime, crowded with saints' days and church holidays. The National Convention's adoption of the revolutionary calendar in 1793, one year after the proclamation of the Republic and the abolition of the monarchy, symbolized the Revolution's complete break with the culture of the past. It symbolized the creation of the Revolution's new citizen. The revolutionary calendar would produce an entirely new "framework of memory" to establish habits of the heart and mind appropriate to the new age.[29] The new calendar would be more rational. Its festivals would commemorate the Revolution. And it would be based on nature rather on Christian history.[30] These grand goals were interconnected, but it soon became clear that the overarching aim of a complete break with the past was too ambitious. As the years wore on, the French people became more insistent on celebrating Sundays and Catholic holidays, which doomed the entire revolutionary calendar. It was finally abolished in 1806 under Napoleon.

The new calendar, like much else in revolutionary France, was to be based on the more rational decimal system. Originally there were to be ten months divided into units of ten, ten-hour days. The months ultimately expanded back to twelve, but the Convention maintained a uniform thirty days for each month, and a ten-day "week," culminating on the *décadi* as the day of rest. There were five extra, or "epagomenal" days at the end of the year (six in leap years), which were individual holidays that bore the collective name *Sansculottides*. Robespierre himself successfully argued for rearranging the order of these holidays so that the first would be a festival of "virtue."[31]

The most significant of the decimal innovations, by far, was the replacement of the Christian Sabbath with the *décadi*. This was an extremely unpopular move that always required coercion, supplemented by pitiable efforts to make the day attractive by reading new laws, announcing new discoveries, agricultural methods, births, marriages, and adoptions.[32] In a 1795 warning to Holland, Burke, with typical prescience and typical lack of success, connected the rational program of the *décadi* with its profound rupture with tradition:

> It is not in my power to prevent the grand Patron of the reformed church, if he chuses it, from annulling the Calvinistick Sabbath, and establishing the Decadi of Atheism in all his states. He may even renounce and abjure his favorite mysticism in the temple of reason.[33]

Fairs, markets, post offices, and theaters were ordered closed on the *décadi*, and government officials could rest only on that day. Even after the end of the Terror, during the neo-Jacobin bid to regain control of the revolution in 1798, officials were told to avoid the old Christian holidays when scheduling markets and fairs. The message was clear: the revolution must be irreversible.

The new calendar commemorated the revolution's break with the old regime in the most deliberate way conceivable. The last day of the calendar year became September 21, the day on which the monarchy was abolished, followed by the proclamation of the Republic on the next day. Year One dated from September 22, 1792, the first day of the Republic. The original architect of the calendar, Romme, associated the old calendar with the evils of royalty, "fanaticism" (by which he primarily meant the church), and the persecution of philosophy.[34] Romme delighted in pointing out that the Republic's birth coincided with the equinox under the zodiacal sign of *la Balance* (Libra), thus providing a heavenly equality of light and dark to correspond to the Republic's proclamation of "civil and moral" equality. The Revolution's social regeneration seemed written in the stars.

Romme's proposed calendar was based on the history of the French Revolution up to 1793. A great shortcoming of his proposal was that the names for the months (*Jeu de Paume, la Bastille*) and days (pike, cockade) would not translate well across national boundaries. In the debate on the calendar, Bentabole warned the Convention about the limits of a calendar based on the history of one people or group. Unlike Muhammad's project of introducing a new calendar to separate Islam from the rest of the world, he said, "we wish to unite all peoples through fraternity."[35] Although the revolutionary festivals could enforce national unity in France, the political goals of the calendar should be universal in scope.

The Convention realized that undertaking significant calendrical reform would be a powerful sign that there was no turning back to the past. The Convention was not just instituting new annual holidays, as significant as those were, it was reconceiving time altogether, from the year down to the day, and from the week up to the month. Its calendar abolished the past. Ultimately it was based on nature rather than history, and Romme's historical nomenclature was replaced by Fabre d'Églantine's beautiful names for the months—Floréal (April 20–May 19), Fructidor (August 18–September 21), and so on. Still, by beginning the year on September 22, the first day of the French Republic, the calendar was unalterably French rather than universal. Ironically, the technical difficulties created by forcing the new year to coincide with the autumnal equinox contributed to the confusion, unpopularity, and ultimate failure of the calendar.[36]

Nevertheless, to revolutionaries like Fabre in the fall of 1793, early in the Terror and in the midst of a de-Christianization movement, the possibilities for purging the errors of the past and rejuvenating the nation seemed limitless. The first words of Fabre's report to the Convention (October 24, 1793) link political regeneration with the reform of the calendar.[37] The lies and prejudices of throne and altar sully every page of the Gregorian calendar, he says. It is not enough for the new calendar to be more precise. The visions of ignorance must give way to the realities of reason, and the prestige of the priest to the truth of nature.

Fabre gives the old religious calendar its due. By associating St. John's Day with the harvest and Rogation Days with spring, the priests said, in effect, "We priests are the ones who have made the fields green again . . . and refilled your granaries: believe us, respect us, obey us, enrich us, otherwise we will use our hail and thunder to punish you for your disbelief, laziness, and disobedience." Whether the old calendar actually contained that message or not, the new one certainly taught comparable revolutionary ones. It was accompanied by enforcement measures that discredited the old religious festivals, especially Christmas, Easter, and Lent.[38] Revolutionary officials dealt with disbelief, laziness, and disobedience through coercion. With even greater rigor than the revolutionary festivals, the new calendar provided a monthly and even daily structure for sorting out acceptable cultural patterns from counterrevolutionary ones.

Road to Terror—From Celebrants to Suspects

The Festival of the Supreme Being occurred throughout France about one year into the Terror. Two days after the festival, on June 10, 1794, Robespierre and his faction inaugurated the "Great Terror" with the infamous "Law of 22 Prairial." This law punished the enemies of the people by raising mere denunciation to the level of formal charges, eliminating the rights to counsel and the examination of witnesses, and making acquittal or death the only legal outcomes. After six weeks of this repression, on 9 Thermidor (July 27), Robespierre himself was arrested. He was executed the following day, and the Law of 22 Prairial was repealed on August 1. The Terror was over, at the cost of perhaps a half-million arrests, about 16,600 capital sentences, and tens of thousands dead of terroristic massacres, drownings, and other means.[39]

Some have found Robespierre's simultaneous promotion of a religious festival and the Terror puzzling. How could the same man simultaneously promote "the sweet knot of universal fraternity," while denouncing, imprisoning, and putting to death his allies of only a few months before, such as Georges Danton and Camille Desmoulins?[40] It seems hypocritical that Robespierre could condemn Catholic priests as "greedy, cruel, [and] implacable," while turning a blind eye to the merciless destruction of farms, women, and children in Lyons and the Vendée earlier in 1794.[41] Yet the charge of hypocrisy is the one of which Robespierre is least guilty. He is known to history as "the Incorruptible," and his manner of life was simple. Robespierre was living out, in the most unswerving way, the implications of the revolutionary view of virtue and knowledge. The deficiency of Enlightenment reason would be overcome by a new ordering of time, supported by a new system of weeks, months, and festivals. The weakness of virtue would be supported by terror.

Robespierre had explained why terror was the support for revolutionary virtue earlier in 1794, in his speech of 17 Pluviôse (February 5). At the outset of the speech Robespierre argued that the new republic demanded new virtues. The base and cruel passions will be chained, he proclaimed, whereas new laws will awaken generous and benevolent passions.[42] These laws will not be written on marble or stone, he continued, but on the hearts of all men. Unlike Socrates' art of the dialectic, which is written on the soul and submits to questions in the uncertain search for truth, Robespierre is quite certain that the regenerated citizens will see the truth as the Incorruptible sees it. The new citizen will substitute integrity and principle for outmoded forms of honor and custom, while greatness of soul will replace vanity: "[A]ll the virtues and miracles of the Republic [will replace] the vices and ridiculous practices of the monarchy."

Robespierre is not merely talking about reform, even reform on a large scale. His program, in the 1794 speeches, conceives a new structure for law and social relationships altogether. We must not allow ourselves to become the "dupe of words," he warns, and lavish our consolations on those who have died in the Terror. To punish oppressors is mercy; pardoning them is barbarism.

> The first maxim of our polity should be that we lead the people by reason and the enemies of the people by terror. If the wellspring of popular government in peacetime is virtue, its wellspring during revolution is simultaneously virtue and terror."[43]

Numerous commentators have noted that the Terror gave French citizens a clear choice: they could suspect others or become suspects themselves.[44] The death penalty for hoarders went into effect in the summer of 1793, and terror was made the "order of the day" on September 5. The measure that epitomized the Terror was the "law of suspects" (September 17, 1793), which made it a crime to fail to show one's devotion to the republic. But if the law existed only on the heart, rather than in a written document, how could one know the requirements of citizenship in the new republic? How could one obey the law and avoid suspicion? How could one ever know how to please the new authorities? Robespierre dismissed all such questions: "to destroy an abuse, it suffices to point it out. It's enough for us to name it, on behalf of the fatherland."[45]

Robespierre gives a brilliant justification for keeping the suspect in a perpetual state of uncertainty. In his important speeches of 17 Pluviôse and 18 Floréal, he insists that the revolution is "sublime," which (as I explained in the previous chapter) means that it defies rational representation. Sublime meanings go beyond the existing canons of rationality. To fall outside the language of the Revolution, comments Marie-Hélène Huet, is to fall into terror. She writes:

> [I]f the Revolution is to realize the sublimity and virtue that [make] up its very definition, it must transcend not only the sensible presentation of ideas but also the representation that is part and parcel of language itself. It must transcend "the abuses of language," which are always capable of betraying the meaning and truth of the sublime . . . Liberty, this sublime idea, should not have to defend its own cause. Language cannot be trusted.[46]

Robespierre seems to think that he is only denouncing treasonable words, tyrannical words, false, unjust, and vicious words. But his program had made language itself a suspect. Calendars and festivals, once instituted, did not defend themselves in words. They provided their own justification in images, gestures, and movements that distinguished citizens from counterrevolutionaries. It was therefore no accident that the Great Terror followed the Festival of the Supreme Being. They were all part of the same sorting mechanism. Robespierre had seen beyond the rationalism of the Enlightenment into the place where mysticism mingles with politics.[47]

Having concentrated all social, religious, political, and judicial power into one place, however, it transpired that only a god could have finally discriminated between the just and the unjust. Fabre, Robespierre, and Romme had a vision of taking their people beyond the fragmentation of Enlightenment. By failing to acknowledge the shortcomings of that vision, they led them into terror.

As the Terror began rising to its height in early 1794, Fabre met the guillotine during France's first passage through the month of "Germinal" (1794), which he had named to remind the people of the rising of the sap in March and April. In the weeks that followed, Robespierre overstepped his power as he drove the Terror to a boiling point. He was executed during the first "Thermidor," the month named for the heat of July and August. Romme followed a year later, when he cheated the guillotine by committing suicide after receiving the death sentence.

La Régénération du Peuple Moderne: Codifying Conduct and Disciplining Dissenters

I hope the first chapters of this book have shown my sympathy with much of the postmodern skepticism toward epistemological rationalism. I believe Robespierre and the calendrical reformers saw correctly that politics demands resources that go beyond the limits of empirical and rational knowledge. However, when shorn of traditional and religious limits and coupled with radical ideology and institutional power, a potent combination of ritual, virtue, and discipline develops. That combination deludes many, especially in today's education establishment, into thinking they can suppress free speech, ignore due process, and establish new rituals in their quest to "regenerate the people" under their control, to use Fabre's phrase.

The rest of this chapter will do more than list examples of excessive political correctness. I hope to explain why postmoderns gravitate to new festivals and disciplinary mechanisms in support of the virtues envisioned by their favorite political ideologies. Like other critics of political correctness, I hasten to observe that efforts to control thought are not limited to the left and that no one has set up a guillotine.[48] But no one set up a guillotine during the Red Scare of the 1950s either. That fact has done nothing to diminish more than forty years of commentary detailing that era's self-imposed censorship, the loss of institutional security, the abridgement of civil liberties, and the abuse of power. This story is similar. As the examples of the 1950s highlighted abuses from the right, today's examples come mostly from the left, whose political thought has generally allied itself most often with postmodernism, and whose adherents occupy the strongest positions of institutional authority in the university.

Like the actors in the first part of this chapter, the more recent part of this story begins with critiques of the past, followed by the awareness that rational knowledge will not create a new humanity, as demanded by the reigning ideologies. Codes then attempt to sort acceptable people from unacceptable ones, and dissenters are punished. New festivals and holidays try to establish new social rhythms, but, to the frustration of those in charge, the transformation is never complete.

An example from the area of sexual orientation may serve as a starting point. In 1992 the Mayor David Dinkins of New York and Joseph Fernandez, Chancellor of the city's public schools, enthusiastically promoted a new curriculum titled *Children of the Rainbow*.[49] Although the 443-page guide was billed as a multicultural curriculum, its section called "Fostering Positive Attitudes Towards Sexuality" proved to be a lightning rod for opposition. This section encouraged teachers to present homosexuality as normal, beginning in materials for first graders. Of the two hundred parents from Queens District 28 who showed up at a winter meeting to air their concerns about the curriculum, only about a quarter were white. In other words, they represented the truly multicultural character of New York City. The school board of their even more diverse neighbors in Queens District 24 had already rejected the curriculum—only to be suspended by the Chancellor. Although a few parents at the meeting expressed outright prejudice against homosexuals, most of them simply did not want their schools to teach that homosexuality was normal. Some called the curriculum indoctrination or brainwashing. One woman commented, "'What they're trying to do is take our children and form them into their ideal perfect society. So what if in ten years from now or twenty years from now they have a different ideal perfect society? And who's going to be raising our children's children? Us? Or the schools? These are our children.'"

This woman's comments were a protest against the coercive power of the mayor and the chancellor. She saw the curriculum as an attempt to establish a new social order by authoritative governmental figures. By adopting a curriculum that conformed to a certain ideology, however, the schools (these parents believed) were overstepping their social role and intruding into areas properly reserved for the family and religious institutions. Embedded in the curriculum, of course, was the clear message that past teachings about sexuality, including those of most of the parents of Queens District 28, were wrong.

A mere critique of the past, however, is rarely adequate for the most radical voices, as we have already seen. Moreover, the power of public school officials is tempered by the influence of families, neighborhoods, religious institutions, and electoral politics.

A truly transformative social order requires more control. It must be backed by a code, an enforcement mechanism, and ultimately, a calendar. The universities, relatively sheltered and autonomous, have offered greater scope for these experiments in recent years. By the 1990s, many universities had revamped freshman orientations and student life programs to serve particular visions of tolerance and diversity; they had developed harassment codes to enforce the new order. The critiques in response were not long in coming.[50]

When Timothy George was accepted as a resident adviser for a Cornell undergraduate dorm in 1990, his nine-day training session consisted of numerous seminars and role-plays designed to establish his identity as a "privileged person" and quash any dissent from multicultural or gay ideology.[51] On the first Sunday of training, he asked to be excused from a session to attend mass. "When he observed that his own diversity was not being recognized," writes Richard Bernstein, "he was told that his accusation was unfounded":

> "That day was gay day," he continued, "and they brought in members of ZAP, which is the gay, lesbian, and bisexual group. They were very nice people," Tim said, "but in the end they showed us explicit sex movies, first one of lesbians and then one about gay men . . . .

> "While it was playing, two people went around taking pictures of the RAs' reactions." This was apparently done to examine facial expressions to make sure that nobody was harboring any homophobic squeamishness while watching the film.

Beginning with Bernstein and continuing up to the present, one can find story after story of students and faculty who have been disciplined yet are unable to discover the charges against them. They are often unable to obtain information about the procedures under which their case will be considered or confront their accusers in a public forum.[52] Many have been threatened with formal dismissal proceedings, forced to leave their posts through more subtle coercion or disciplined in other ways. Some have fought back successfully, almost always facing long odds against an institution that pretends to value academic freedom. All this, at a time when studies show that students have a positive view of diversity.[53]

The parallels from history help us understand why diversity workshops, harassment policies, freshman orientation programs, and efforts to remove dissenters from campus have become codified at the historical moment when they are least needed. In France during the 1790s, revolutionary discipline actually intensified as the risks to the Revolution diminished.[54] Robespierre did not justify his actions as a temporary historical expedient. His justification lay in the creation of a new humanity. Revolutionary discipline became the mode of separating the unfit from the true citizens. To deviate from the vision, or even to tolerate apolitical expressions of citizenship, as Danton discovered, was to become an enemy. To be sure, isolated incidents of racism, sexism, and intolerance occur occasionally on U.S. campuses. The usual perpetrators, though, are rarely persons or groups with significant institutional power. They often come from disturbed or anonymous individuals, or from sophomoric groups whose offense is often bad taste or ignorance, rather than overt racism. The relevant point, however, is this: even if these incidents were to disappear entirely, the disciplinary mechanisms would always be needed to sort out those who have the new virtues engraved on their heart from those who do not.

It is striking that one of the most forceful defenders of campus codes is the postmodern theorist Stanley Fish. In his candid book, *There's No Such Thing as Free Speech* (1994), the premier deconstructionist of the United States writes as if free speech defenders either neglect or discount the political and historical traditions surrounding that right. Under his hands, merely placing his subject—free speech itself—into its political and historical context casts suspicion on it.[55] Like all deconstructionists, he is able to find a key that shows how the value in question—here, free speech—subverts itself:

> It is the job of the First Amendment to mark out an area in which competing views can be considered without state interference; but if the very marking out of that area is itself an interference (as it always will be), First Amendment jurisprudence is inevitably self-defeating

and subversive of its own aspirations. That's the bad news. The good news is that precisely *because* speech is never "free" . . . we must take responsibility for our verbal performances.

"Responsibility," in turn, justifies coercive codes for speech and behavior, according to Fish. Indeed, he maintains that ideological constraints actually generate speech in the first place. The only alternative to his own position that Fish seriously considers throughout the chapter is one that would defend hate speech. You are either a defender of speech codes or a defender of hatred, according to Fish's logic: you must ally yourself with the white supremacist bigotry of David Duke or accept Fish's critique of free speech.

Fish's argument opens with a lame attempt at humor: "Nowadays the First Amendment is the First Refuge of Scoundrels.—S. Johnson and S. Fish," he writes in paraphrase of a famous line from Boswell.[56] Fish's humor may obscure the crucial sorting function of his argument, but it is clear that he considers those who claim the protection of the first amendment are scoundrels— *scélérats*, in French, to use one of Robespierre's favorite censures:

> And when someone observes, as someone surely will, that antiharassment codes chill speech, one could reply that since speech only becomes intelligible against what isn't being said . . . the only question is the political one of which speech is going to be chilled, and, all things considered, it seems a good thing to chill speech like "nigger," "cunt," "kike," and "faggot."

Given the sorting function of Fish's view of virtue, it is no wonder that students like George must be disciplined. More broadly, Christian student groups that teach that sexual intimacy should be reserved for a husband and wife are silencing other possibilities, and therefore they must be silenced. In the two decades since George's run-in, many campuses have attempted to do just that.[57]

Neither the postmodern thought of Fish nor the hypermodern French revolutionary ideology can provide a workable practice of freedom. For them, freedom dissolves into power: "someone is always going to be restricted next," writes Fish, "and it is your job to make sure that the someone is not you."[58]

Once the virtuous citizens have been sorted out from the scoundrels, the institutional use of power, in the form of codes, holidays, and calendars, makes complete sense. A word like *cunt* which violated Fish's code in 1994, is now a favored term in workshops on "Vagina Day," the most recent holiday of radical feminism. Notice the intellectual and political consequence of Fish's reasoning: those who couple strong social commitments with an extreme postmodern suspicion of knowledge can change the definitions of virtue and vice almost at will. Once they gain power, they are impervious to the rational appeal of a dissenter. And dissenters—those who do not have the laws of postmodern ideologies written on their heart—are bound to get into trouble.

Ultimately, Fish's combination of postmodern epistemology and extreme political commitment collapses in on itself. Those who suspect that rationality is little more than a mask for power find it difficult to compromise or to see their own weaknesses once they come to assume power themselves. They may come to find themselves in a situation parallel to that of Fish himself, two years after he wrote his critique of free speech. Fish was executive editor of the journal that failed to spot a hoax masquerading as a genuine commentary on science, as I explained in the previous chapter. When Fish was caught, he refused to acknowledge his error and reacted with anger.[59] Most of the public simply laughed.

If compromise is difficult, however, university leaders also find it unpleasant to discipline their opponents. Discipline is hard on those who exert it as well as those who receive it. It would be much more effective if everyone simply enjoyed the Vagina Day festival. But not everyone does. The Festival of the Supreme Being was supposed to be a happy occasion. The newly constituted French citizenry was supposed to celebrate their new virtues joyfully. But the official festivals were so boring that participation fell off.[60] The revolutionaries thus anticipated the problem encountered by their postmodern descendants: what do you do when people do not want to come to the party? Ultimately, discipline becomes the fulfillment of the utopian festival, in both revolutionary and postmodern times.

New Holidays and Calendar Reform in Revolutionary and Postmodern Times

The revolutionary and postmodern ideologue recognize a deep truth: festivals have a persuasive power far beyond merely rational arguments. It is one thing to deliver arguments for a new concept of the citizen and society. By contrast, getting people to participate in parades, songs, and spectacles involves them in performing new roles, symbolic of the new order. Holiday activities model, if they do not actually create, new citizens for a new society. New festivals thus finesse the problem of making rational defenses of the codes and disciplinary procedures needed to restrain dissenters. The new citizen learns by doing.

A new calendar goes further still. The way we mark time tells us a great deal about ourselves, perhaps more than the laws we create, the money we spend, and the beliefs we profess. Although forums, lectures, and books can promote new ideals, if we then return to Christmas, Passover, and the Fourth of July, what changes have we really made? A truly transformative, new order that wishes to compete with the political and religious order of the past will create a new calendar.[61]

Here is why: rational, political programs are always disputable, always open to contradiction, change, or defeat. To create the humanity that will dwell permanently in their new order, new rituals, holidays, and saints are needed. These new social rhythms will then establish loyalties that are beyond dialogue and dispute. During Black History Month, we are not asked to debate affirmative action. We are asked to celebrate diversity. During Women's History Month, we do not reconsider the question of abortion. We are asked to wear a ribbon. On the last Sunday in June, we are asked to march for gay pride, not to engage the serious questions of sexuality.

The verbs are important: celebrate, wear, and march. These actions go far beyond purely intellectual functions. They either presuppose rational assent to an ideology or bypass rationality altogether, especially when the young are required to participate. Celebrating a value, wearing a ribbon or costume, and marching for a cause ratify a value. Nevertheless, in the broader view of knowledge taken by this book, they also contribute to what we know. They involve the emotions in the service of supposed truths, like the hymns of Isaac Watts, and are occasions for storytelling, like the narratives of Daniel Defoe. In the case of Earth Day celebrations, they even promote a more personal relationship to nature, like the poetry of Christopher Smart.

In addition, whether we sympathize with the recent holidays or criticize them, they have much in common with traditional holidays. Christmas, Passover, and the Fourth of July are emotional events, surrounded by rituals and stories that defy complete explanations, or metanarratives. If the parents are Christians, Jews, or patriotic Americans, they want their children to participate in these traditions from their earliest youth, before they can reason. They want them to establish literal "seasons" of their own lives according to a general pattern that the parents have found to be good.

As the French found, however, a deep transformation of social reality is not only difficult; it is extremely untidy. Then as now, new festivals and calendars inevitably become sorting mechanisms, and those in power have to decide how severely they will discipline dissenters. A recent Vagina Day celebration at Roger Williams University in Rhode Island will illustrate both the goals and the problems encountered by the most radical calendrical reformers.[62]

In the week or so before Vagina Day, celebrated on February 14, a participating university will typically be blanketed by flyers (reading "My Vagina is Flirty," "My Vagina is Huggable," etc.), followed by a series of workshops on the orgasm, empowerment, and so on. Students receive vagina-shaped lollipops, and the school's women's center typically offers institutional support. The centerpiece of the holiday is a presentation of *The Vagina Monologues*, a play in which men appear primarily as rapists and clitoridectomists. In the play, sexual pleasure is removed from its relationship to romantic love and raised to an end in itself.

Since February 14 really has no religious or national significance, Vagina Day (however radical in intent) is a relatively minor calendrical reform.[63] Still, it is no accident that its climax comes on Valentine's Day, the traditional holiday for celebrating romantic love in all its various forms. By contesting that holiday, Vagina Day does more than simply interrupt the older way of thinking about romantic love. On the hundreds of campuses where the Vagina Day College Initiative has been carried out, participants literally have no time to engage older views of romance or relations between the sexes. The holiday is designed to promote a new model for sexual relations, as the promoters of Vagina Day make clear.[64] By reordering time, the Vagina Day Initiative actually reduces intellectual diversity about sexual love: It captures institutional space and time for its purposes only. It substitutes the diversity of Western thought about love, from the sexual passion of the ancients through medieval courtly love and the Renaissance reconciliation of love with marriage, with its thoughts alone.

At Roger Williams University, the College Republicans decided to question their school's 2005 celebration of Vagina Day. They countered by initiating "Penis Day," complete with mock-flyers and a satirical *Penis Monologues*. A friendly phallus, Testaclese, paraded around campus and was even embraced by the university provost (who thought he was hugging a mushroom). Although the school proclaims its commitment to diversity, the College Republicans were told to stop distributing their flyers and keep their mascot off campus.[65] When they refused, the Testaclese costume was confiscated and locked up. Two students, Monique Stuart and Andy Mainiero, received letters of reprimand and were placed on probation by the Office of Judicial Affairs. The College Republicans were suspended for a year, unable to operate as a club, hold events, or receive a budget.[66]

As in the French Revolution, an institutional commitment to a new cultural order may require that dissenters be sorted out and dealt with. Occasionally this discipline has successfully invoked the law: in 2003 a Canadian teacher was suspended from his post for writing a letter to the editor that homosexual orientation could be changed, and a Swedish pastor was convicted of violating his country's hate-speech law for preaching against homosexuality.[67]

Unlike these high profile cases, however, dissent is generally quashed peacefully and silently on U.S. university campuses through the force of majority opinion. "As long as the majority is doubtful," wrote Tocqueville on the lack of independent thought in the United States, "one speaks":

> but when it has irrevocably pronounced, everyone becomes silent and friends and enemies then seem to hitch themselves together to its wagon. The reason for this is simple: there is no monarch so absolute that he can gather in his hands all the strength of society and defeat resistance, as can a majority vested with the right to make the laws and execute them.[68]

There is no more irrevocable pronouncement than an institutionally sanctioned holiday. Moreover, even if a numerical majority on campus may not support the holiday in all of its aspects, few individual students or faculty have the time, resources, or social support to express disagreement. Tocqueville, of course, was speaking of American society as a whole, not the sheltered world of the university campus. Yet it is instructive that this observer of the United States, whose extended family had been decimated by guillotine forty years before, warns that the mild despots most likely to undermine U.S. democracy would resemble "school-masters," who would keep its citizens in a perpetual state of childhood. This "tutelary power," he concludes, "willingly works for their happiness; but it wants to be the unique agent and sole arbiter of that . . . [C]an it not take away from them entirely the trouble of thinking and the pain of living?"

Each of the new months or holidays promoted by recent social reformers has its unique history. Each has a different place along a continuum of ideological commitment. The histories of Black History Month and the Martin Luther King Jr., holiday are rather moderate in political terms. The first "Negro History Week" in 1926 (the origin of Black History Month) was sponsored in the week of February closest to the birthdays of Abraham Lincoln and Frederick Douglass.[69] Negro History Week thus aimed at high-lighting the contributions of blacks to a shared U.S. culture, not at presenting an utterly new vision of race and U.S. history. With few individual exceptions, all sides of the political spectrum now revere the achievement of Martin Luther King in reforming U.S. society. Moreover, King and many other African American reformers have such deep roots in U.S. religious and political traditions that the holiday and the month can never successfully present themselves as offering a revolutionary break with the past.

Kwanzaa has much more radical origins. Some of its advocates continue to promote extreme ideological goals, whereas others have moderated their tone and ambitions over the years. Established in 1966, Kwanzaa offers African Americans a seven-day festival on the final days of the year in response to the "cultural and economic exploitation perpetrated against us during . . . the Christmas season."[70] In 1999 journalist Tony Snow reported that the "official Kwanzaa web site" (which is now rather tame) claimed that Kwanzaa should help create "conditions that would enhance the revolutionary social change for the masses of Black Americans." On that site, the holiday's originator, Maulana Karenga, still warns that "nothing should be advocated or practiced which violates the original spirit, basic purpose and essential concepts which informed the creation and practice of Kwanzaa."[71]

One of the founders of Earth Day is equally visionary, though more open to synthesizing his views with other political and religious visions.[72] John McConnell insists that Earth Day should be celebrated as a global holiday on the vernal equinox. Lifting a page from Romme, McConnell argues that the equality of day and night can serve as a model of balance and equality for the holiday's comprehensive goals: eliminating poverty and initiating "peace, justice, and the care of Earth."[73]

Whether they ultimately succeed or not, the originators of these new holidays understand that the ordering of time reflects our most profound cultural expressions of the sacred. Sociologist Émile Durkheim taught that classifying our experience in terms of sacred or profane was essential to human understanding.[74] Because we experience nature only in time, the ways we divide time, from the year and the months down to the week and the day, reflect deep cultural values. Through our sabbaths and holidays, we turn "nature" into "culture," by interrupting the temporal continuity of nature. Kwanzaa's use of the days after Christmas through New Year's Day may thus seem like a brilliant choice. These seven days seem like the odds and ends of the old year—*epagomenal* days, to use the technical term—and many modern Americans already treat them as holidays. Similarly, Earth Day's McConnell made much of the rare 2005 coincidence of Palm Sunday with the vernal equinox to promote his holiday: the resurrection of Christ and the resurrection of Nature seemed an appealing way to market Earth Day. But one of the key sociological insights in this area is that truly sacred human activities must take turns, both with normal activities and with each other. They cannot occur simultaneously.[75] No one who seriously celebrates Easter will combine it with Earth Day; Kwanzaa's proximity to Christmas will forever make it a weak rival to a powerful religious and national holiday.

Nevertheless, Karenga and McConnell have a deep, instinctual comprehension of these matters. In this, they parallel the French revolutionaries and their critics. Like the architects of the French revolution, modern calendar reformers like Karenga, McConnell, and Eve Ensler, the driving force behind Vagina Day, hope that their movements communicate a significant rejection of the past.

The only recent U.S. calendar change in any way comparable to the French reforms was the 1983 institution of Martin Luther King, Jr. Day as a new national holiday. In that act, controversial enough in its day, the U.S. Congress and President Ronald Reagan recognized that the country had rethought its past history and its future commitments to racial equality. Yet even in this instance, the U.S. action was far less ambitious than those of the French Convention. The Convention was not just instituting new annual holidays, as significant as those are. It was reconceiving time altogether. The Martin Luther King Jr. holiday does not attempt to do anything remotely similar to that. Nor do month-long celebrations, such as Women's History Month. The national promoters of Women's History Month have some radical goals, but that month is still "March" to the rest of the world. When Women's History Month is accompanied by teaching kits and group observances (in a school setting for instance), it takes on additional institutional power, to be sure. But it will always be interrupted by Lent, St. Patrick's Day, and that most anticipated of academic holidays, spring vacation.

If their power does not rise to the level of the revolutionaries', however, the instincts of today's activists are remarkably similar, down to the level of the gestures and costumes they adopt for their festivals. They defend the exclusion of traditional holidays and place a premium on being seen at the correct celebrations. A threat of violence, whether real or symbolic, is often just below the surface. They even carry sacred objects that embody their values, as the celebrants in the revolutionary festivals did, and their vision is carried as much by style as substance.[76]

On the morning of the annual Gay Pride March in 2005, a Minneapolis radio host took a call from a listener who complained that his workplace promoted gay and lesbian issues during June but had refused to allow similar recognition for Christmas. The radio commentator was unmoved. The Christmas season starts in October, she said, and is hardly unreported. So what if the workplace is the one venue where Christmas not acknowledged? Although she refused to admit the power of institutional promotion of Gay Pride Month and the exclusion of the Christian holiday, her listeners got the point: institutional establishment of a new virtue justifies the exclusion of the old.

As in the Festival of the Federation, it is important to be seen at the Minneapolis Gay Pride March. A St. Paul congresswoman waved her way down the 2005 Minneapolis procession, along with candidates for governor, legislature, and the park board. The AIDS quilt was displayed and revered in a way that recalled the French federative banner—the main relic and sacred object of that revolutionary festival. There was particular tension in the 1790 Festival of the Federation to see if priests would use the Eucharist in some way to bless the revolution. Some of the marchers in Minneapolis have been from gay Catholic movements, urging the Eucharist for practicing homosexuals, against the directives of their hierarchy. The threat of violence, largely symbolic in the 1790 marches, is symbolic in the Gay Pride March as well: the fall of the Bastille was present but in the background of the federative festivals; similarly, the Stonewall riots provide the background for Gay Pride marches. Symbols of the old regime were degraded during some of the French festivals—a monkey dressed as a bishop or the figure of William Pitt carried on a donkey—which finds its parallel Gay Pride marchers dressed in bright red, as mock Catholic cardinals, or celebrants whose tee shirts proclaim obscenities directed at public officials. Particular hairstyles, costumes, even ways of walking—the parallels are almost without limit—show one's endorsement of a new social order. Every detail works toward a unanimity of feeling, behavior, and thought, to the exclusion of alternatives.

For many years, students who have disagreed with feminist, multiculturalist, or gay ideology have been diagnosed with "resistance" to their professors, rather than granted the right to arrive at legitimate differences of opinion. [77] Scholarly papers recommend ways of treating resistance; allowing students to come to conclusions that differ from the teacher's ideology is generally not among the options.[78] Like the French revolutionaries, however, those who enforce the postmodern virtues have come to realize that coercion cannot succeed by itself. They must support their social vision with celebration and discipline. The phrase <i>Celebrate Diversity</i> now represents something of a catch-all exhortation: if celebrants at the Gay Pride March do not clap loudly enough, they are encouraged to celebrate; to boost attendance at the diversity rally, students are told to celebrate.

Ultimately the French revolutionary festivals died of boredom. The nature of man and society would not conform to their model of a new social vision. Citizens cannot pretend forever. I suspect that something similar will happen in our own day. Society will change, of course, but its shape will never conform to the ideological vision of the postmodern celebration. You cannot force people to party.

6

TRADITION AS A WAY OF KNOWING
IN EDMUND BURKE AND
HANS-GEORG GADAMER

In my teaching I often encounter students who say that we can never escape our prejudices. They are not just criticizing the prejudices of the past as outworn beliefs that have been put behind us. They are also including their own opinions, frequently prefacing their comment with a phrase like, "Speaking from my own biased point of view. . . ." Earlier in my career this troubled me. "Why bother with school at all," I wondered, "if your education cannot penetrate to the level of your deepest beliefs?" Now, however, I think my students are on to something important, something that goes beyond the modern assumption that the best learner is someone who approaches his subject as a blank slate, or someone who sees her past as a weight to be cast off.

It is not as though the modern assumptions have vanished. When the speaker at a recent Ivy League commencement congratulated the graduates for having left behind many of the prejudices with which they entered college, I looked around at the parents there, wondering how they took this estimate of their childrearing. College curricula often encourage students to "wrestle with [their] own prejudices and biases" and urge students to think critically.[1] Rare is the U.S. school that acknowledges the value of rooting one's critical thought in a tradition.[2]

155

These trends are a result, in part, of the power of majority opinion: it is difficult for anyone, including academics, to buck the antitraditionalist tide. In part, they reflect the lingering Enlightenment assumptions held by baby boomers, who will continue to run U.S. institutions for a few more years. Many of these men and women still accept the Enlightenment assumptions that reject forms of knowing that do not measure up to rationalistic or empirical standards.[3] The next generations, however—Gen X, the millenials, and their successors—have not accepted their parents' critique of the past. They are unlikely to believe, as some baby boomers did, for instance, that it is wise to raise children entirely outside of a religious tradition so that they can choose a particular religion freely, on the basis of pure intellectual assent. In my opening example, my students were not just acknowledging the cultural and personal *limits* with which they entered any conversation, they were also affirming the *value* of their background for acquiring new knowledge. Their instincts are generally sound, I believe. Moreover, if assumptions need to be challenged, as of course they must, one such assumption is whether it is desirable or even possible to lay aside one's past at the outset of any serious learning. The first chapter of this book has already established the difficulty of doing this, for if we gain knowledge from the past stories of which we are a part, then our past is a necessary resource in acquiring new knowledge. The second chapter, on worship, suggested an increased openness to tradition in the emergent church's use of icons and liturgies.

This chapter will look at a division within postmodern thought on how to approach the past. On the one hand, many dominant postmodern thinkers have regarded past writings with suspicion. The "hermeneutics of suspicion" has become a methodological tool in many postmodern approaches to literature, from feminism to postcolonial and new historicist treatments, which typically assume that a primary task of interpretation is to uncover and criticize the prejudices embodied in earlier literature.[4] On the other hand, Hans-Georg Gadamer, whose emphasis on the limits to knowledge has certain affinities with postmodern thought, has done more than any recent thinker to show the necessity of embracing one's history and even the "prejudices"—or prejudgments—with which we enter any discussion.[5]

First, however, I will go back to the eighteenth century to look at a set of questions surrounding tradition in Edmund Burke's critique of the French Revolution. I will begin with a significant aesthetic issue, literary allusion, and then move to a historical one, the British Constitution. The Constitution was crucial to Burke's view of history and politics, and allusion is one of his major rhetorical tools, though neither one comes close to exhausting Burke's aesthetic practice nor historical thought. These two issues are central, however, to an understanding of tradition in Burke's thought. I will then examine the role that Burke gives to "taste" as a standard for judging how new elements may be incorporated into tradition. Finally, I will move to Gadamer to show how he picks up and extends the Enlightenment debate over tradition and knowledge.

Burke's Use of Allusion:
Learning through the Literary Tradition

Before Edmund Burke published his *Reflections on the Revolution in France* in November 1790, his political ally Philip Francis questioned the timing and the taste of his manuscript. It was beneath him, Francis warned, for Burke's volume to target a mere Unitarian divine, Richard Price, who had delivered a prorevoluntionary sermon likening the French Revolution to the Revolution of 1688.[6] Burke's book would provoke a pamphlet war, he predicted, and his defense of the Queen Marie Antoinette would lay Burke open to unnecessary attack. In the book, Burke describes his first sight of the future queen of France at Versailles (in 1773) as a "delightful vision" and compares her to "the morning-star, full of life, and splendor, and joy":

> I thought ten thousand swords must have leaped from their scab-bards to avenge even a look that threatened her with insult.—But the age of chivalry is gone . . . —That of sophisters, oeconomists, and calculators, has succeeded; and the glory of Europe is extinguished for ever.[7]

Francis' letter had been brutal: the lines on the queen were "pure foppery," he charged, and compared Antoinette to Messalina, the famously licentious wife of the Roman emperor

Claudius.[8] In reply, Burke was equally uncompromising: "I know nothing of your story of Messalina," he wrote to Francis:

> Am I obliged to prove juridically the Virtues of all those I shall see suffering every kind of wrong, and contumely, and risk of Life, before I endeavour to interest others in their sufferings? . . . What, are not high Rank, great Splendour of descent, great personal Elegance and outward accomplishment, ingredients of moment in forming the interest we take in the Misfortunes of Men? The minds of those who do not feel thus, are not even Dramatically right. "What's Hecuba to him, or he to Hecuba, that he should weep for her?" Why, because she was Hecuba, the Queen of Troy, the Wife of Priam, and sufferd [sic] in the close of Life, a thousand Calamities! I felt too for Hecuba, when I read the fine Tragedy of Euripides upon her Story: and I never inquired into the Anecdotes of the Court or City of Troy before I gave way to the Sentiments which the author wished to inspire.[9]

Not surprisingly, the passage on Marie Antoinette stayed, and Francis' predictions were proved true.

A great deal is going on in this letter to Francis. Burke is fully aware of the rumors concerning the queen, of course, but unwilling to concede anything to them. He chooses not to "know" them as Francis does and rejects any responsibility for proving the queen's character "juridically," that is, by the rational and empirical methods required by a legal inquiry. By disagreeing with Francis over "Messalina" and substituting "Hecuba," Burke signals a disagreement over the past and its meaning for the present. He locates their dispute in the area of tradition: which is the proper ancestor for Marie Antoinette? Francis and his allies are thinking of Marie Antoinette-as-Messalina, in a tradition that might be labeled "queenly profligates." Burke's allusions to Euripides and *Hamlet* place her in a tradition of "queens whose reign is unjustly destroyed." Both are legitimate traditions: some queens were profligates; others were unjustly destroyed. Marie Antoinette may even belong in both traditions. Burke knows that there is not a single unitary tradition that all knowledgeable people must accept.[10] But which is most applicable to 1789–1790? That is the choice he lays before Francis—and us.

Burke's choice of one tradition over the other involves many simultaneous modes of thought—political and historical analysis, judgments of taste, and literary criticism. Although these all rely on reason, they cannot be settled with reference to a rational or empirical method. Burke's chooses to direct our attention to the queen's "high rank" and "misfortunes," which allude to Aristotle's famous discussion of tragic figures in the *Poetics*. This in turn leads him to the character of Hecuba as developed by Euripides and modified by Shakespeare. When he says, "The minds of those who do not feel thus, are not even dramatically right," Burke is refusing to separate aesthetics from rational political knowledge—a separation assumed in the epistemology of many Enlightenment figures like Thomas Paine, as I will explain. By alluding to Hamlet's speech on the fictional Hecuba (*Hamlet* Act 2, scene 2, vv. 534–91), Burke takes matters a step further. Remarking on the player's ability to work up tears for a fictional queen, Hamlet reproaches himself for not having revenged his father's death. Burke is thus suggesting that we, like Hamlet, deserve reproach if we cannot feel for the calamities that have befallen the French political order. Something is missing from our education if we have not learned such feelings. It is worth noting that Burke's exemplary figure comes from fiction—Hamlet—rather than from the historically verifiable figure chosen by Francis, Messalina. Someone who compares the political fortunes of the Queen of France during 1789 and 1790 to Messalina rather than to Hecuba has a deficient imagination, Burke suggests, along with bad taste and inadequate historical judgment.[11]

That may sound like a lot for a couple of allusions to bear. It may seem impossible to decide whether Burke was justified in applying aesthetic categories from Aristotle and a speech from Shakespeare to contemporary French royalty. These are typical of the difficulties in reading Burke today. He deploys a wealth of allusion. He has an astonishing command of seventeenth- and eighteenth-century poetry, the English Bible, William Shakespeare, John Milton, numerous French authors, and the literatures of Greece and Rome. The difficulties of this passage continue to mount, as Burke closes his lament for the age of chivalry with an allusion to Horace's "Art of Poetry."

> The precept given by a wise man, as well as a great critic, for the construction of poems, is equally true as to states. *Non satis est pulchra esse poemata, dulcia sunto.* There ought to be a system of manners in every nation which a well-formed mind would be disposed to relish. To make us love our country, our country ought to be lovely.[12]

How convincing are the aesthetic categories, activated by Burke's allusion to Horace, in establishing a contrast between the cold and tasteless political philosophy of the revolutionaries with the cultural inheritance he is defending? To clarify the issues raised by Burke's use of allusion, we need a deeper understanding of how that literary tool works. How does allusion create new meaning— new knowledge—through its relationship to tradition?

Literary allusion is more than a direct reference to a past work. Well deployed, an allusion activates the meaning of an older work and gives it new life within the structure of a new work.[13] What is more, a good allusion alters the meaning of the older work as well. For those who know both sources, the older work never looks quite the same again. Perhaps the example of biblical literature will help. In Western culture the most influential set of literary allusions are those in the Christian Scriptures that refer to the Hebrew Bible. Whether it is David as a type of Christ or parallels between Passover and the Passion narratives of the Gospels, Christian allusions to the Hebrew Scriptures created new meanings for the early followers of Christ—and simultaneously turned the Hebrew Bible into the Old Testament.

The meaning of Burke's allusion to Horace goes far beyond Burke's short explanation of the Latin quotation. The reference brings to mind Roman civilization at its height. It calls attention to Burke's own Horatian sententiousness in the chiastic assertion that ends the paragraph: "to make us love our country, our country ought to be lovely." What is more, it subtly makes the "beautiful" elements of a peaceful society stand out against the terrifying, "sublime" elements of revolution: a peaceful, beautiful society rests on manners; by contrast, a revolution keeps the threat of violence just below the surface, well within the peripheral vision of its opponents.[14]

Allusion is also more than an attempt to establish authority by appealing to the past. Allusion is a literary tool, not a logical or legal technique. It tries to expand the meaning of an event with reference to the past, but only the reader or hearer can decide the validity of the allusion. An allusion attempts to mediate the present by the past. In deploying an allusion, a writer is lifting up part of a past tradition, making his or her readers conscious of it and requiring those readers to reflect on it. That reflection occurs in a new, present-day context, whose meaning the writer hopes to clarify with reference to the past. The clarification succeeds or fails according to the reader's judgment. To return to a biblical example, some will recognize the New Testament allusions to Christ as the Passover Lamb without accepting that particular meaning. Burke's strategy in the Horatian allusion is to illustrate the barrenness of revolutionary political rhetoric in hopes that his readers will recognize the rich beauty of his alternative. Accepting the validity of that connection, however, remains up to the reader.

Allusion, therefore, presupposes reflection on tradition. It neither presupposes an uncritical acceptance of tradition, nor makes history its final authority, as Burke's critics sometimes charge.[15] Allusion does, however, presuppose that our consciousness of the present has a history that we must acknowledge. We cannot step outside of history, into an objective realm—of abstract universal rights, the state of nature, or any nonhistorical space—to gain pure political knowledge. If we could, there would be little reason to study the past and absolutely no reason to allude to past works.

Francis thought Burke was alluding to the wrong literary and historical characters. It was probably not important to Francis that one character was historical, whereas the other was literary. He would likely agree with Burke's assumption that one can learn as much from the fictional Hecuba as from the factual Messalina. Others in the late eighteenth century, however, would make all such literary knowledge either irrelevant or strictly subordinate to the rational knowledge that one can derive from history. We have already seen this approach to knowledge in Daniel Defoe's ambivalence over *Robinson Crusoe*. For Thomas Paine, fact was the opposite of fiction. For Burke, by contrast, both fiction and non-fictional accounts could be true or false, depending on the taste with which they were presented.

Burke's more radical opponents, such as Paine, deny the validity of his style altogether. He contests Burke's impassioned account of the "October days" (October 5–6, 1789), when Louis XVI and Marie Antoinette were forced from Versailles to Paris by a mob of Parisian women. "This is neither the sober style of history," writes Paine, "nor the intention of it."[16] Burke should lay aside his theatrical style and "recollect that he is writing history, and not plays; and that his readers will expect truth, and not the spouting rant of high-toned exclamation."

Paine is making a much more radical critique of Burke than Francis had done. Francis disputes Burke's taste but not his decision to use literary art. For Paine, it is artfulness itself that is questionable: "[H]e degenerates into a composition of art, and the genuine soul of nature forsakes him."[17] Paine's rationalism brings him to the point of opposing nature and art. He goes on to ridicule the historic authority of the British crown as a mere "metaphor, shown at the Tower for six-pence or a shilling a-piece." Communication between two such men could hardly occur. Their approaches to knowledge are irreconcilable.

Paine's claims for his own writings are similarly radical. After his own account of the October days, Paine concludes that if his version of the facts is true, they "show the *necessity* of the French revolution," as if his historical analysis were akin to a geometrical proof.[18] Paine sets out his criteria for truthful writing in this section of *The Rights of Man*: "Before anything can be reasoned upon to a conclusion, certain facts, principles, or data, to reason from, must be established, admitted or denied."[19] One begins with a principle, analyzes the facts, and ends by concluding the necessity of an event. It is all rational, all scientific—yet impossible for Paine himself to follow. Far from engaging Burke in a discussion of the history of the English Revolution of 1688—the basis for Burke's critique of the French Revolution—Paine immediately turns to the creation of Adam and the state of nature.[20] Having promised an analysis based on historical fact, then, he produces a rationalistic argument based on an imagined or prehistorical age. He draws many conclusions about natural rights, civil rights, equality, the authority of the present over the past, and political authority, none of which may be confirmed by appeal to historical data.

Burke's use of allusion provides a key to his different mode of understanding. Even his harshest critics grant that his style is artful. Far from adopting Paine's extreme rationalist opposition between art and a true knowledge of society and human nature, however, Burke sees the one as inseparable from the other. "Art is man's nature," he declares in his *Appeal from the New to the Old Whigs* (1791).[21] In this declaration, he denies the Enlightenment assumption that one can abstract human nature from the historic, artificial conventions that have become part of social life. Abstracting humanity from social life, in his view, does not reveal the state of nature; it reveals our capacity for inhumanity.[22]

Although this sketch may clarify Burke's critique of Enlightenment theories of the state of nature, social contract, and natural rights, it does not take us far in a positive direction. Burke's positive alternative is still a long way off. How does Burke's allusive style really work? How does he make readers conscious of the past and cause them to reflect on its meaning for the present? If allusions are not deployed as authorities, in the way that Paine's "facts" demand to be, what claims do they have on the present? How does allusion create knowledge from the literary tradition?

Some have argued that Burke uses his literary knowledge, especially his knowledge of learned languages, as a weapon in the debate over the French Revolution.[23] The French Revolution was a bourgeois revolution of citizens against gentlemen, and this argument maintains that Burke uses his Latin to exclude middle-class aspirants from political leadership—men Burke ridicules as attorneys, hairdressers, hack writers, and tallow chandlers.[24] There is some truth to this view. He was often carried away with the power of his own rhetoric. Still, to charge that Burke's use of literary allusion functions primarily as a class weapon is misleading and reductive. Previously in his career, Burke had deployed allusions in his passionate speeches and pamphlets on America and Ireland, where his defense of those two peoples cannot be construed as having a class basis.[25] In addition, revolutionary writers and artists (or those viewed favorably by the revolutionary side) were fully capable of contesting Burke's way of incorporating the past into the present, and often satirized his rhetoric with allusions of their own.[26] Finally, the charge distinguishes unnaturally between Burke's use of Latin allusions and the ones derived from English and biblical literature. We may find them different in kind, but Burke did not. They all represented a "choice of inheritance" from the past, to use Burke's own language, and the Bible in particular was used by all sides in the debate. Burke had been galvanized into writing the *Reflections* by a sermon that used biblical allusion to link the French Revolution with the Revolution of 1688, the basis of the constitutional framework that Burke cherished. He knew that the literary tradition was contested ground, and his epistemological purpose was clear: by reviving certain parts of that tradition in particular, imaginative ways, he intended to supply the knowledge that contemporary English society most urgently needed.[27]

Burke's allusive strategy comes from his deep sense of a people's rootedness in the past. "Society is indeed a contract," he writes, in grudging acknowledgment of the influence of social contract theory. But contrary to the revolutionary implication that contract theory grants supreme authority to the present generation, he continues:

> [I]t is not a partnership in things subservient only to the gross animal existence of a temporary and perishable nature. It is a partnership in all science; a partnership in all art; a partnership in every virtue and in all perfection. As the ends of such a partnership cannot be obtained in many generations, it becomes a partnership not only between those who are living, but between those who are living, those who are dead, and those who are to be born.[28]

Burke here affirms that we belong to history; our consciousness of the present is brought into being by the past. To consider the person primarily as an individual, rights-bearing creature, with no relation to his or her cultural history is, for Burke, literally inhumane.

Allusions to the writings of the past are particular ways of incorporating the culture of the past into the present. Not everything is brought forward. Much is forgotten; everything is altered by the process. The choices, omissions, and alterations represent the writer's rational deliberation and his unconscious inclinations. Unlike the scientific tradition, moreover, where the knowledge that is preserved depends on the consensus of an entire community, the literary tradition gives an individual writer the privilege and responsibility of selecting from the past, based on his or her own taste, imagination, and wit.[29] Allusion gives new life to the literature of the past, creating new knowledge in the process. Burke's allusions generally try to create a sympathetic connection between past and present. They try to show an unbroken cultural continuity from classical to modern times, often by way of contesting contemporary Enlightenment doctrines.

In a difficult passage from his *Appeal from the New to the Old Whigs*, for instance, Burke alludes to Virgil at the end of a refutation of the theory of consent as the basis for all political authority. "Duties are not voluntary," he asserts:

> Men without their choice derive benefits from that association [within civil society]; without their choice they are subjected to

duties in consequence of these benefits; and without their choice
they enter into a virtual obligation as binding as any that is actual.
Look through the whole of life and the whole system of duties. Much
the strongest moral obligations are such as were never the result of
our option. I allow, that if no supreme ruler exists, wise to form, and
potent to enforce, the moral law, there is no sanction to any contract,
virtual or even actual, against the will of prevalent power. On that
hypothesis, let any set of men be strong enough to set their duties
at defiance, and they cease to be duties any longer. We have but this
one appeal against irresistible power—

> *Si genus humanum et mortalia temnitis arma,*
> *At sperate Deos memores fandi atque nefandi.*[30]

In the quoted passage from Virgil, Ilioneus (the eldest com-
rade of Aeneas) is objecting to Dido about the hostile reception
the Trojans received in Carthage. The Trojans have lost their last
resources, and their fleet is largely destroyed. Ilioneus is driven to
implore the queen for mercy, if not out of her respect for Trojan
arms or for humanity itself, then because of her respect for the
gods. Burke's allusion depends on the reader to recognize that, in
a revolutionary situation like that of contemporary Europe, when
a set of "men [is] strong enough to set their duties at defiance,"
the community is powerless to enforce social obligations. Like
the band of shipwrecked sailors under Aeneas, society is driven at
such times to implore its fellow citizens to remember the divine
structure of the moral world.

The allusion does not argue for that structure; it appeals to
the hearer's sympathy. The allusion does not explain the basis for
natural law, which binds mythical Trojans with Carthaginians, and
historical Romans to the English and French; it tries to create sympathy for the communities of the past, historical and fictional, where
natural law was accepted. In his next sentence, Burke acknowledges
that the "disciples of the Parisian philosophy" will not accept his
reasoning. He thereby implies that the allusion will fall on deaf ears
as well as understanding ones. Allusion is a mode of knowing that
works by persuasion rather than force, by beauty rather than logic.
Without receptive sympathy in the reader, the allusion can impart
no knowledge. With it, the reader may begin to question contemporary Enlightenment beliefs regarding the source of duties, and
learn something from tradition about the basis for morality.

Burke's Constitutionalism: Learning through Historic Traditions

Paine creates a memorable phrase to deride Burke's belief in the British Constitution when he ridicules the "musty records and mouldy parchments" of the past.[31] Paine's low opinion of the past—his assumption that looking into the "musty records" of the past will do little to advance the cause of a just society—is a common one in the Enlightenment, a I explained in the chapter on Jonathan Swift and technology. To add one more example to those discussed previously, Marquis de Condorcet's "Report on Education" (1792) concluded that the new French citizen's education should altogether avoid classical learning (which was "full of errors") and rely on natural sentiment and secular reason alone to teach moral principles.

This negative attitude toward the past was not held by all of Burke's opponents during the debate on the French Revolution, however. Burke's ire had been sparked by a sermon before "the Revolution Society," which had met for the express purpose of commemorating the Glorious Revolution of 1688. In that sermon, Richard Price, the object of Burke's attack, had given a respectable argument that the Revolution's continuing significance called for greater religious tolerance and more equal Parliamentary representation.[32]

Many readers are surprised at the long historical discussion of the Revolution of 1688 that opens Burke's *Reflections*. Parliament tossed out King James II, invited William and Mary to the throne, and explained its actions with the "Declaration of Right" (1689). Burke's strategy is to begin with a direct, historical response to Price. Everyone agrees that the Revolution of 1688, which was largely peaceful, had enormous historical significance. It established the principles of separation of powers and the authority of the legislative branch in checking the monarch.[33] It clearly established the rule of law as against the divine right of kings and recognized a Bill of Rights.

For Burke's antagonist, however, the Revolution was significant for establishing "three fundamental rights" that the French were now putting into practice across the Channel:

    a. To choose our own governors.
    b. To cashier them for misconduct.
    c. To frame a government for ourselves.[34]

Although Burke mentions the United States only rarely from this point in his career on, it was certainly possible to defend the American Revolution in terms of these three rights, as Price and Paine did at the time. Moreover, these principles could be derived from an authority who was virtually unassailable at the time of Burke's writing, John Locke, whose *Second Treatise on Government* (1689) could accommodate radical readings of both the American and the Glorious Revolutions.[35]

The Revolution of 1688 was the founding event of Burke's Whig party, the point of departure from which Burke's political self-understanding was derived. He could no more admit that the French Revolution was a legitimate child of this event than a modern liberal could agree that the New Deal shared the political principles of European fascists, or a modern conservative could consent in equating the 2001 "USA PATRIOT Act" with the Alien and Sedition Acts of 1798. When Price made the connection between the French Revolution and the historical origins of Burke's party, a debate was inevitable.

It is a mark of success on the part of Paine, Price, and other critics of the *Reflections*, that Burke is forced to return to the debate over history throughout his antirevolutionary writings. The title of Burke's *Appeal from the New to the Old Whigs*, published in August 1791, contrasts his "old Whig" interpretation of 1688 with that of the "new" Whigs, who had driven him from his party that spring.[36] About 15 percent of the *Appeal* consists of transcripts from the trial of Henry Sacheverell in 1709–1710, in which Whigs and Tories debated the meaning of the Revolution of 1688. As a whole, this lengthy pamphlet is Burke's effort to interpret the events of 1688 and the Declaration of Right as consistent with the tradition of the "ancient constitution" of Britain. Necessity required Parliament to remove James II to preserve the "original contract of the British state," Burke argues, as against the rights-based interpretation given by Price, Paine, Mary Wollstonecraft, and others. Burke is especially stung by Paine's remarks on the irrelevancy of "musty records," and he responds with an attack on Paine's mode of Enlightenment knowing:

> It is current that these [old Whig] politicians knew little of the rights of men; that they lost their way by groping about in the dark, and fumbling among rotten parchments and musty records. Great lights they say are lately obtained in the world; and Mr. Burke, instead of

shrowding himself in exploded ignorance, ought to have taken advantage of the blaze of illumination which has been spread about him.[37]

Knowledge that comes from a historic tradition does not come in a blaze of light. It is partial; the methods of acquiring it cannot be fully articulated. Paine's confidence in the strength of his defense of the French Revolution is virtually the opposite of the diffidence that Burke expresses regarding his own knowledge. "I never desire to be thought a better Whig than Lord Somers," writes Burke of one of the principal actors in the Revolution of 1688,

> or to understand the principles of the Revolution better than those by whom it was brought about. . . . We know that *we* have made no discoveries, and we think that no discoveries are to be made in morality, nor many in the great principles of government, nor in the ideas of liberty, which were understood long before we were born, altogether as well as they will be after the grave has heaped its mould upon our presumption and the silent tomb shall have imposed its law on our pert loquacity.[38]

Burke is overstating for effect, of course. His career up to that point had been that of a reformer—arguing for reform of British policies toward America, Ireland, and India and for a reform of the system of political patronage. In these reforms, however, Burke understood himself as perfecting the nature of the British Constitution, not as discovering fundamentally new political knowledge.[39]

It is clear that Burke realizes the futility of his arguments to overcome the objections of his opponents. His revolutionary detractors will continue to believe that a rational statement of the facts shows the necessity and justice of the French Revolution. As he expected, the "new Whigs" treated his style with contempt and few were interested in his historical arguments. As the decade wore on, Burke expressed exasperation at the ease with which revolutionaries came to their theory-based conclusions, compared to the difficulty he faced in attempting to revive the English historical tradition to his generation:

> We have discovered, it seems, that all, which the boasted wisdom of our ancestors has laboured to bring to perfection for six or seven centuries, is nearly or altogether matched in six or seven days, at the leisure hours and sober intervals of Citizen Thomas Paine.[40]

Paine used the past to prove his present positions and had no interest in the past for any other reason. Burke was bound to the past—to its communities, its histories, its cultural achievements—in a much deeper sense. "He had, in the highest degree, that noble faculty whereby man is able to live in the past and in the future," wrote the nineteenth-century historian Thomas Babington Macaulay of Burke's imagination.[41] "Living in the past" would be a reproach for many Enlightenment thinkers. Not for Burke. Burke needed the past to make sense of his—and Britain's—present identity and possible future direction.

Burke's imaginative constitutionalism ultimately forced some of his contemporaries to question their Enlightenment assumption of progressively superior knowledge, particularly after the Terror of 1793–1794. Perhaps his most powerful defense of traditional knowledge comes in an extended metaphor of a landed estate, one of many metaphors from landscape architecture that enrich his antirevolutionary writings. "You will observe," he writes to the original French recipient of his *Reflections*, Charles-Jean-François Depont,

> That from Magna Charta to the Declaration of right, it has been the uniform policy of our constitution to claim and assert our liberties, as an *entailed inheritance* derived to us from our forefathers, and to be transmitted to our posterity; as an estate specially belonging to the people of this kingdom without any reference whatever to any other more general or prior right. By this means our constitution preserves an unity in so great a diversity of its parts. We have an inheritable crown; an inheritable peerage; and an house of commons and a people inheriting privileges, franchises, and liberties, from a long line of ancestors.
>
> This policy appears to me to be the result of profound reflection; or rather the happy effect of following nature, which is wisdom without reflection, and above it. A spirit of innovation is generally the result of a selfish temper and confined views. People will not look forward to posterity, who never look backward to their ancestors. Besides, the people of England well know, that the idea of inheritance furnishes a sure principle of conservation, and a sure principle of transmission; without at all excluding a principle of improvement. It leaves acquisition free; but it secures what it acquires. Whatever advantages are obtained by a state proceeding on these maxims, are locked fast as in a sort of family settlement; grasped as in a kind of mortmain for ever. By a constitutional policy,

working after the pattern of nature, we receive, we hold, we transmit our government and our privileges, in the same manner in which we enjoy and transmit our property and our lives. The institutions of policy, the goods of fortune, the gifts of Providence, are handed down, to us and from us, in the same course and order. Our political system is placed in a just correspondence and symmetry with the order of the world, and with the mode of existence decreed to a permanent body composed of transitory parts; wherein, by the disposition of a stupendous wisdom, moulding together the great mysterious incorporation of the human race, the whole, at one time, is never old, or middle-aged, or young, but in a condition of unchangeable constancy, moves on through the varied tenour or perpetual decay, fall, renovation, and progression . . . In this choice of inheritance we have given to our frame of polity the image of a relation in blood; binding up the constitution of our country with our dearest domestic ties; adopting our fundamental laws into the bosom of our family affections; keeping inseparable, and cherishing with the warmth of all their combined and mutually reflected charities, our state, our hearths, our sepulchers, and our altars.[42]

Burke conceives politics in spatial and architectural terms here: the Constitution is likened to an entailed estate, improved over the years and transmitted to future generations for their enjoyment. The spatial implications of this metaphor could not be more different from the revolutionaries' way of thinking. By 1789, maps drawn up by the National Assembly divided France into a rational grid of rectangular "departments" to diminish local attachments and increase national pride.[43] But "[n]o man ever was attached by a sense of pride, partiality, or real affection, to a description of square measurement," Burke wrote. "He will never glory in belonging to Checquer N° 71."[44] It is typical of Burke's sympathetic imagination that his metaphor shifts almost imperceptibly from an estate at the beginning to a blood relative by the end. The family that inhabits the estate belongs to its history and vice versa. The shift humanizes the estate metaphor, which feeds into Burke's larger reflections on the mutually reinforcing powers of social institutions and nature. The knowledge that Burke gains from the historical tradition derives from those powers, acting together. The "principle of improvement" that he wishes to convey is natural because the process of "perpetual decay, fall, renovation, and progression" is natural. It is social in that the present generation must decide what constitutes true improvement as opposed to mere innovation. Even so unpromising a term as "mortmain," the "dead hand of the past" so derided by antitraditionalist writers, is converted into a potent symbol of the way in which past generations transmit life-giving benefits to the present.[45]

This is all appealing, at least to many sensibilities. But in what way is it true? How can one *know* that Burke's analysis represents a valid, reliable, or true picture of the way of incorporating the past into the present?

Is There No Disputing Taste?

Burke's Political Aesthetics, Tradition, and Prejudice

If one is looking for certain knowledge, or still more, a *method* that guarantees certain knowledge, one is likely to be attracted to a revolutionary politics, not to Burke's historic constitutionalism. It is revolutionary to believe that that one can begin with an epistemologically sound political theory (of the state of nature, natural rights, the consensual basis of authority, etc.) and then shape the actions of a state accordingly. Reading history with this method in mind is equally revolutionary and for the same reasons.[46]

The political knowledge to which Burke aspired was founded on a different form of critical judgment altogether—it was founded on taste. "Taste" has an effete ring to our ears, especially if it is associated with eighteenth-century men in wigs, women in constricting dresses, and arts that value form over the artist's self-expression. To many, it seems aristocratic, frivolous, inflexible, and in a word, *false*. But taste, for Burke, is not about the cut of knee-breeches. In his hands, taste is a form of imaginative judgment that unites political, aesthetic, and social reality. This mode of judgment is ultimately more democratic than the Enlightenment alternative practiced by Paine and others because it incorporates "those who are dead, and those who are to be born," along with the present generation in its search for a sustainable society. Burke's standard of taste is also more serious than contemporary Enlightenment rationality, because it is better able to record the tragedies of political life.[47] What I wish to focus on, however, is the flexibility of Burke's mode of political judgment, compared to the rigidity of his Enlightenment detractors.

This book has discussed the continued narrowing of the view of knowledge as the Enlightenment proceeded. In the most significant philosophical treatment of the imagination in the late eighteenth century, Immanuel Kant's *Critique of Judgment* (1790), the knowledge gained from the imagination is distinctly substandard, inferior to the products of the understanding. For Kant, "taste" is in service to the understanding. Taste is a mode of judgment that subjects the imagination to the understanding. The artist may use his imagination freely only with the understanding that nothing he produces really matters as knowledge. The good and the true have been cut off from the beautiful.[48]

Burke's place in this history is complicated by the fact that he wrote a youthful aesthetic work, *A Philosophical Enquiry into the Origin of Our Ideas of the Sublime and Beautiful* (1757), whose somewhat rigid principles are sometimes at odds with his mature rhetorical practice. In particular, the second edition of the *Enquiry* (1759) includes an introductory essay "On Taste," which tries to establish absolute principles of judgment apart from particular examples.

A number of recent interpreters have focused their attention on the relation between Burke's aesthetic theory and his politics.[49] Although they come at the issue in a variety of ways, all agree that, unlike most of his political opponents, Burke's political conclusions incorporate aesthetic judgment along with history and political philosophy. They also agree that Burke defends taste as an alternative to the Enlightenment mode of political judgment. Like most of the other figures in this book, Burke's approach to knowledge was at odds with the dominant trends in Enlightenment culture, and his detractors were excellent at ridiculing him. Paine's criticism of Burke, for expressing concern for the aristocracy while allegedly ignoring the suffering of the French nation, still resonates: "He pities the plumage, but forgets the dying bird."[50]

What is missing from these interpretations, however, is an explanation of how Burke's approach to history differs epistemologically from that of his opponents. Burke's aesthetics cannot be reduced to a method. Unlike the "necessary" outcomes of Paine's methodical analyses, the outcomes of Burke's approach always require judgment. Where the revolutionaries offer certainty, Burke requires prudence. Where their approach offers a prescribed method, Burke demands flexibility.

In focusing on the "flexibility" of Burke's standard of taste, I do not mean to deny the moral and philosophical principles at the core of his thought. Burke believed in an underlying natural law, capable of recognition by all nations, which provided a moral center to the social world.[51] He did not believe, however, that human laws followed straightforwardly from natural law in the way that Paine derived civil rights from natural rights.[52] The flexibility in Burke's thought runs through his political, moral, and aesthetic judgment:

> Nothing universal can be rationally affirmed on any moral, or any political subject. Pure metaphysical abstraction does not belong to these matters. The lines of morality are not like the ideal lines of mathematics. They are broad and deep as well as long. They admit of exceptions; they demand modifications. These exceptions and modifications are not made by the process of logic, but by the rules of prudence. Prudence is not only the first in rank of the virtues political and moral, but she is the director, the regulator, the standard of them all.[53]

Burke's historic constitutionalism required a flexible form of judgment. A method that proceeds from principles to facts and back again cannot provide the practical wisdom required by the politician. It is too mechanical and too tied to consistency of approach to allow the politician the leeway he needs; its dedication to consistency makes it unfit for the complexities of political life. "An ignorant man, who is not fool enough to meddle with his clock," Burke writes, "is however sufficiently confident to think he can safely take to pieces, and put together at his pleasure, a moral machine of another guise, importance, and complexity, composed of far other wheels, and springs, and balances, and counteracting and co-operating powers."[54] In other words, it is the revolutionaries' theory—the theory based on the natural rights of man—that is inflexible. Its metaphysical truths cannot accommodate themselves to the actual moral and political realities of life.

The politician, as Burke conceives him, is a "philosopher in action."[55] As such, the virtue he needs most is not consistency but prudence. Prudence has an old-fashioned sound today, but it is nothing more or less than the practical wisdom of knowing how to apply one's principles in varying circumstances. Burke agreed with the classical and medieval traditions that prudence was the highest political and moral virtue because it alone could restrain reason, the highest human faculty.[56] Practical wisdom comes slowly, by thoughtful comparisons of past experience with present needs, and by reflection on one's own experience. The politician must avoid the tempting certainty of Enlightenment political reason, Burke thinks. He must educate his judgment so that he can know, within the bounds that limit all human knowledge, how best to respond to contemporary circumstances. The best word for this form of judgment, as applied to Burke's practice, is *taste*.

Some have seen Burke's emphasis on taste as irrational or worse.[57] The resurgence of interest in Burke's aesthetics, however, has led most interpreters to see that Burke's taste is a reasoned alternative to the narrower rationalism of his opponents. Recalling his allusion to *Art of Poetry*, one can see that Burke incorporates Horace's long meditation on literary taste into his art of politics.[58] Terms like *balance*, *decorum*, *equipoise*, and *harmony* appear in highly significant contexts in Burke. For example, like other great eighteenth-century stylists, Burke often suspends the most significant words of his periodic sentences until the end, as he does in the final words of the *Reflections*. He is one who "wishes to preserve consistency," he writes in the book's concluding paragraph, but is willing to vary

> his means to secure the unity of his end; and, when the equipoise of the vessel in which he sails, may be endangered by overloading it upon one side, is desirous of carrying the small weight of his reasons to that which may preserve its equipoise.[59]

"Reasons" are of metaphorically small weight in the final nautical metaphor of this work. They may produce a systematic consistency—which may in turn lead to political shipwreck—unless they are flexible enough to shift according to circumstances. The ship of state needs the "equipoise" that a prudent leader supplies by his good judgment.[60] Paine and Price proclaimed their rational consistency in defending both the American cause in the 1770s and the French Revolution in 1789. It takes good judgment—taste—based on contingent historical circumstances and principle, to understand the Burke's reasons for defending the Americans and opposing the French revolutionaries.

Burke's standard of taste applies to his traditionalism generally, not just to his incorporation of literary and aesthetic elements into his thought. It guides the historic constitutionalism that undergirds his political practice. Still, ambiguity persists when judging whether a given principle fits a historical circumstance. Uncertainty remains when estimating whether a past event finds an echo in a present situation. To join the two is an exercise in decorum, not in pure reason.[61] The judgment one makes is based on reflection on past practice, which can never be obtained by the pure theorist and never fully articulated even by the practical politician.

Burke is sometimes willing to spell out the differences he has with his opponents, as his critique of "pure metaphysical abstraction" shows. At other times, he is dismissive. "The author of the Reflections has *heard* a great deal concerning the modern lights," he writes in the *Appeal*, "but he has not yet had the good fortune to *see* much of them."[62] At still others, Burke is so deeply aware of the split between his approach to knowledge and that of his Enlightenment opponents that he sometimes writes as if he has given up his prerogative to speak of reason or truth at all. His judgment—based on prudence and taste—is simply too far removed from their rationalistic approach. He defends the "musty records" ridiculed by Paine. He embraces the "moral sentiments, [which are] so nearly connected with early prejudice as to be almost one and the same thing," against the "perfectly systematic" revolutionary truths, which "boldly draw the conclusions to the destruction of our whole constitution in church and state."[63] If it comes down to a choice between prejudice and the contemporary Enlightenment approaches to truth, he goes so far as to defend prejudice—the epistemological target of the Enlightenment critique:

> You see, Sir, that in this enlightened age I am bold enough to confess, that we are generally men of untaught feelings; that instead of casting away all our old prejudices, we cherish them to a very considerable degree, and, to take more shame to ourselves, we cherish them because they are prejudices; and the longer they have lasted, and the more generally they have prevailed, the more we cherish them . . . Many of our men of speculation, instead of exploding general prejudices, employ their sagacity to discover the latent wisdom which prevails in them. If they find what they seek, and they seldom fail, they think it more wise to continue the prejudice, with the reason involved, than to cast away the coat of prejudice, and to leave

nothing but the naked reason; because prejudice, with its reason, has a motive to give action to that reason, and an affection which will give it permanence. Prejudice is of ready application in the emergency; it previously engages the mind in a steady course of wisdom and virtue, and does not leave the man hesitating in the moment of decision, skeptical, puzzled, and unresolved. Prejudice renders a man's virtue his habit; and not a series of unconnected acts. Through just prejudice, his duty becomes part of his nature. Your literary men, and your politicians, and so do the whole clan of the enlightened among us, essentially differ in these points.[64]

Burke was not the only writer of his age to worry about that the Enlightenment critique of prejudice was claiming more than it could deliver. Five years before the *Reflections*, in 1785, the German philosopher Moses Mendelssohn had warned against "this sham enlightenment . . . where everyone ridicules prejudices, without distinguishing what is true in them from what is false."[65] Voltaire had given lip service to the defense of "universal and necessary prejudices" in his immensely popular *Philosophical Dictionary* (1764), but he defines prejudice as "an opinion *without* judgment" (a definition Burke would never have accepted), and he limits acceptable prejudices to the opinions that parents teach their children.[66] In an influential German pamphlet titled "On Enlightenment," published in 1788, Andreas Riem ridiculed any who would dare to question the progress that his own age had achieved. Subjecting past traditions and prejudices to critical examination was, for him, the essence of enlightenment:

> From the wild uncultured man who locks up the powers of his spirit inside himself and who, tyrannized by the prejudice of eternal rituals, does not develop them, to the European who in dumb obstinacy persists in his prejudices—have not all the smarter, more enlightened peoples and human beings reached a higher level than they, a level envied by short-sightedness and prejudice? If your understanding remains within the borders of custom you will become as laughable to the more enlightened people as the miserable Chinese, who gaze astonished at the works of enlightenment, without assimilating them into their arts and sciences.[67]

In an otherwise excellent treatment of Burke's place in the debate over prejudice, James Schmidt comments that Burke "is faced with the unpleasant alternative of defending prejudices *because* they are prejudices or of conceding the Enlightenment's position and granting that we ought to cherish prejudices only insofar as they have proven to be reasonable and thus *deserving* of our affection."[68] This does not capture Burke's view. Burke criticized the "blind, unmeaning prejudices" that simply ratified the world as it happened to be.[69] Nevertheless, Burke believed that prejudice finds its place within the irreducibly historical setting from which one sets out on the quest for knowledge. The historical, political, and aesthetic traditions of which one is a part cannot be eradicated. Nor can they be reduced to principles that promise to guide any neutral observer to the proper decision.[70] By "prejudice," Burke means a judgment that is made before all the facts can be known. In his view, moreover, *all* of the facts relevant to a difficult political decision can *never* be fully known by an objective observer. That is the nub of the epistemological difference between Burke and his enlightenment opponents. True judgment can never be a matter of applying abstract principles objectively and exhaustively to individual cases. It involves much more subtle, far-ranging decisions about how to interpret the present as a whole in light of the past as a whole.

These issues of interpretation, or hermeneutics, are also central to the philosophy of Hans-Georg Gadamer. Indeed he says that the issue of prejudice, understood in its historical complexity "is the point of departure for the hermeneutical problem."[71] Gadamer refers specifically to Burke's "critique of the Enlightenment" in this context, and sets himself the task of justifying "true prejudices" by "rational knowledge"—a task which (he admits) can never be fully completed. He is aided in this project by the more neutral connotations of the German word for prejudice, *Vorurteil*, which implies "prejudgment" or a decision "given beforehand." The kind of reason that confirms these "prejudgments," as Gadamer explains, is not the same as Enlightenment rationalism, for it everywhere acknowledges its historical origins and therefore its limits; it incorporates the judgments of taste; and it is willing to live with ambiguity. These could be descriptions of Edmund Burke's practice. In the final section, I hope to show their value for our own age.

Hans-Georg Gadamer: Resuscitating Tradition in the Postmodern Era

Like their Enlightenment ancestors, many recent schools of literary interpretation have been built on their claim to uncover the prejudices and hidden assumptions of the past. Whether it was from the perspective of Marxism, Freudian analysis, or a Nietzschean scrutiny of the genealogy of a text's historical, political, or moral assumptions, a "hermeneutics of suspicion" has united these critics in their method of literary interpretation.

It is remarkable, therefore, that major interpreters from each of these strands have either moved toward approaches that emphasize the older texts themselves or have cast doubt the approach that brought them fame. Harold Bloom, previously known for his Freudian interpretations, is now strongly associated with an attachment to texts that he unhesitatingly calls *The Western Canon*: "For many years I have taught that Freud is essentially prosified Shakespeare," he has written, in a revealing reversal.[72] The former Marxist critic, Frank Lentricchia, has confessed that he simply stopped reading literary criticism because of the critics' assumption of moral superiority over the writers they were supposed to be explaining. Lentricchia realized that he loved literature, not criticism, and he went back to the "veil-piercing books" that propelled him out of his narrow world.[73] Two leading New Historicist critics, Stephen Greenblatt and Catherine Gallagher, conclude somewhat regretfully that the success of their approach has led to the "widespread disenchantment with the project of ultimate demystification" itself. The questions raised by the New Historicism, they say, has led to a "cynical edge" among some.[74]

In this context, the hermeneutics of Hans-Georg Gadamer (1900–2002) provides a helpful perspective on the work of Burke. Like the practice of Burke, Gadamer's theory emphasizes that we bring prior understandings to the interpretation of each new text. But unlike the "masters of suspicion," Gadamer's interpreter gains new knowledge from the *interplay* among the text, tradition, and the "fore-understanding" we bring to our reading.[75]

Gadamer accepts neither the Enlightenment notions of objectivity, nor the extreme postmodern attitude of suspicion with respect to the works of the past. In *Truth and Method*, first published in 1960, he revived the philosophical enterprise of encountering persons and traditions as truly "other"—truly different from oneself. Apart from a personal encounter with these others, there is no way to learn the significant things these persons and traditions have to teach us. The primary way this occurs, Gadamer explains, is through our interpretation of older or "traditionary" texts. The study of interpretation—hermeneutics—is thus central to his entire work. Gadamer's approach differs from the Enlightenment attempt to eliminate the personal element and seek for the objective truth. It differs as well from many postmodern theories that interpret language as primarily an expression of power or an exaltation of the individual's will.

For Gadamer, as for Burke, tradition is something that we belong to and yet is "other" than ourselves.[76] Where Burke stressed the element of belonging, Gadamer introduces the equally important element of difference. To encounter tradition fully is to encounter elements of both the alien and the familiar.[77] Both elements are crucial to an increased understanding of oneself and the world. Gadamer reaches back to the term *Bildung* for this growing self-understanding, noting that its German connotations embrace education, personal development, character formation, and culture. Bildung is "the properly human way of developing one's natural talents and capacities," he writes.[78] "To recognize one's own in the alien, to become at home in it, is the basic movement of spirit, whose being consists only in returning to itself from what is other." In the process of development, then, the individual grows beyond his or her own natural existence to experience the social world that is constituted by "custom and language," and then returns to realize one's mature identity.

The first step in this process is not to purify one's consciousness of the prejudices that have been part of one's social world, as Riem maintains and as Francis Bacon had argued in the sixteenth century.[79] The first step is to recognize that one's consciousness owes itself to history. Gadamer writes that genuine experience is the experience of one's own finitude, particularly the limits imposed on one's powers by one's historicity.[80]

The mind cannot manage its own origins; it is not the perfect master of its destiny. Instead, it brings its experiences, history, and prejudices into the present as a "horizon" that makes up one's range of vision.[81] The traditions of the past, and particularly the texts of the past, provide another horizon, an alternative to one's own vantage point. Personal development—education, or Bildung—occurs when one is able to put one's prejudices at risk through an encounter with traditionary texts.[82] One is not trying to recreate the past through this encounter, as certain historicists have tried to do.[83] Nor does one interpret older texts to "interrogate" the past from the superior vantage point of the present, as many postmodern interpreters do. Still less does one abandon one's own past, or "fore-meanings," as Gadamer calls them, that one brings to a text:[84]

> Rather, a person trying to understand a text is prepared for it to tell him something. That is why a hermeneutically trained consciousness must be, from the start, sensitive to the text's alterity. But this kind of sensitivity involves neither "neutrality" with respect to content nor the extinction of one's self, but the foregrounding of one's own fore-meanings and prejudices. The important thing is to be aware of one's own bias, so that the text can present itself in all its otherness and thus assert its own truth against one's own fore-meanings.

True understanding, then, occurs when there is a "fusion of horizons" of past and present. The traditional text creates a tension with a reader who is conscious of his or her own "horizon," history, perspectives, and prejudices. Gadamer explains this process as "the interplay of the movement of tradition and the movement of the interpreter."[85] We begin our interpretation on the basis of our past traditions. In addition, we participate actively in reshaping that tradition with every act of interpretation. Understanding involves allowing one's horizon to change under the pressure of this interpretative encounter with the text.

When and how are we required to reshape our "horizon"? To refer to the major issue raised in this chapter, how does Burke know that the principles put forth by the revolutionary writers are foreign to British political self-understanding? What is the basis for Burke's judgment? At this point, Gadamer's explanation of the faculty of taste—a much fuller and more self-consciously philosophical concept than one finds in Burke—becomes crucial for seeing how tradition becomes a way of knowing.

Gadamer specifically criticizes the Enlightenment narrowing of reason to exclude the epistemological significance of taste. Kant "denies taste any *significance as knowledge*," he writes. "In taste nothing is known of the objects judged to be beautiful, but it is stated only that there is a feeling of pleasure connected with them a priori in the subjective consciousness."[86] Gadamer profoundly disagrees with this view. "The concept of taste undoubtedly implies a *mode of knowing*," Gadamer writes. "The mark of good taste is being able to stand back from ourselves and our private preferences."[87]

To be sure, taste is not a matter of judging individual cases on the basis of universal principles.[88] It will not produce unanimity of judgment, consistency across all observers, or a methodical guide to truth. To demand these would restrict taste to a narrow sphere, Gadamer believes. Taste is a way of knowing how the part properly fits into the whole, he says, and must therefore consult a range of cultural realities before making its judgment. Moreover, taste operates within a community.[89] Because communities are always being affected by new trends in morality, politics, and manners and in the arts, taste is needed to judge a broad array of social reality. It cannot be limited to a separate aesthetic realm, as Kant believed.

Burke's view of the British Constitution—his assumption that it had generally produced a free, ordered society—was the "whole" from which he viewed every "part." This prejudice, or prejudgment, formed the basis of his horizon. When a reform seemed an appropriate addition to that whole, such as granting more civil rights to Irish Catholics, for instance, Burke labored to show the reform's fitness, using all of the constitutional, historical, and literary tools at his disposal.[90] When Burke considered a reform at odds with the constitutional tradition—such as Price's notion that the Revolution of 1688 gave British citizens the right to choose their own governors and frame a government for themselves—his criticism was similarly wide ranging. History, metaphor, allusion, and political principles all merge into a whole, whose rhetorical effectiveness depends on good taste. He did not separate his political arguments from their rhetorical presentation, as if the first alone were rational and the framework merely decorative. His defense of the Constitution was of one piece—aesthetic, political, and historical.

Burke was intensely aware of the historical nature of his prejudice in favor of the Constitution. To use Gadamer's terms, he knew that his horizon was not just constructed from the histories of England, Ireland, Scotland, and Wales, but from more sources in Western culture than he could name. Along with English legal authorities like Edward Coke, John Selden, Matthew Hale, and William Blackstone he treats Horace, Virgil, and Shakespeare as contemporaries because, in the most important sense, they *are* his contemporaries.[91] They are part of the tradition that he eagerly engages in conversation with the present. When he alludes to those writers, he puts his prejudice for the Constitution at risk, for they will inevitably modify it: "[T]radition exists only in constantly becoming other than it is," Gadamer writes. Similarly, Burke's imaginative reconstruction of the Constitution also modifies that tradition.[92] The "entailed inheritance" that Burke used as an image of the Constitution is in a perpetual cycle of "decay, fall, renovation, and progression," after all, so it is no surprise to find him participating in that process.

Gadamer emphasizes that tradition is not inert. Tradition exists only it as is "affirmed, embraced, [and] cultivated," which means that everyone who engages his or her tradition does so with a certain degree of freedom.[93] Moreover, the person who looks back to the preservative function of tradition is using reason, though in a way that differs from that of a reformer who has only the future in view. "[W]e are always situated within traditions," Gadamer writes, and (whether we acknowledge it or not), tradition is active in all change.

Burke's critique of the revolutionary understanding of politics began with a prejudice in favor of the British Constitution—"wisdom without reflection," as he called it. Should rational reflections lift one's views out of the realm of prejudice altogether, and into the realm of objectivity, as critics of Burke and Gadamer have argued?[94] I do not think so. Reflection is itself part of an intellectual tradition that predates the Enlightenment, Gadamer writes, and it is no more possible to step outside of that tradition than to step outside of language itself.[95] After reflection establishes the rational value of a traditional practice, Burke recommends that one "continue the prejudice, with the reason involved, [rather than] cast away the coat of prejudice and to leave nothing but the naked reason." Why? Because prejudice motivates action and arouses affection.[96]

The difference between Burke and Gadamer, on the one hand, and the Enlightenment on the other, is contained in the title of Burke's book: *Reflections on the Revolution in France*. A reflection does not contain its own source of light—or enlightenment. Such light as it has comes from another source, and perhaps from many other sources. Declaring one's liberation from the past would be like liberating an individual spark from a fire and expecting it to create a blaze all on its own. Reflection, by contrast, implies the individual's insufficiency; it implies the necessity of inviting others, past and present, to mediate our understanding of contemporary life.[97] What it sacrifices to simplicity, it gains in taste, and what it loses in certainty, it adds in wisdom.

7

RECONCILING THE HEART WITH THE HEAD IN THE POETRY OF WILLIAM COWPER AND THE THOUGHT OF MICHAEL POLANYI

In my last physics class—the one that convinced me that I had no higher calling in that field—we derived Einstein's famous equation $e=mc^2$ from a purely mathematical and theoretical chain of reasoning. I could follow the formulas, but they meant nothing to me because I could not sense the brilliant relationships that the various steps signified. I did not really participate in those classes with true comprehension—even though I could have repeated the derivations methodically. Did I understand what Einstein had done? No. Beyond seeing that a little matter translates into a large amount of energy, I could not reflect personally on the physical and mathematical relationships that our chain of reasoning had described. I could not "indwell" them, to use a term from the lexicon of the chemist-philosopher Michael Polanyi (1891–1976). And without that indwelling, as Polanyi writes, formulas "inevitably spread out into a desert of trivialities."[1]

I am not criticizing my teachers, of course. I had simply reached the end of my ability to pursue physics. Without any intuitive or personal connection to the next problem our class approached, the problems seemed inert and unconnected. Previously, a certain kind of relationship had bound me together with my fellow students, teachers, and the material. There was an implicit faith that each new acquisition of knowledge would deepen our understanding of how electromagnetism and mechanics explained the workings of nature. Nature, of course, was the external authority that confirmed or contradicted our attempts at understanding. And when I could no longer personally understand nature's confirmations of how the world worked, further advances in my knowledge of physics were impossible.

Unlike their Enlightenment forebears, many modern scientists have embraced a personal element as crucial to their research. Knowledge is attained by persons, Polanyi emphasized, and scientists are personally committed to what their fields of knowledge claim to explain. In practice, research scientists exercise personal judgments about what kind of knowledge to pursue, which guides their empirical or theoretical inquiries. Their research includes an unspoken, "tacit knowledge," whose intuitions cannot be reduced to a method.[2]

This chapter begins by focusing on William Cowper (1731–1800), the most widely read poet and hymn writer of the final decade or so of the eighteenth century. Cowper protested the elimination of the personal element of knowledge in the Enlightenment. He saw that Enlightenment figures had discounted the epistemological significance of one's commitment to and passion for the objects of knowledge. He protested the Enlightenment effort to separate the advancement of knowledge from one's personal participation in that knowledge. At the end of the chapter, I will show how Polanyi draws together and extends similar critiques of the Enlightenment in his ambitious philosophy of personal knowledge.[3]

Cowper shows as great an awareness of Enlightenment approaches to knowledge as his contemporary, Edmund Burke. Both writers were acutely aware of the claims being made for modern methods of acquiring scientific, historical, and even theological knowledge. Like Burke, Cowper criticizes them for failing to understand their proper limits. He knew he was on the losing side of the cultural shift that was occurring, and yet (also like Burke) he also knew he represented cultural institutions that were still the objects of powerful critiques. Cowper's positive contribution to an alternative to Enlightenment knowing differs from Burke's, however, in that his emphasis on the personal element of knowledge largely avoids the entanglements of history, tradition, and prejudice.

Cowper's Struggle for Mental Health

Because William Cowper's critique of the Enlightenment concerns one's personal relationship to knowledge, one must confront the sad and bizarre elements of his biography. Cowper battled madness throughout his adult life, and even when sane, he was often deeply depressed. After an early breakdown and suicide attempt in 1763, he thought he had committed the unforgivable sin;[4] then followed an eighteen-month stay in a mental asylum, St. Albans, run by a forward-looking physician, Nathaniel Cotton, who was an evangelical Christian. Sometime during the summer of 1764, Cowper experienced a conversion, and about a year later he left Dr. Cotton's care.[5]

Observers of Cowper sometimes attribute the gloom of his final twenty-seven years to the Calvinist doctrines he embraced in 1764.[6] But Cowper's first bout of melancholy occurred in 1753. His 1763 insanity and suicide attempts occurred a year before his conversion, and his emotional recovery was closely associated with his conversion. "To this moment," Cowper writes of his suicide attempt, "I had felt no concern of a spiritual kind. . . . I was as much unacquainted with Christ and all His saving offices as if His Blessed Name had never reached me."[7]

Cowper's 1763 insanity was brought on by the prospect of appearing before the House of Lords. He had been nominated by his uncle Ashley Cowper (who held the office of Clerk of the Parliaments) to become Clerk of the Journals in the House of Lords. Earlier, in 1756, Ashley had forbidden a match between Cowper and his daughter, Theadora, and his offer of this sinecure seven years later almost certainly implied his approval of Cowper as a future son-in-law. Cowper had a legal education and with moderate effort he could have passed this test. But the prospect of exposing himself to examination in the House of Lords overwhelmed Cowper:

> To require my attendance at the Bar of the House that I might there publicly entitle my self to the office was in effect to exclude me from it. . . . They whose spirits are formed like mine, to whom a public exhibition of themselves upon any occasion is mortal poison, may have some idea of the horror of my situation; others can have none.[8]

In 1773, when he had his most serious breakdown, Cowper was suddenly confronted with the actual prospect of marriage to Mary Unwin. This would mean constantly exposing his full identity to a wife. When Mrs. Unwin was widowed 1767, she and Cowper had moved to a house in Olney at the invitation of John Newton, who was at that time the little known rector of the village. Though Cowper's household provoked gossip, the presence of Mrs. Unwin's daughter, Susanna, gave it sufficient respectability to continue for a number of years. The growing friendship between Mrs. Unwin and Cowper led to their engagement, but the issue did not become pressing until Susanna's own marriage prospects forced the issue.[9] In late January or early February of 1773, Cowper had a fateful dream, in which he heard God say, "It is all over for you—you have perished."[10] Cowper tried to commit suicide again, abandoned poetry for about four years, and came to believe that he was the unique example of a member of the elect whom God condemned to hell.[11] He retained this belief to the end of his life. Cowper made another suicide attempt in 1787 and suffered yet another significant breakdown in 1794.

I believe that Cowper's fear of self-exposure—whether before the House of Lords, a prospective wife, or God—is a thread that links Cowper's bouts of madness and attempts at suicide. The most terrifying forms of exposure, of course, were his encounters with God; in them one sees his mental illness in its most intense form.[12]

Cowper's mental illness prevented him from participating in the spiritual commitments that he continued to affirm. In other words, he retained the intellectual armory of orthodox Christianity, but after that breakdown he could not attend worship, go to a prayer meeting, or even say grace at meals.[13]

After 1773 he was rarely able to shake off his sense of unworthiness, notwithstanding the ministrations of numerous friends: his famous spiritual director, John Newton, the slave-trader turned evangelical preacher, who gave him a place to live and encouraged his hymn writing; his caring cousin, Lady Hesketh, who revived their friendship through her correspondence; the Unwin family, with whom he began living in 1765; and a lively younger woman, Lady Austen, who encouraged his epic poem, *The Task* (1785).

Although he writes honestly about religious doubts and anxieties in the *Olney Hymns*, composed in the early 1770s, autobiographical poems about his personal dealings with God after 1773 are rare. When he does treat this subject in verse, Cowper honestly records the terror and dread it caused him. In "Truth" (1782), for instance, an unnamed sinner who sounds much like Cowper experiences God as "the tempest howling in the trees." He dreads "[t]he scrutiny of those all seeing eyes."[14] Later in the poem, when mental illness results in a character's suicide, Cowper writes that

> Such lunacy is ignorance alone;
> They [the jury and coroner] knew not, what some bishops may not know,
> That scripture is the only cure of woe. . . .

But Cowper himself did not experience this cure after 1773, at least not for long. Of his dreams in 1792, he writes: "Death, Church yards and carcases, or else thunder storms and lightnings, God angry, and myself wishing that I had never been born . . . I live a life of terrour."[15]

In his poems of the 1780s, Cowper often emphasizes the crucial relationship between one's knowledge and one's commitments. In the satirical poems of that period, he criticizes those who would separate the two. In *The Task*, his deepest intellectual affirmations regarding nature and friendship are intimately linked to his personal commitments. It is no wonder that his inability to experience the harmony of spirit and mind in religious matters endangered his mental balance.

It is profoundly sad to read Cowper's accounts of his rejection by God:

> Hatred and vengeance! my eternal portion,
> Scarce can endure delay of execution,
> Wait, with impatient readiness, to seize my
> Soul in a moment.[16]

Those lines, unpublished in his lifetime, probably come from the period of his 1773 breakdown. His last English poem is bleakest of all. In "The Cast-away" (1799), Cowper compares God's refusal to save him with the inability of a ship to turn and rescue a man who has been swept overboard:

> No voice divine the storm allay'd,
> No light propitious shone
> When snatch'd from all effectual aid,

We perish'd, each, alone;
But I, beneath a rougher sea,
And whelm'd in deeper gulphs than he.[17]

In these autobiographical poems, being alone with God is unutterably terrifying. Suffering under his deranged belief in God's condemnation, yet unable to die, Cowper lived in a "deeper gulf" than the one that sent the drowned man of the poem to his death. He ends the poem "Hatred and Vengeance" lamenting that he cannot die and must endure being "[b]uried above ground."

At this distance, we cannot accurately diagnose Cowper's mental illness. But as I will show, we do know from his verse that Cowper never believed one could separate personal commitments from one's knowledge of theology, nature, or politics. We know that after his major breakdown in 1773, Cowper took pleasure in nonreligious commitments and activities—friendships, poetry, gardening, and the care of animals—which brought him periods of relative health.[18] We also know that from 1773 on, he could not sustain a unity between the religious truths he continued to profess and his personal, lived experience. Whether that disunity itself was part of the cause or the effect of mental illness, we do not know. In any case, it must have been maddening.

Despite his mental illness, Cowper's poems during his final twenty years are, with rare exceptions, delightful. Whether their mode is satirical, reflective, elegiac, or spiritual, they are entirely sane, often witty, and nearly always reflective. By common consent, Cowper's letters from this same period place him among the finest epistolary writers in a century of great correspondents.

Cowper's poetic achievement, both before and after his major breakdown, offers important alternatives to Enlightenment approaches to knowledge. In fact, even his battle with insanity may indicate some clues about the importance of finding connections between personal knowledge and other forms of knowledge. In 1817, Samuel Taylor Coleridge, who considered Cowper the greatest modern poet, called him the first who "combined natural thoughts with natural diction; the first who reconciled the heart with the head."[19] The reconciliation that eluded Cowper in life, that is to say, was evident in his verse, particularly in his late, epic-length work, *The Task*, which Coleridge singled out for praise.

As Coleridge indicates, Cowper realized that the Enlightenment had split the personal knowledge of the heart from the rational knowledge of the head. Cowper did not primarily satirize that split, like Swift, or even question it, like Smart. Cowper knew that the Enlightenment genie was out of the bottle. His contribution was, first, to diagnose the dimensions of that split; and, second, to find a language that (to modify Coleridge slightly) combines the knowledge of the heart and head.

For the purposes of this chapter, Cowper's work may be divided into three periods: 1771–1772, when he wrote most of the *Olney Hymns*; the early 1780s, when he wrote the lengthy poetic satires that appear in his *Poems*, 1782; and 1783–1784, when he wrote *The Task*.

In the *Olney Hymns*, where Cowper's theme is clearly and exclusively religious, the expression of doubts and anxieties becomes part of his process of spiritual discovery. In the early 1780s, his satires offer an explicit critique of the Enlightenment separation of intellectual from personal knowledge. In the reflective *Task*, Cowper achieves a language for harmonizing his personal commitments and the knowledge he affirms.

"Philosophy Baptiz'd": Cowper's Alternative to Enlightenment Knowing

Combining Faith and Doubt in Olney Hymns

In the years after his conversion and before his 1773 breakdown, Cowper's poetic work was limited to hymnody, primarily the poems printed in *Olney Hymns* (1779). The idea for the hymnbook was Newton's, who also involved Cowper in prayer meetings and pastoral duties in and around Olney. Cowper was little suited to the public exposure this brought, and his cousin, Lady Hesketh, blamed Newton's hymn project for Cowper's lapse into insanity: it "kept him in a *constant fever*," she wrote. "Only imagine a man of his Genius dwelling incessantly on this one Subject!"[20] Cowper had written sixty-six hymns before his breakdown. When it became evident that his recovery would be a lengthy one, Newton brought the project to completion, completing more than four times as many hymns as Cowper.

Cowper's contributions to *Olney Hymns* are no more the spiritual autobiography of Cowper than Isaac Watts' hymns are an account of the earlier hymn writer's life. The hymns were written for public use, to be expounded (not sung) during prayer meetings and religious instruction.[21] Still, Cowper's hymns explore themes of doubt and anxiety, along with faith and spiritual assurance. Regrettably, Cowper was ultimately unable to reconcile these elements to a life of faith. In an early account of his conversion, in fact, he gives a rather objective, rational explanation for his faith. In a letter, written to the same cousin who later criticized Newton, he writes that the truth of Scripture is established by the fulfillment of prophecy.[22] Cowper is telling her that one—anyone— can point to particular historical events, match them to biblical prophecies, and logically conclude that the Bible must be true. Clearly Cowper himself had not been converted this way when he was under the care of Cotton. The letter's mode of establishing the truth of Scripture is one peculiarly suited to Enlightenment rationalism—logical, built on evidence, open to all observers, indifferent to the person making the observations. There's nothing wrong with it, and none of the eighteenth-century Christians in this book believed Christian truth was *contrary* to evidence or observation. But those elements did not produce faith in Cowper. As he writes twenty years later in *The Task*, it was the personal, Christ-like touch of Cotton at the St. Alban's asylum during 1764 that nurtured him back to mental health and "bade me live."[23]

There is a mixture of faith, doubt, and personal commitment in *Olney Hymns* that is probably closer to typical modes of theological inquiry than Cowper knew. The best of these hymns approach their subject matter with unflinching honesty:

> Our faith is feeble we confess,
> We faintly trust thy word;
> But wilt thou pity us the less?
> Be that far from thee, Lord!
>
> Remember him who once apply'd
> With trembling for relief;
> "Lord, I believe, with tears he cry'd,
> O help my unbelief."[24]

Yet Cowper fully never developed a way of embracing his own doubts or acknowledging the role of uncertainty in the search for theological knowledge. He gives voice to it in *Olney Hymns* but even there he often seems to think that doubts are to be overcome and left behind. In a song too personal for *Olney Hymns*, Cowper recounts his recovery from madness more as he imagined it than as he actually experienced it:

> All at once my chains were broken,
> From my Feet my Fetters fell,
> And that Word in Pity spoken,
> Snatch'd me from the gates of Hell.
> Grace Divine, how sweet the Sound,
>
> Sweet the grace which I have found.
> Since that Hour in Hope of Glory,
> With thy Foll'wers I am found,
> And relate the wondrous Story
> To thy list'ning Saints around.[25]

Nevertheless, some of Cowper's hymns achieve greatness precisely by their acknowledgment of the mysteries of God's ways, the fleeting nature of religious fulfillment, and the spiritual dryness that often accompanies the believer. "God moves in a mysterious way" begins with the sublime imagery of God planting "his footsteps in the Sea / and rid[ing] upon the Storm." But the fourth stanza acknowledges the difficulty of comprehending God's ways:

> Judge not the Lord by feeble sense,
> But trust him for his grace;
> Behind a frowning providence,
> He hides a smiling face.[26]

The hymn goes on to liken God's purposes to a fragrant flower but acknowledges that its bud "may have a bitter taste."

The combination of the sweet and the bitter may be seen in "Sometimes a Light Surprizes," where short periods of spiritual fulfillment are followed by dryness:

> Sometimes a light surprizes
> The christian while he sings;
> It is the LORD who rises {Lord in small caps}
> With healing in his wings:
> When comforts are declining,
> He grants the soul again
> A season of clear shining
> To cheer it after rain.[27]

As a great poet and close student of Cowper, Donald Davie, has written, "the crucial word in it is the first. 'Sometimes'—only sometimes, not always, not even very often!"[28] Numerous other hymns recount the speaker's difficulty in loving God or trusting that his prayers will be heard.[29] Cowper does not usually single out a cause (such as sin in the believer's life) for the transitory nature of spiritual contentment. Instead, he explores the actual, personal experience of the life of faith and gives voice its ambiguities and mysteries.

Another well-known hymn, "Oh for a closer Walk with God," takes the speaker from spiritual contentment into the desert:

> Where is the Blessedness I knew
> When first I saw the Lord?
> Where is the Soul-refreshing View
> Of Jesus in his Word?[30]

The speaker goes on to lament the "Aching Void" left by the memory of that time. He fears that the divine spirit of rest may never return. The hymn is moving not because the speaker finds fulfillment in the end, but because of the moving pleas and questions that accompany the walk of faith.[31]

During this part of his life, Cowper's hymns conveyed religious uncertainty and religious knowledge simultaneously. His deep reflection on the Christian life, like that of Watts, produced work that has been used and considered valid by many generations of believers since his day. The popularity of the hymns testifies that many of their singers affirm the combination of faith and anxiety they find in them.

What Cowper could not see after his 1773 breakdown, was that if belief is part of religious knowledge, so, too, is doubt, as I will explain in the last part of this chapter.[32] He could see the role of personal experience in many other forms of knowing, but because of his 1773 breakdown and continuing mental illness, Cowper was never again able to assimilate his experience with the religious convictions he continued to hold.

Personal Commitment and Knowing: Cowper's 1782 Poems

After his catastrophic breakdown, Cowper recovered his sanity in the late 1770s by turning to the care of animals, carpentry, gardening, friendship, and poetry. For the purposes of this chapter, the chief interest of the long satirical verse in his 1782 *Poems* is Cowper's development of an approach to knowledge that arises from personal commitment—an approach that *The Task* would demonstrate even more powerfully. At many points Cowper contrasts his approach to the detached, impersonal view of knowledge in his day. Many of his insights into nature, society, and religion arise from his alternative to contemporary Enlightenment thinking.

Yet although his verse continues to affirm Christian truth, Cowper could no longer take part in religious activities, as he had before the breakdown. To make matters worse, Cowper's satirical poems of 1782 attribute unhappiness to deficient piety:

> Throw tints and all away,
> True piety is chearful as the day,
> Will weep indeed and heave a pitying groan
> For others woes, but smiles upon her own.[33]

Hints of his personal troubles appear in this verse as well, but he is unable to mine them to good effect. His long poem "Conversation," published in 1782, contains a sad self-reference in his lines on "The Christian, in whose soul, though now distress'd, / Lives the dear thought of joys he once possess'd." But the next lines offer cold advice rather than reflective consideration of the dark night of the soul:

> The song of Sion is a tasteless thing,
> Unless when rising on a joyful wing
> The soul can mix with the celestial bands,
> And give the strain the compass it demands.[34]

Despite these sad elements, Cowper's verse affirms the value of personal commitment to the discovery of knowledge. What he could merely write about in religious matters, he experienced in the areas of his life that provided him with mental balance. But write about it he did. A few weeks after the 1782 *Poems* appeared, Cowper expressed his belief that the reviewers would "undoubtedly reprobate the doctrines [and] pronounce me Methodist."[35] Two years later, he expressed hope that the ailing Samuel Johnson, a fellow believer, would yet produce a work to "give proof, that [for] a man of profound learning . . . to embrace the gospel, is not evidence either of enthusiasm, infirmity, or insanity."[36]

Cowper's satires criticize the corruptions of learning, wealth, politics, and religion in ways comparable to other eighteenth-century writers. Moving beyond an ordinary critique, however, Cowper finds the root problem in a narrowing concept of reason:

> Then truth is hush'd, that heresy may preach;
> And all is trash that reason cannot reach.[37]

"Reason," here is that of the late eighteenth-century Enlightenment. The truths of religious faith "hardly find a single friend" in this intellectual climate, as he writes a few lines later. Cowper's verse warns that criticism of tradition is often being replaced by a blind prejudice that favors the present without any recognition of the moral failures of the day. Cowper saw that personal vanity, greed, and lust were only too quick to fill the vacuum that arises from separating knowledge from the personal commitments that make up our personal lives. Either those commitments come to have no validity, or new forms of learning, such as philology in the passage below, justify one's basest desires:

> Hence the same word that bids our lusts obey,
> Is misapplied to sanctify their sway.
> If stubborn Greek refuse to be his friend,
> Hebrew or Syriac shall be forc'd to bend;
> If languages and copies all cry, No—
> Somebody proved it centuries ago.[38]

Cowper is satirizing the notion that the tools of modern learning, such as philology, can be neutral. He sees that what masquerades as an objective, detached method actually ends up ratifying virtually any belief one wishes.

Cowper was clearly aware that Christian faith was being banished to the irrational or the merely subjective—even by contemporary religious leaders. The "two grand nostrums" of contemporary free thinkers, Cowper writes, are "[t]hat scripture lies, and blasphemy is sense."[39] The Enlightenment religious leaders satirized in Cowper's verse still have a role for Jesus: he was a man who came to eliminate the prejudices from Judaism. He intended to create a religion that was entirely accessible to the unaided reason. In other words, their Jesus had something like the religion of Voltaire in mind: cool, commonsensical, non-miraculous. Many churchmen, meanwhile, had quietly given up believing that their faith was true, as opposed to being merely comforting. According to a fictional churchman in Cowper's verse,

[D]iffering judgments serve but to declare
That truth lies somewhere, if we knew but where.[40]

This enlightened clergyman has acquiesced to the split between knowledge and personal commitment.

Cowper considered his poems to be a "vehicle of true knowledge," but in the world of the late eighteenth century, they had to compete with those who separated religious, political, and scientific knowledge, while putting aesthetic experience in yet a different category.[41]

Although the satires in the 1782 *Poems* usually attack general ills rather than individuals, they are by no means impersonal. Nor does Cowper set himself apart from his subject matter. In this, Cowper differs from Voltaire, one of the individuals he does attack. The effect of Voltaire's wit is to leave him looking shrewd and skeptical, whereas the subject he satirizes is made to seem trivial or brutal, ignorant or unenlightened. In Voltaire's *Philosophical Dictionary*, for instance, Solomon comes off looking ridiculous:

> The first work attributed to him is that of Proverbs. It is a collection of maxims, which sometimes appear to our refined minds trifling, low, incoherent, in bad taste, and without meaning. People cannot be persuaded that an enlightened king has composed a collection of sentences, in which there is not one which regards the art of government, politics, manners of courtiers, or customs of a court.[42]

Although both Cowper and Voltaire are satirists, their literary modes differ markedly, primarily because their approaches to knowledge are so different. Voltaire undertakes no commitment that could embarrass him with its vulgarity or threaten him with its lack of refinement. He stands far off. He invites us to ridicule his object—Solomon in this case. He draws our attention and applause to himself. Cowper satirizes this aspect of Voltaire by looking at it from the horizon of Voltaire's death.

> He begs their flatt'ry with his latest breath;
> And, smother'd in't at last, is prais'd to death![43]

Fairly or not, Cowper criticizes Voltaire for using his skill primarily to establish his reputation as a wit. The ultimate goal of poetic reflection for Cowper is not to establish his reputation. What he seeks is "divine communion."[44] This goal is most evident in Cowper's relation with his landscapes, and yet it is also evident in his verse on society. In his satire "Retirement," he describes David as a model for personal, inner transformation.[45] During his exile from Saul, David embraces both the expression of the inner life (through the Psalms he wrote) and a model of loving action. David becomes a great king through the communion he achieves between his personal piety and outward actions.

The eight long satirical poems of 1782 continue the process of assembling Cowper's alternative to Enlightenment ways of knowing. Where the *Olney Hymns* acknowledged the role of uncertainty, these poems highlight the role of personal experience and criticize the Enlightenment ideal of detachment. The preface to Cowper's 1782 *Poems*, written by Newton, spells out the situation: "little is considered as deserving the name of knowledge, which will not stand the test of experiment."[46] Newton clearly believes that Cowper's poems communicate knowledge, and that this knowledge is of a particular type—"experimental." Cowper's verse "aims to communicate his own perceptions of the truth, beauty, and influence of the religion of the Bible," Newton continues, and this experiment has shown that "we found *ourselves* described [in Scripture].—We learnt the causes of our inquietude—we were directed to a method of relief—we tried and we were not disappointed." Experiment, then, is the epistemological meeting ground between truth and personal experience, and Cowper's 1782 *Poems* provide a record of these "experiments." Cowper himself had used the term in a similar way to refer to his and his brother's evangelical conversions: "There is that in the nature of salvation by grace when it is truly and experimentally known which prompts every person to think himself the most extraordinary instance of its power."[47]

It remains to see how Cowper incorporates and deepens his personal experience into a distinctively reflective way of knowing in *The Task*.

Reflection and Discovery in The Task

In Cowper's verse, the poet is a discoverer of truth, not a creator. Although he laments the lack of originality in contemporary poetry "[w]hate 'er we write, we bring forth nothing new"— Cowper's goal is to find new language for known religious truths: "'Twere new indeed, to see the bard all fire, / Touch'd with a coal from heav'n assume the lyre."[48] As much a nature poet as Wordsworth, Cowper's poems even give a "pre-intimation of immortality," according to Newton—a phrase that may have lodged in Wordsworth's imagination.[49] Nevertheless, Cowper is hardly the poet to claim that his language or imagination are, in themselves, creative tools. "I might have preached more Sermons than ever [Archbishop] Tillotson did, and better," he wrote his cousin in 1786, "and the world has been still fast asleep. But a Volume of Verse is a fiddle that puts the Universe in motion."[50] Verse puts the universe in motion, but it neither supplants nor competes with the truths of the sermon or the scientific treatise. His practice is completely opposed to that of an Enlightenment thinker like the Marquis de Laplace (1749–1827), who believed that knowing the forces and positions of all entities at a given time could theoretically produce certain knowledge of their past and future positions.[51] Although his emphasis on beauty implies a unified vision of truth, Cowper recommends no single mode of inquiry for obtaining it. His verse in the 1780s makes use of many fields of knowledge. Even theology yields to botany, history, moral philosophy, political science, and psychology, when appropriate.

In rejecting the Enlightenment attempt to detach the personal realm from the scientific one, Cowper's *Task* emphasizes the role that intuition plays in acquiring knowledge. This intuitive, reciprocal relationship between the observer and the natural world gives fullness to the experience of "nature" in the final book of that poem:

> There is in souls a sympathy with sounds,
> And as the mind is pitch'd the ear is pleas'd
> With melting airs or martial, brisk or grave.
> Some chord in unison with what we hear
> Is touched within us, and the heart replies.[52]

Even more broadly, the poem finds truth when natural observation, morality, and beauty are reconciled in one's inner life and outward experience.

The accumulation of observable facts may have a connection with wisdom and truth, Cowper writes, but only under certain conditions. The detached intelligence that knows all universal forces and positions in Laplace's theory could never achieve wisdom. True knowledge must be internalized. It must pass through serious reflection. As an example, consider this winter scene, where Cowper rises from a description of a late robin to a broader reflection on observation itself:

> The red-breast warbles still, but is content
> With slender notes and more than half supress'd.
> Pleased with his solitude, and flitting light
> From spray to spray, where'er he rests he shakes
> From many a twig the pendent drops of ice,
> That tinkle in the wither'd leaves below.
> Stillness accompanied with sounds so soft
> Charms more than silence. Meditation here
> May think down hours to moments. Here the heart
> May give an useful lesson to the head,
> And learning wiser grow without his books.
> Knowledge and wisdom, far from being one,
> Have oft times no connexion. Knowledge dwells
> In heads replete with thoughts of other men,
> Wisdom in minds attentive to their own.[53]

The mere accumulation of knowledge is trivial beside a wise apprehension of nature, Cowper maintains. The wise observer, whether poet or scientist, does more than merely locate, identify, describe, and analyze what he or she observes. Instead, he or she "dwells" in observations meditatively over so long a period that hours seem to be mere moments. Only by establishing such a personal connection does the observer have the possibility of discovering a language for nature that will, over time, command broad intellectual assent.

Cowper's nature poetry often cultivates connections between knowledge of the natural world and other forms of knowledge. After an epic catalogue of flowers in the final book of *The Task*, for instance, Cowper concludes:

> These have been, and these shall be in their day.
> And all this uniform uncoloured scene
> Shall be dismantled of its fleecy load,
> And flush into variety again.
> From dearth to plenty, and from death to life,
> Is Nature's progress when she lectures man
> In heav'nly truth; evincing as she makes
> The grand transition, that there lives and works
> A soul in all things, and that soul is God.[54]

Cowper sets out his discoveries for others to confirm or even dispute. His jasmines and woodbines are part of Nature's "lecture," after all, and immediately after this passage he criticizes deist and pagan notions of nature. His is a poetry that is intensely personal without being merely subjective, reflective without being private.

The quoted selections from *The Task* illustrate Cowper's approach to nature, but he summarizes the significance of internalizing the objects of knowledge much earlier in the poem as well. True advances in knowledge, as Cowper explains them, come from periods of "retirement," a term that had served as the title of his final 1782 poetic satire. Retirement does not mean flight from business to the countryside or an indulgence in mere feeling, both of which he satirizes. Retirement is the meditative posture of an active, reflective observer, someone who is "studious of laborious ease":

> He that attends to his interior self,
> That has a heart and keeps it; has a mind
> That hungers and supplies it; and who seeks
> A social, not a dissipated life,
> Has business. Feels himself engaged t'atchieve
> No unimportant, though a silent task.[55]

The "business" of this observer, if one takes *The Task* as a whole, is to achieve the wisdom that comes from connecting his experience of nature, social life, beauty, and religion. This is the "silent task" that Cowper names. Retirement moves from a withdrawal of worldly pleasures, early in *The Task*, to suggest the "never-ending rest" of the Sabbath as the poem nears its end.[56] In so doing, religious and natural knowledge mix with belief and participation in worship, and with a delight in beauty. Rest, participation, and beauty, in other words, form part of the epistemology of Cowper's *Task*. The poet ultimately uses rest to connect his knowledge of nature with its beauty and the "word" of its creator. " 'Love kindles as I gaze,' " he says to an imagined angelic choir:

> "I feel desires
> That give assurance of their own success,
> And that infused from heav'n, must thither tend."
> So reads he nature whom that lamp of truth
> Illuminates. Thy lamp, mysterious word!
> Which whoso sees, no longer wanders lost

> With intellects bemazed in endless doubt,
> But runs the road of wisdom.[57]

Although each person will have his or her own way of cultivating the contemplative rest that gives rise to insight, for Cowper it comes through "Friends, books, a garden, and perhaps his pen, / Delightful industry enjoyed at home."[58] Unlike Voltaire, whose reflections often lead him to spurn the world, Cowper's reflective stance draws him back to the world. Unlike the deism that Voltaire promoted, the God of Cowper's verse was no mere "artificer" or clockmaker, who created Nature, gave it laws, and then abandoned it.[59] In words that recall the critique of Christopher Smart, he protested against the inactive deity of Newtonian mechanics.

> Some say that in the origin of things
> When all creation started into birth,
> The infant elements receiv'd a law
> From which they swerve not since. That under force
> Of that controuling ordinance they move,
> And need not his immediate hand, who first
> Prescrib'd their course, to regulate it now.
> Thus dream they, and contrive to save a God
> The incumbrance of his own concerns, and spare
> The great Artificer of all that moves
> The stress of a continual act, the pain
> Of unremitted vigilance and care,
> As too laborious and severe a task.[60]

Cowper is not just criticizing the deist's God. He is criticizing the way that the deist's knowledge distances him from God. Increased natural knowledge, Cowper maintains, brings one into a closer, personal relationship to the Creator. Cowper's critique, in other words, particularly focuses on the lack of commitment in deism. There is no commitment between the deist's God and his creation, and no commitment between the deistic observer and God. They are all detached from the other. This detachment, if it were truly practiced, could never produce the intuitions that are central to further discovery.

Cowper realizes, of course, that one can observe nature without perceiving its underlying order or beauty. One can even perceive its order without recognizing a creator: "[N]ever yet did philosophic tube / That brings the planets home into the eye . . .

Discover him that rules them," he writes.[61] What's missing from this observer is any connection between his astronomical observations and the rest of creation. This astronomer is content with mere "instrumental causes," Cowper continues a few lines later. His observations are all external, unconnected with his inner life or the deep order that binds all creation together.

Cowper moves from external observation to internal knowledge in his meditations on society as well as on nature. After a long discussion of political liberty in book five of *The Task*, Cowper moves to "a liberty unsung / By poets, and by senators unpraised."[62] This is the "liberty of heart, derived from heav'n." In an even more far-reaching passage, he names the judge Matthew Hale (1609–1676) as a man whose knowledge of the law combined personal integrity and an acute understanding of his field. In the following passage, which links Hale with John Milton and Sir Isaac Newton, Cowper calls this kind of knowledge "philosophy baptized." The term *philosophy* refers to all of the fields of learning they represent, as I have explained elsewhere in this book. "Science" (in the lines that follow) draws on its broad pre-Enlightenment connotations, drawing law, literature, and physics into a unity:

Philosophy baptiz'd
In the pure fountain of eternal love
Has eyes indeed; and viewing all she sees
As meant to indicate a God to man,
Give *him* his praise, and forfeits not her own.
Learning has borne such fruit in other days
On all her branches. Piety has found
Friends in the friends of science . . .
Such was thy wisdom, Newton, childlike sage!
Sagacious reader of the works of God,
And in his word sagacious. Such too thine
Milton, whose genius had angelic wings,
And fed on manna. And such thine in whom
Our British Themis gloried with just cause,
Immortal Hale! for deep discernment praised
And sound integrity not more, than famed
For sanctity of manners undefiled.[63]

Each of these men pushed the bounds of his "science" into areas that the poetry, legal practice, and natural science of their day could not imagine. They were examples of personal commitment and integrity and intellectual genius. The knowledge that they acquired depended on these personal elements, as Cowper sees, and cannot be reduced to impersonal methods or formulas.

Cowper's poetry was working back to a reconciliation of the heart with the head, as Coleridge later wrote. To articulate the significance of the personal element for modern science, however, required a different kind of thinker. Its most convincing description arises from a twentieth-century scientist-turned-philosopher, Polanyi, who testifies to the power of experience, commitment, and beauty in assembling an alternative to the epistemology of his own day.

"Indwelling," Commitment, and Beauty in Michael Polanyi's *Personal Knowledge*

The Enlightenment belief that the advance of knowledge requires us to detach ourselves from the objects of knowledge, criticized by Cowper, became a source of intolerable irritation to chemist Polanyi. Polanyi, whose research in physical chemistry had come to the favorable notice of Albert Einstein in 1913, was a younger member of the group of brilliant scientists who worked in Berlin in the 1920s, including Albert Einstein, Max Planck, Erwin Schrödinger, and others.[64] Polanyi's departure from scientific research to philosophy was hastened by his horror at the justifications for harnessing science to the power of the state by Soviet Russia and Marxist apologists in the West.[65] The destruction of yet another world war, fought by the most intellectually advanced nations in history, forced Polanyi to give his full attention to the nature of knowledge. "Why did we destroy Europe?" he began asking, and in 1948, he left chemistry for good to concentrate on the philosophical and social questions that so concerned him.[66]

Polanyi named many epistemological elements as contributors to the disasters that had befallen the West: a quest for universal reason where truth is detached from social ritual, the abandonment of the intellectual value of legal traditions, and the submission of the individual to the state.[67] For the purposes of this chapter, I will focus on Polanyi's critique of the Enlightenment's understanding of scientific discovery. In place of its goal of scientific detachment, he constructs a postcritical alternative that validates "personal knowledge": commitment to a set of beliefs, intuition, and a necessary role for beauty.

As Polanyi saw it, Western science had made a tragic choice during the Enlightenment: in seeking to detach personal biases from scientific investigation, it actually eliminated the basis for a commitment to the human person. Polanyi's most sustained enquiry into his subject, *Personal Knowledge*, rejects this detachment at the outset.[68] He realized that the process of modern scientific discovery had *never* been an impersonal enterprise, from Johannes Kepler's seventeenth-century discoveries through Einstein's theory of relativity.[69] Polanyi criticizes the ideal of objective scientific knowledge, understood as the assumption that scientific progress comes from detached observation according to an identifiable method. Instead, he says, we must acknowledge an "intuition of rationality in nature . . . [as an] essential part of scientific theory."[70]

Polanyi argues that one must acknowledge the specifically human element in scientific discovery. "It is not words that have meaning," after all, "but the speaker or listener who means something by them."[71] The equations of Kepler, Newton, or Einstein mean nothing by themselves, without "the ubiquitous participation of the scientist in upholding [their] affirmations." At the beginning of this chapter, I wrote that I could no longer participate in science in this way. I saw that repeating the formulas on the board would become a mere "desert of trivialities," as Polanyi says. By contrast, the true scientist participates personally and even passionately in both the certainties of his or her science and the uncertainties at its frontiers. Even in the routine observations of a physician, Polanyi writes, the feelings of intellectual satisfaction or personal responsibility (though sometimes dormant) are present.[72]

Polanyi gives a striking name to this way of participating in scientific discovery: he calls it "indwelling." He contrasts indwelling to an objective approach that pretends to hold its methods at arms length, believing nothing and committed to nothing:

> When we accept a certain set of pre-suppositions and use them as our interpretative framework, we may be said to dwell in them as we do in our own body. Their uncritical acceptance for the time being consists in a process of assimilation by which we identify ourselves with them. They are not asserted and cannot be asserted, for assertion can be made only *within* a framework with which we have

identified ourselves for the time being; as they are themselves our ultimate framework, they are essentially inarticulable.[73]

Over time, dwelling in the epistemological framework of one's field of knowledge produces an intuitive grasp of its contours. The "inarticulable" or tacit elements of this framework, which is essential to new discoveries, cannot be reduced to a formula or set of procedures. Polanyi describes the transmission of this art of discovery as something passed "by example from master to apprentice," and he compares scientific research to the craft of violin making:

> It is pathetic to watch the endless efforts—equipped with microscopy and chemistry, with mathematics and electronics—to reproduce a single violin of the kind the half-literate Stradivarius turned out as a matter of routine more than 200 years ago.

> To learn by example is to submit to authority. You follow your master because you trust his manner of doing things, even when you cannot analyze and account in detail for its effectiveness. By watching the master and emulating his efforts in the presence of his example, the apprentice unconsciously picks up the rules of the art, including those which are not explicitly known to the master himself. These hidden rules can be assimilated only by the person who surrenders himself to that extent uncritically to the imitation of another. A society which wants to preserve a fund of personal knowledge must submit to tradition.[74]

This quotation summarizes three elements of Polanyi's view of the process of discovering new knowledge: personal commitment, indwelling, and intuition. The apprentice is committed to his or her craft. He believes in the validity of many elements of its knowledge structure without being able to articulate them. Both apprentice and master "indwell" their craft to learn, master, and advance it. Their knowledge gives them intuitive or tacit knowledge of what tool to use, how to hold it, what pressure to use, and so on—little of which may be reduced to an explicit procedure.

Each of these elements is evident in the poetry of Cowper, as we have seen, and both men stress their importance to an age that has forgotten them. A fourth element in the work of both Cowper and Polanyi is the role that beauty plays in the discovery of knowledge.

A great scientific theory, writes Polanyi, "has an inarticulate component acclaiming its beauty, and this is essential to the belief that the theory is true."[75] He stresses the essentially human aspect of this part of his framework by adding that no animal can appreciate the intellectual beauty of science. Louis De Broglie first ascribed wave qualities to particles in motion "purely on the basis of intellectual beauty," he writes, and Einstein's assumption that beauty was "a token of reality" enabled him to discover new consequences of relativity.[76] Einstein's theories have "a beauty that exhilarates and a profundity that entrances us," he writes. But Polanyi moves beyond exhilaration, and in a discussion of crystallography, identifies the epistemological significance of beauty. Crystallography establishes an

> ideal of shapeliness, by which it classifies solid bodies into such as tend to fulfill this ideal and others in which no such shapeliness is apparent . . . Next, each individual crystal is taken to represent an ideal of regularity, all actual deviations from which are regarded as imperfections. This ideal shape is found by assuming that the approximately plane surfaces of crystals are geometrical planes which extend to the straight edges in which such planes must meet, thus bounding the crystal on all sides . . . [H]owever widely the crystal specimen deviates from the theory, this will be put down as a shortcoming of the crystal and not of the theory.[77]

Polanyi sees in crystallography "the formalization of an aesthetic ideal," which brings the domain of art criticism close to that of science.

Scientific discovery implies a bridge from the uncertain to the certain. That bridge is rational, to be sure, but it comprises the aesthetic pleasure of admiration along with the observations of the senses:

> To say that the discovery of objective truth in science consists in the apprehension of a rationality which commands our respect and arouses our contemplative admiration; that such discovery, while using the experience of our senses as clues, transcends this experience by embracing the vision of a reality beyond the impressions of our senses, a vision which speaks for itself in guiding us to an ever deeper understanding of reality—such an account of scientific procedure would be generally shrugged aside as out-dated Platonism: a piece of mystery-mongering unworthy of an enlightened age.[78]

The "reality beyond the impressions of our senses" is not something that can be proven or described by empirical science. It is part of an intuitive framework that provides the basis for all discovery.

Beauty then rounds out the elements that make up Polanyi's "fiduciary program" of scientific discovery, which he offers as an alternative to the Enlightenment's view of a detached scientific method. This program embraces artistic and religious discoveries and scientific ones, as Polanyi recognizes, and he names Augustine as the first to see that belief is before all knowledge. Polanyi calls Augustine the first postcritical philosopher because he recognized that all knowledge presupposes commitment. When Augustine wrote "unless you believe, you will not understand," he was acknowledging that no seeker can operate outside of a "fiduciary framework."[79] To take the next step and advance knowledge, the seeker must indwell the practices that guide the scientific, religious, aesthetic, or other assumptions of his or her field. Indwelling, in turn, produces intuition in a thoughtful person, which enables him to have an "intimation of approaching nearer towards a solution" to the problems at hand.[80] The entire process resembles the creation of a work of art, for there is a "fundamental vision of the whole" whose beauty (however uncertain) is essential to the conviction of truth.

Polanyi's fiduciary program attempts to provide a postcritical approach to knowledge that recovers the strengths of pre-Enlightenment knowing without sacrificing the undisputed gains of the Enlightenment.[81] His alternative envisions an epistemology in which certain unproven beliefs could be "tacitly taken for granted in the days before modern philosophic criticism reached its present incisiveness."[82] As I have explained, Cowper saw the necessity of these elements as well, though he did not give them the philosophical coherence that Polanyi achieved.

By recognizing the role of belief, Polanyi by no means embraced dogmatism, which he identified with medieval Catholicism and modern political ideologies. Belief has its hazards, he admits: "[T]he possibility of error is a necessary element of any belief bearing on reality."[83] Doubt always accompanies one's investigations, and mistaken beliefs must fall before the test of reality as other fellow explorers contribute their findings. "We may firmly believe what we might conceivably doubt; and may hold to be true what might conceivably be false."[84] Scientific exploration involves a good deal of guesswork, he wrote, and scientific propositions retain their conjectural character even after the scientist is convinced of their truth.

After writing his *Olney Hymns* and his 1773 breakdown, Cowper was not able to record a positive role for doubt in his own meditations. Sadly, his mental illness left him in no doubt that he was damned. However much progress he made toward articulating an alternative to Enlightenment approaches to knowledge, the meditative characters who appear frequently in Cowper's later work have few doubts.

The fiduciary program depends on yet a final element that is emphasized equally by Cowper and Polanyi: this is the element of repose and meditation that the poet called *retirement*, and the scientist *rest* and *contemplation*. Discovery does not usually occur "at the peak of mental effort," Polanyi writes, "but more often comes in a flash after a period of rest or distraction."[85] In Cowper's verse, poetic discovery arises in periods of retirement. It emphatically does not come at the end of a string of empirical observations, logical deductions, or witty insights, but after a time of reflective quiet.

Polanyi mentions the process of writing poetry several times in *Personal Knowledge*, highlighting its ability to modify one's framework of knowledge, its power of indicating tacitly more than it can state, and its requirement to pause amid uncertainty before settling on the right line.[86] Perhaps the best illustration of how poetic and scientific discovery may be linked within Polanyi's thought, however, comes from the Harvard chemist Dudley Herschbach, who shared the 1986 Nobel prize with Polanyi's son, John. Herschbach knew Michael, and he stresses the element of imagination in his own research. The typical tasks of introductory chemistry courses are so unlike what a leading creative scientist does, says Herschbach, that he has his beginning students write poems:

> I assign them to write poems, because I say that's much more like doing science than the ordinary academic exercises. You see, when you're doing frontier science, you're not concerned in the first place whether you're getting it right . . . [A]t the outset you're concerned more [with] "are you asking a good question? Have you found a perspective or an approach that is likely to give you a new view of things that would tie together things that hitherto had seemed unrelated

or confusing or out of joint?" . . . And writing a poem is like that. There's no concern with whether it's right or wrong. There's a concern, "does this give you some more or less vivid view, snapshot or insight . . . that you don't get in the ordinary humdrum of prose?"[87]

As personal as this process is, it is not merely subjective. Cowper and Polanyi were not subjectivists. Their work continually referred to a reality outside of themselves, whose comprehension requires the best, most rigorous examination of nature, society, and self: "[P]ersonal knowledge in science is not made but discovered," writes Polanyi, "and as such it claims to establish contact with reality beyond the clues on which it relies. It commits us, passionately and far beyond our comprehension, to a vision of reality."[88] For Cowper, reclusive and melancholy though he was, poetry involved him in contemporary moral campaigns against slavery and for more humane treatment of animals; in numerous social debates over marriage, gambling, and education; and in the intellectual discussions about deism, history and the natural sciences.

Not everything that Cowper or Polanyi wrote was true, but the same goes for every one of the figures mentioned in this book. There never has been a formula for truth, as these men teach us. But there is an approach to reality, human and natural, in which we begin to indwell the truths that we perceive, thereby connecting our observations with our deepest personal commitments and leading to new discoveries. Of course we can reject all of this and pretend that faith never intersects knowledge, when knowledge really counts. In that case, we'll never have to expose our full self to truth. But that way madness lies.

CONCLUSION

This book began by searching for approaches to knowledge that are more coherent and humane than the ones the twentieth century inherited from the Enlightenment. By the end of the eighteenth century knowledge had fractured along many different lines—natural science had separated from theology, theology from history, and history from literature, just to name a few of the fissures I have attempted to describe. No longer could "science" be used to describe general human knowledge, as it was before the eighteenth century; no longer could "philosophy" include natural science, as it had in earlier decades.

Throughout the seven chapters of this book, several common themes have emerged among the critics of the Enlightenment, both from the eighteenth century and our own time. These critics often stress the significance of the communal search for knowledge as opposed to Immanuel Kant's Enlightenment challenge to the individual, "dare to know!" They urge attention to the past, whether through tradition or narrative, as opposed to the Enlightenment's self-confident orientation to the future. They often embrace some version of personal or relational knowledge, as opposed to the Enlightenment's belief that insights that aspire to knowledge must spring from an impersonal, objective method. Somewhat to my surprise, nearly all of them emphasize an aesthetic element

211

to knowledge, whether in the form of beauty or good taste, as opposed to the more narrowly rationalistic or empirical boundaries to Enlightenment epistemology.

Each of these themes aims at coherence rather than fragmentation. Each implies connections among different approaches to knowledge rather than the specialization. Yet the specialization of knowledge since the Enlightenment had undeniably led to great intellectual advances. In light of this, perhaps we should simply palliate the evils of fragmentation without trying to cure them. Certainly if the cure looks like a twenty-first century version of Maximilien Robespierre's ideology, combining a powerful understanding of social rhythms and an equally powerful misunderstanding of one's own capacity for evil, I would opt for fragmentation. But part of the appeal of the postmodern ideologies is their perception—correct, in my view—that our cultural concepts of human nature need reinforcement, whether from social rhythms or some other nonrationalistic resources. Man seeks for unity, social and temporal, to feel at home in the world. If our culture cannot provide some version of this unity, people will be all the more likely to listen to the false promises of the next Grand Inquisitor.

Beyond the negative consequences of an extreme postmodernism, there are positive reasons for pursuing broader, more unified approaches to knowledge as represented in this book. I have already hinted at one of them: they can help us feel more at home in the world. The relational and aesthetic emphases of Christopher Smart, John Polkinghorne, William Cowper, and Michael Polanyi, for instance, give epistemological weight to the experience of the wonder and beauty of the natural. Without rejecting the stupendous gains of modern science, they urge us to embrace a personal commitment to the objects of one's knowledge. Instead of isolating scientific achievement in the laboratory, they locate it in a human process that begins with the individual's awe at the world, rises to understanding, and continues in a form of "indwelling" the significance of one's knowledge.

If these scientists and poets help us feel welcome in space, a number of this book's philosophers and prose writers extend that welcome to time. Edmund Burke, Hans-Georg Gadamer, Daniel Defoe, and the narrative theologians reacquaint us with the epistemological validity of past traditions and older narratives. These writers urge us to go beyond the critical gaze of the Enlightenment and look at these sources of knowledge with a "second naiveté." Seeing fresh relations between older stories and our own can strengthen the "history-like" character of narrative. Seeing new links between one's own community and past traditions can put political controversies in a broader perspective than can be managed by a rationalistic application of ahistorical rights to political problems.

Finally, the connections fostered among the broader forms of knowledge that I have described in this book are more likely to give rise to wisdom than the fragmented, specialized forms of knowledge that have dominated the West since the Enlightenment. Defoe and the narrative theologians cannot confirm the historical veracity of scriptural stories, but they offer a way of connecting one's individual life to those stories as generations of readers have discovered. Jonathan Swift and Wendell Berry cannot offer an alternative to educational technology, but they remind us that our educational practices are intimately connected to our view of the human soul. Whatever wisdom is, they urge, it has to do with connecting knowledge to human life, not about accumulating more data.

All of this discussion of unity and coherence, however, may be somewhat misleading. The thinkers discussed sympathetically in this book do not offer a single, unified alternative to the Enlightenment. They typically offer analogies among various forms of knowledge—between science and theology, for instance—rather than an integration of the two. Although I have tried to show that these analogies offer a more coherent relation between the human knower and the objects of knowledge, they do not add up to a single epistemological framework, so far as I can see. They do not aspire to challenge the Enlightenment on its own terms. Far from offering certainty, the analogies among the languages of science, poetry, and theology, suggested by Smart and Polkinghorne, require a type of faith. Although they cannot be accused of harboring an irrational enthusiasm of the sort derided by John Locke, their analogies rest on a trust that our experiences of awe and joy in nature will find an answer in a rational description of the natural order.

This analogical mode of imagining, exploring, and reasoning is common to most of the figures in this book. Previously I quoted narrative theologian Garrett Green, who remarks that "as" may be considered the "copula of the imagination." He was explaining how a believer's life may be viewed as an individual instance of typical biblical plots and characters. But he also noted that this mode of imagination is common to the natural scientist and the poet as well. We might add that it is necessary to the political philosopher and historian. Burke and Gadamer cannot give us a scientific method for discriminating between good and bad prejudices. Instead, they introduce us to traditions that make up "the wardrobe of a moral imagination," in Burke's words, "which the heart owns, and the understanding ratifies."[1] These can help us distinguish valid reforms from foolish innovations, but they will never eliminate the need for the judicious taste that knows when and how to use traditions.

Although I have agreed with much of the postmodern critique, there are many aspects of it that I find lacking. Many postmodern figures continue to embrace power of the individual, albeit in a form that differs from that of the Enlightenment. They continue to endorse the individual's mastery over language and time that, in my view, blinds them to their own inevitable moral and political shortcomings. The figures I have treated sympathetically also have their shortcomings, of course, and I trust I have acknowledged them. But I have also tried to indicate the self-correcting resources among them. Their individual explorations are tempered by a strong emphasis on relationship; their sense of mastery by an openness to mystery. By following their inquiries within the mysteries of one's relationships to society, nature, and God, I hope I have indicated some profitable ways for seeking the fullness of knowing that we need in the decades ahead.

NOTES

Introduction

1. Edmund Burke, *Reflections on the Revolution in France* [1790], vol. 8 of *The Writings and Speeches of Edmund Burke*, ed. Paul Langford and P. J. Marshall (Oxford: Clarendon, 1981), 138.

2. Max Horkheimer and Theodor Adorno, *Dialectic of Enlightenment*, trans. John Cumming (New York: Herder and Herder, 1972), 93.

> The instrument by means of which the bourgeoisie came to power, the liberation of forces, universal freedom self-determination—in short, the Enlightenment, itself turned against the bourgeoisie once, as a system of domination, it had recourse to repression . . . finally, the antiauthoritarian principle has to change into its very antithesis—into opposition to reason, the abrogation of everything inherently binding.

3. Among many excellent treatments of the Enlightenment, three particularly notable ones in this context are those by Louis Dupré, *The Enlightenment and the Intellectual Foundations of Modern Culture* (New Haven: Yale University Press, 2004); Isabel Rivers, *Reason, Grace, and Sentiment: A Study of the Language of Religion and Ethics in England, 1660–1780*, 2 vols. (Cambridge: Cambridge University Press, 1991, 2000); and Joseph Levine, *The Battle of the Books* (Ithaca: Cornell University Press, 1991). Dupré's work strongly emphasizes science, arguing that the Enlightenment conception of "reason" itself is a mental construction of its particular time period—not a universal or objective standard. Isabel Rivers focuses on the tension between reason and grace in her

215

first volume, and reason and sentiment in the second. Levine's study explains how the proponents of modernity argued that modern learning outpaced ancient achievements in every field, while the ancients argued the opposite. Levine's conclusion, roughly stated, is that the moderns won the battle with regard to the "cumulative" forms of learning (which include the natural sciences, archeology, philology, and certain approaches to history) whereas the ancients claimed that the literature of antiquity retained its claim to superiority. Still other fields (notably philosophy) remained in dispute.

4. Alasdair MacIntyre, "Epistemological Crises, Dramatic Narrative, and the Philosophy of Science," in *Why Narrative? Readings in Narrative Theology*, ed. Stanley Hauerwas and L. Gregory Jones, 89–110 (Grand Rapids: Eerdmans, 1989), 144.

5. Voltaire, "Laws," sec. 4, in *Philosophical Dictionary*, trans. by William Fleming, *The Works of Voltaire* (Paris: E. R. Dumont, 1901), 11:99.

6. Not all proponents of Enlightenment were politically radical, however, as James Schmidt shows in his description of the leading Enlightenment figures of Berlin. See the introduction in *What Is Enlightenment? Eighteenth-Century Answers and Twentieth-Century Questions* (Berkeley: University of California Press, 1996), 12–13.

7. Thomas Paine, *The Rights of Man, Part II* in *Thomas Paine: Political Writings*, ed. Bruce Kuklick (Cambridge: Cambridge University Press, 1989), 258. Paine uses the phrase "regeneration of man" in Part I (1791) on p. 127.

8. Maximilien Robespierre, *Discours*. Edited by Marc Bouloiseau and Albert Soboul. Vol. 10 of *Œuvres de Maximilien Robespierre*, ed. E. Déprez and E. Lesueur, 10 vols. (Paris: Presses Universitaires de France, 1910–1967), 358, 357.

9. Horkheimer and Adorno, *Dialectic of Enlightenment*, 117–19.

10. The paragraph that follows draws on a useful summary of critiques by James Schmidt in the opening paragraph of his introduction to *What Is Enlightenment?* (1). His list includes political critiques by James Q. Wilson, Leszek Kolakowski, and Richard Pipes; the critique of foundationalism by Richard Rorty; Isaiah Berlin's critique of the Enlightenment neglect of the tragic nature of moral conflict; and the ethical critiques of Charles Taylor and Alasdair MacIntyre.

11. Richard Rorty, *Philosophy and the Mirror of Nature* (Princeton: Princeton University Press, 1979), 359. See Roger Lundin's analysis of Rorty, in *The Culture of Interpretation* (Grand Rapids: Eerdmans, 1993), 35.

12. David Harvey, *The Condition of Postmodernity* (Cambridge, Mass.: Blackwell, 1990), 56–57.

13. In Neale Donald Walsch, *Conversations with God: Questions about the Language of the Soul* (San Bruno, Calif.: Audio Literature, 1996), for instance, "God" tells author "You are the creator of your own reality . . . You think it into being. This is the first step in creation. God the

Father is thought. Your thought is the parent which gives birth to all things. . . . You can be, do, and have whatever you desire."

14. "[P]ostmodernism," writes Gerald L. Bruns, "is simply the crisis of rationality or enlightenment brought on by those who would level the genre distinction between philosophy and literature and who are determined to confound the logical differentiations among science, morality, and art" (8). See Gerald L. Bruns, "Along the Fatal Narrative Turn: Toward an Anarchic Theory of Literary History," *Modern Language Quarterly* 57, no. 1 (1996): 1–21.

15. William Cowper, "Expostulation," 108–9 in *The Poems of William Cowper*, ed. John D. Baird and Charles Ryskamp (Oxford: Clarendon, 1980), 1:299.

Chapter 1

1. Following convention, I will refer to *The Life and Strange Surprizing Adventures of Robinson Crusoe* (1719) by its common name, *Robinson Crusoe*. Quotations from the two sequels come from *The Works of Daniel Defoe*, ed. G. H. Maynadier, vol. 2: *The Farther Adventures of Robinson Crusoe*, and vol. 3: *Serious Reflections During the Life and Surprising Adventures of Robinson Crusoe* (New York: George D. Sproul, 1903).

2. In this chapter, I will leave aside classical literature, but similar issues had surfaced somewhat earlier in the criticism of Greek and Roman texts. See Levine, *The Battle of the Books*. In this book, Levine explains how the new fields of philology and archeology, as they developed in the seventeenth century, began to cast doubt on the authority of Homer and other ancient writers. What began as a critique of Homer's knowledge of astronomy and natural history developed into a more radical, Enlightenment questioning of the humanist assumption that ancient literature could serve as a guide to life.

3. To take just one example from Hans Frei's seminal work, *The Eclipse of Biblical Narrative: A Study in Eighteenth and Nineteenth Century Hermeneutics* (New Haven: Yale University Press, 1974), 66: "[t]he shift in the interpretation of the biblical narratives which came to a climax in the eighteenth century had been gradual and complex. . . . [Johannes] Cocceius obviously did not realize that he was on his way toward a separation of history and story."

4. Quoted in Pat Rogers, ed., *Defoe: The Critical Heritage* (London: Routledge, 1972), 20.

5. Frei, *Eclipse*, 1. Garrett Green writes that "the dominant thrust of apologetics since the European Enlightenment," for both theological liberals and conservatives, has been "directed toward rescuing the Bible from fictional status," from Garrett Green, "'The Bible As . . .' Fictional Narrative and Scriptural Truth," in *Scriptural Authority and Narrative Interpretation*, ed. Garrett Green, (Philadelphia: Fortress, 1987), 81.

Green's essay is a sustained examination of two Enlightenment assumptions: the identification of the literal sense of the Bible with its historical veracity and the identification of the fictional with the untrue. He rejects both assumptions.

6. Green, "'The Bible As . . .,'" 79–81. My next two sentences are indebted to these pages in Green's essay as well.

7. For treatments of the way Puritan literature shaped Defoe, see G. A. Starr, *Defoe and Spiritual Autobiography* (Princeton: Princeton University Press, 1965) and J. Paul Hunter, *The Reluctant Pilgrim: Defoe's Emblematic Method and Quest for Form in "Robinson Crusoe"* (Baltimore: The Johns Hopkins University Press, 1966).

8. Four years before the publication of *Robinson Crusoe*, a character in Defoe's "The Family Instructor" (1715) upbraids her sister for wasting time by attending and reading plays (204). Even earlier, as J. Paul Hunter points out, Defoe's preface to *The Storm* (1704) had denounced fiction as a lie, imposture, and sin against truth, *The Reluctant Pilgrim*, 119.

9. It was not only Puritans who had difficulty reconciling fiction and truth in the late seventeenth century. In the opening paragraphs of her 1688 novel *Oroonoko*, which is set in Surinam, Aphra Behn insists that she was an eyewitness to "a great part" of the events she recounts and received the rest directly from Oroonoko himself. Subtitled *The History of the Royal Slave*, *Oroonoko* nevertheless freely mixes fabulous elements of romance and the tall tale, along with events Behn may have witnessed— or heard about—during her stay in Surinam.

10. Defoe, *Serious Reflections*, xii. John Bender explores Defoe's statement with respect to eighteenth-century views of the penitentiary in the second chapter of *Imagining the Penitentiary: Fiction and the Architecture of Mind in Eighteenth-Century England* (Chicago: University of Chicago Press, 1987). Paula Backscheider discusses Defoe's imprisonment in *Daniel Defoe: His Life* (Baltimore: The Johns Hopkins University Press, 1989), 131.

11. The Puritan Gosson himself does not complain about poetry because it is fictional, but because it tends to produce wanton behavior. He applauds the ancient poetry of Homer and others for its role in teaching justice and providing examples of worthy lives—sometimes under the guise of fiction. I believe J. Paul Hunter somewhat overstates the Puritan "suspicion of anything fictional," which he attributes to "the Puritan conception of the world and events as emblematic. . . . For the Puritanism of the late seventeenth century," he writes, "fiction simply falsified the detailed world of fact and event—and thereby obscured the clear message that God wrote for men in 'real' happenings," *The Reluctant Pilgrim*, 115. He quotes Defoe's contemporary, Charles Gildon, who criticized *Robinson Crusoe* because "'the Christian Religion and the Doctrines of Providence are too sacred to be delivered in Fictions and Lies,'" *The Reluctant Pilgrim*, 118. But Gildon, who had migrated from

Catholicism to deism to orthodox Anglicanism, declares himself "far from being an Enemy to the Writers of Fables," and (like Gosson) he rests his critique of particular fictional works on whether they produce "some useful Moral," quoted in Rogers, ed., *Defoe*, 44; see Hunter, *The Reluctant Pilgrim*, 20. As I have already pointed out, nervousness about fiction that one sees in Behn (who was hardly a Puritan) shows that the difficulty of reconciling realistic fiction to truth was widespread.

12. Two prominent examples of this treatment of the novel can be found in Ian Watt, "*Robinson Crusoe* as a Myth," *Essays in Criticism* (April 1951): 95–119; and in Michael McKeon, *The Origins of the English Novel, 1600–1740* (Baltimore: The Johns Hopkins University Press, 1987).

13. See Hunter, *The Reluctant Pilgrim*, 108–13, for instance.

14. Hunter also notes Robinson's "Everyman" quality, *The Reluctant Pilgrim*, 128.

15. McKeon, *The Origins of the English Novel*, 323; Watt, "*Robinson Crusoe* as a Myth," 105–6. See also McKeon's dismissive description of Crusoe's use of the Bible as "bibliomancy," *The Origins of the English Novel*, 317.

16. William Wilson, *Memoirs of the Life and Times of Daniel Defoe* (New York: AMS Press, 1973), 3:442–43; see also Rogers, ed., *Defoe*, 91.

17. Wilson, *Memoirs of the Life and Times*, 3:442; see also Rogers, ed., *Defoe*, 91.

18. It may be more accurate to consider the Scriptures as two different grand narratives, depending on whether one is considering the Hebrew Scriptures or the Christian Bible. This modification does not change the force of the postmodern critique.

19. Martin Kreiswirth provides a good explanation of Lyotard's "grand narratives" in "Trusting the Tale: The Narrativist Turn in the Human Sciences," *New Literary History* 23, no. 3 (1992): 642 and 655, n. 38. The list of the Christian, Enlightenment, and Marxist grand narratives comes from Jean-François Lyotard's *Le Postmodern expliqué aux enfants* quoted in Geoffrey Bennington, *Lyotard: Writing the Event* (New York: Columbia University Press, 1988), 161. Lyotard has a more philosophical list of grand narrative subjects in *The Postmodern Condition: A Report on Knowledge* (Minneapolis: University of Minnesota Press, 1984), xxiii, including "the dialectics of Spirit, the hermeneutics of meaning," etc.

20. Lyotard, *The Postmodern Condition*, xiii. All quotations from Lyotard are from this book, unless noted. This paragraph also draws on Kreiswirth, "Trusting the Tale," 642.

21. Kreiswirth, "Trusting the Tale," 642; David Carroll, *Paraesthetics: Foucault, Lyotard, Derrida* (New York: Routledge, 1987), 159; Bennington, *Lyotard*, 113.

22. Richard Rorty, *Contingency, Irony, and Solidarity* (Cambridge: Cambridge University Press, 1989), xiv.

23. Rorty, *Contingency*, 28; emphasis added. Harold Bloom popularized the concept of the "strong reader" in *A Map of Misreading* (New York:

Oxford University Press, 1975), 3–26. Rorty identifies the "strong reader" as someone who uses knowledge for self-creation. For Bloom, however, there is no fully autonomous self-creation, for all creations reveal a relationship to another creator.

24. Kelly James Clark questions the basis for Rorty's moral "anti-realism" in "Fiction as a Kind of Philosophy," in *Realism and Antirealism*, ed. William P. Alston (Ithaca: Cornell University Press, 2002), 280–94.

25. Kreiswirth, "Trusting the Tale," 642. In his 1992 article, Kreiswirth goes on to note that Frederic Jameson's foreword to Lyotard's *Postmodern Condition* endorses the grand narrative of Marxism to "underwrite future social justice," ("Trusting the Tale," 644; he is referring to page xix of the foreword to *The Postmodern Condition*). For all their interest in historical conditions and irony, postmoderns seem peculiarly blind to the irony of linking Marxism to social justice, even after the fall of the Berlin Wall.

26. Richard Rorty, "Freud and Moral Reflection," quoted in Kreiswirth, "Trusting the Tale," 638.

27. Richard Rorty, *Objectivity, Relativism and Truth: Philosophical Papers Volume One* (Cambridge: Cambridge University Press, 1991), 110.

28. This paragraph refers to Lyotard, *The Postmodern Condition*, 18–21.

29. Frei's *The Eclipse of Biblical Narrative* offers the seminal treatment of the Enlightenment's separation of the "literal meaning" of Scripture from other, alleged "biblical truths" which are accessible only through the tools of higher criticism. Both George W. Stroup's *The Promise of Narrative Theology: Recovering the Gospel in the Church* (Atlanta: John Knox, 1981), 140; and George Lindbeck's "The Story-Shaped Church: Critical Exegesis and Theological Interpretation," in Green, *Scriptural Authority*, 164, make similar points.

30. Erich Auerbach, *Mimesis: The Representation of Reality in Western Literature*, trans. Willard Trask (Garden City, N.Y.: Doubleday-Anchor, 1957), 12.

31. Frei, *Eclipse*, 2–3.

32. Stephen Crites, "The Narrative Quality of Experience," *The Journal of the American Academy of Religion* 39 (1971): 295. The next sentence is indebted to Crites, "The Narrative Quality of Experience," 296–97.

33. The term *first naiveté* comes from Paul Ricoeur quoted in Hans Frei in *Theology and Narrative: Selected Essays*, ed. William C. Placher and George Hunsinger (New York: Oxford University Press, 1993), 130. This is part of Ricoeur's response to the "masters of suspicion" (Marx, Freud, Nietzsche), whose hermeneutic is central to postmodern thought. As Frei explains it, Ricoeur distinguishes the precritical first naiveté from both the critical reading of the Enlightenment and the postcritical reading that he favors. Postcritical reading would include a "second naiveté," Frei continues, a "revised literal" sort of reading: "It distances the text from the author, from the original discourse's existential situation and from every other kind of reading that would go 'behind' the text

and 'refer' it to any other world of meaning than its own, the world 'in front of' the text." Frei calls this a "hermeneutics of restoration," which distinguishes it from postmodern approaches. To approach Defoe's text with a "first naiveté" is untenable, for every reader knows that *Robinson Crusoe* is a fiction. But the narrative theologians also make us question the postmodern belief that one can and must create an autonomous self apart from the narratives of others. They show us a different, more satisfying way of listening to the text, whether biblical or literary.

34. The explanation of early historical criticism in this paragraph is dependent on the opening fifty pages of Frei's *Eclipse of Biblical Narrative*. George Stroup has a similar discussion in *Promise of Narrative Theology*, 140.

35. Frei, *Eclipse*, 66–69.

36. See Stanley J. Grenz and John R. Franke, *Beyond Foundationalism: Shaping Theology in a Postmodern Context* (Louisville, Ky.: Westminster John Knox, 2001), 58–60. The next sentence is indebted to Grenz and Franke, *Beyond Foundationalism*, 60–63.

37. Green, "'The Bible As . . .,'" 91. See also William C. Placher, "Introduction," in Frei, *Theology and Narrative*, 8.

38. This means that questions of historical veracity are often set to one side by narrative theologians. As Garrett Green writes, "By leaving questions of historicity to the historians (along with the fact-fiction dichotomy that is part of it), theology may hope to achieve a 'second naiveté' that has passed through the fires of historical critical reductionism and learned once again to tell the story on its own terms" ("'The Bible As . . .,'" 91). William Placher puts it somewhat differently: "[N]o doubt the biblical texts provide historical information. But the stories themselves, in their relative indifference to chronology and their occasional inconsistencies, are only loosely related to questions of historical accuracy. Moreover, any residue including only the fragments that a modern historian will glean as historically reliable loses the narrative flow of the texts (particularly evident in the Gospels in the passion narratives) and the full development of the characters the story portrays—and thus loses part of the meaning of the story as story" (Placher, "Introduction," in Frei, *Theology and Narrative*, 8).

39. Stroup, *Promise of Narrative Theology*, 95. The next sentence draws from Stroup, 96–117.

40. Green, "'The Bible As . . . ,'" 89.

41. Rorty, *Objectivity*, 110.

42. Grenz and Franke, *Beyond Foundationalism*, 222.

Chapter 2

1. A major book that describes this movement is Dan Kimball's *The Emerging Church: Vintage Christianity for New Generations* (Grand Rapids:

Zondervan, 2003). For further discussion on the emergent church, see Brian McLaren, "The Strategy We Pursue" (paper presented at The Billy Graham Center Evangelism Roundtable, Wheaton, Ill., April 22–24, 2004). Also see Scott Bader-Saye, "The Emergent Matrix," *Christian Century* 121, no. 24 (2004): 20–27. In this discussion, *emerging*, *emergent*, and *postmodern* are often used interchangeably to define such churches. At this point in time, a single, rigorously defined term seems impossible. Robert Wuthnow discusses the movement's emphasis on art as an avenue for responding to theological mystery in *All in Sync: How Music and Art Are Revitalizing American Religion* (Chicago: University of Chicago Press, 2003).

2. Robert Webber's *Ancient Future Faith: Rethinking Evangelicalism for a Postmodern World* (Grand Rapids: Baker, 1999) discusses the significance of the welcoming, vibrant Christian community as a validation of Christ's continuing presence in the world and his victory over evil (69–70). Grenz and Franke discuss the epistemological significance of community in chapter seven of their *Beyond Foundationalism*. In literary theory, the postmodern critic Stanley Fish has given an influential explanation of the authority of "interpretive communities" as opposed to the authority of an individual, persuasive critic: "There is no single way of reading that is correct or natural," he asserts, "only 'ways of reading' that are extensions of community perspectives," *Is There a Text in this Class?* (Cambridge, Mass.: Harvard University Press, 1980), 16. Ultimately Fish makes the meanings of texts entirely dependent upon their interpretive communities (14). The philosophical issues raised by this issue are taken up more profoundly by Hans-Georg Gadamer (1900–2002) and will addressed in the sixth chapter of this book, on Burke and tradition.

3. Four of the eleven most often reprinted U.S. hymns up to 1860 were by Isaac Watts, but they did not include the three popular ones I have just listed. During this early period, his most popular hymns were "Come we that love the Lord," "Am I a soldier of the cross," "When can I read my title clear," and "He dies the friend of sinners." See Mark Noll, *The Rise of Evangelicalism: The Age of Edwards, Whitefield, and the Wesleys* (Downers Grove, Ill.: InterVarsity, 2003), 275, n. 28, and Stephen A. Marini, "Hymnody as History: Early Evangelical Hymns and the Recovery of American Popular Religion," *Church History* 71 (2002): 273–306.

4. Donald Davie discusses how Watts was influenced by the Polish Jesuit, Matthew Casimire Sarbiewski (1595–1640) in *The Eighteenth-Century Hymn in England* (Cambridge: Cambridge University Press, 1993), 44. Watts' Puritan influences are pervasive, as I hope to show.

5. Watts had begun submitting his hymns to the scrutiny of his own church by 1694, a practice that continued when he became pastor of a leading Dissenting congregation in London in 1702. See Harry Escott, *Isaac Watts, Hymnographer* (London: Independent, 1962), 11, 29–30.

6. "Hymn," in *The New Grove Dictionary of Music and Musicians*, 2nd ed., ed. Stanley Sadie and John Tyrrell (New York: Grove's Dictionaries, 2001), 12:29–31. The article concludes by asserting that the "popularity of Watts' hymns and psalms in his own Independent (later Congregationalist) society amounted to domination for more than a century; among Baptists and Presbyterians it was hardly less. Their influence in America was as great and as lasting as in Britain, and when at length they were admitted into the Church of England, a number of them became, and have remained, among the greatest favorites." In addition to the Wesleyan revival in Britain, this time period would span both the first and second Great Awakenings in America. In *The English Hymn: Its Development and Use in Worship* (Philadelphia: Presbyterian Board of Publication, 1915; Repr., Richmond, Va.: John Knox Press, 1962), Louis Benson reports Jonathan Edwards' 1742 discovery that the congregation in Northampton, Massachusetts was singing nothing but Watts' hymns (163). A century later the prefatory material in the new *Psalms and Hymns* published by the Presbyterian Church in the United States of America concluded that "it would be extremely difficult to furnish a more acceptable version [of the Psalms] than that of Watts" (Philadelphia, 1843).

7. See "Hymn," §IV, 2, in *The New Grove Dictionary of Music and Musicians*, 12:29–31. This article notes that the prejudice against hymns continued in the Church of England throughout the eighteenth century. On the other side of the ecclesiastical spectrum, the Quakers also opposed the introduction of hymns "on the grounds that the singing of other men's words and tunes could not possibly represent that spontaneous speaking from the heart that they conceive to be the only form of worship valid under the New Covenant" (12:30–31). Other treatments of the controversy over hymnody and Watts' role in promoting it include J. R. Watson, *The English Hymn: A Critical and Historical Study* (Oxford: Clarendon, 1997), and Benson's *The English Hymn*.

8. The title of Watts' 1719 work is *The Psalms of David Imitated in the Language of the New Testament*.

9. After this point, my use of the term *hymn* will include Watts' "imitations of the Psalms" and his "hymns," properly so called, unless noted.

10. This sentence and the next are indebted to the long treatment of Watts' influence, found in Benson, *The English Hymn*, 122–218.

11. The definitive account of the Salter's Hall controversy is by Michael Watts, *The Dissenters: From the Reformation to the French Revolution* (Oxford: Clarendon, 1978), 1:374–77. The ministerial candidates doubted the deity of Christ and that the Holy Spirit's deity was equal to that of the Father.

12. The article on Watts in the *Dictionary of National Biography* gives a garbled account of the controversy and Watts' role in it. According to the best records, Watts was either not in attendance at the Salter's Hall

meeting, or his vote was neutral. See T. S. James, *The History of the Litigation and Legislation Respecting Presbyterian Chapels and Charities in England and Ireland between 1816 and 1849* (London: H. Adams, 1867), 709.

13. Arthur Paul Davis discusses the doubts that arose in Watts toward the end of his life in *Isaac Watts: His Life and Works* (London: Independent Press, 1943) 120–26.

14. Locke's modern editor, Peter H. Nidditch, reflects the judgment of many students of the Enlightenment when he makes this comparison at the beginning of his introduction to the *Essay Concerning Human Understanding*, ix. "The message of the *Essay*," he continues, "became deeply diffused among successive generations of philosophers, and of leaders of educated opinion in Britain and abroad."

15. Locke, *Essay Concerning Human Understanding*, 689, 4:18 (hereafter cited as *Essay*.)

16. *The Reasonableness of Christianity*, 1695, reprinted in *John Locke: Writings on Religion*, ed. Victor Nuovo (Oxford: Clarendon, 2002), 108–9, 169; §§43, 199.

17. Nuovo discusses Locke's role in developing an expression of Christianity that was acceptable to the rational, liberal tradition early in the introductions to two of his books, *John Locke and Christianity* (Bristol: Thoemmes Press, 1997) and *John Locke: Writings on Religion*. Nicholas Wolterstorff concludes that Locke's Socinianism is fairly clear from 1690 on, "Locke's Philosophy of Religion," in *The Cambridge Companion to Locke*, ed. Vere Chappell (Cambridge: Cambridge University Press, 1994), 185. Locke's definition of reason (previously quoted, from book 4 of his *Essay*) demonstrated its significance by serving as the basis for John Toland's *Christianity Not Mysterious* (1696), a highly controversial work because of its Socinian tendencies. See J. R. Milton, "Locke's Life and Times," in *The Cambridge Companion to Locke*, 22. Later in this chapter, I will refer to Watts' opinion that Locke was not a Socinian—an opinion that indicates how much Watts' charity outweighed his better theological judgment.

18. See Wolterstorff, "Locke's Philosophy of Religion," 185–87, for a discussion of Locke's "evidentialism." It was not enough for Locke, he explains, that one *have* satisfactory evidence for a theological proposition. One must "know or believe the proposition *on the basis of* satisfactory evidence" (186; emphasis in original).

19. In the chapter on "Enthusiasm" (4:19), added to the *Essay* in the 1700 edition, Locke allows that biblical figures who had themselves seen the evidence of miracles (such as Moses at the burning bush) could legitimately "assert the divine authority of the Message they were sent with" (*Essay*, 705). He admits the use of miracles, prophecies, and the apostles' "plain and direct words" as evidence of the messiahship of Jesus in *The Reasonableness of Christianity*, 113–15; §§55–61.

20. See Wolterstorff, "Locke's Philosophy of Religion," 196–97, for remarks on Locke's foundationalist epistemology of religious belief and its relationship to early modern science.

21. Locke identifies Scripture as "Traditional Revelation," by which he means revelation that is received from others, in contrast to direct, or "Original Revelation": "By the one [original revelation] I mean that first Impression, which is made immediately by GOD, on the Mind of any Man, to which we cannot set any Bounds; and by the other [traditional revelation], those Impressions delivered over to others in Words, and the ordinary ways of conveying our Conceptions one to another" (*Essay*, 690, 4:18).

22. Quotations from the rest of this paragraph come from *Essay* 621, 687–88; 4:10, 17.

23. See *Essay*, 694–95; 4:18 for Locke's description of the proper objects of faith. Locke restricts faith to only those "propositions . . . which are supposed to be divinely revealed" (*Essay*, 693). Given the high degree of interpretation required to derive the rebellion of the fallen angels from Scripture, it is curious that this proposition passes Locke's critical muster.

24. Locke's modern editor explains the *Essay*'s usage of *enthusiasm* by providing the *Oxford English Dictionary*'s definition: "a vain confidence of divine favor or communication" (*Essay*, 837).

25. See Clement Hawes, *Mania and Literary Style: The Rhetoric of Enthusiasm from the Ranters to Christopher Smart* (Cambridge: Cambridge University Press, 1996).

26. Isaac Watts, *The Works of the Reverend and Learned Isaac Watts, D.D.*, ed. David Jennings and Philip Doddridge (London, 1810–1811), 5:556.

27. Locke published a *Second Letter Concerning Toleration* in 1690 and a third in 1692. Fragments of a fourth letter appeared posthumously in 1706. See I. T. Ramsey, ed., introduction to *The Reasonableness of Christianity*, by John Locke (Stanford, Calif.: Stanford University Press, 1958).

28. For an excellent account of the revivals of 1734–1738 in America and the British Isles, see Noll's *The Rise of Evangelicalism*, chap. 3.

29. Geoffrey Wainwright speaks of the connection between intellect and emotion in the liturgy in his magisterial study of worship, *Doxology* (New York: Oxford University Press, 1980), 231. Horton Davies notes the reintroduction of enthusiasm in hymnody in the third volume of his *Worship and Theology in England: From Watts and Wesley to Maurice, 1690–1850* (Princeton: Princeton University Press, 1961), 100.

30. Watts' first two poems on Locke are "To Mr. John Locke, Esq. Retired from Business" and "To John Shute, Esq." (*Works*, 4:460). Both are from book 2 of *Horae Lyricae* (pub. 1706, 1709). Locke resigned from the Board of Trade in June 1700, so presumably the first poem was written shortly after that. The epigraph to the second poem reads "On Mr. Locke's dangerous sickness, some time after he had retired to

study the Scriptures," and is dated "June 1704." Locke died October 28, 1704. The third poem is titled "On Mr. Locke's Annotations upon several Parts of the New Testament, left behind him at his Death" (*Works*, 4:469). Locke's *A Paraphrase and Notes on the Epistles of St Paul to the Galatians, 1 and 2 Corinthians, Romans, Ephesians*, ed. Arthur W. Wainwright (Oxford: Clarendon, 1987), the "Annotations," to which Watts refers, was published between 1705 and 1707. A faulty edition of the Galatians portion appeared in 1705 and was corrected in 1706, when the paraphrases on 1 and 2 Corinthians appeared. Locke's work on Romans, Ephesians, and the Preface was published in 1707. Watts' note to his poem refers to Locke's annotations on Romans 3:25 and 9:5, but it is not clear when he actually wrote the poem. Samuel Johnson insisted on including Watts in his *Lives of the Most Eminent English Poets; With Critical Observations on their Works*, ed. Roger Lonsdale (Oxford: Clarendon, 2006), and although he praises Watts' philosophical works and the poems of *Horae Lyricae*, he has little to say about his hymns.

31. Watts, *Works*, 5:625–28, 526, 544. Christopher Fox discusses the philosophical problem of identity in Locke and Watts in *Locke and the Scriblerians* (Berkeley: University of California Press, 1988). Kenneth MacLean refers to the issues of innate ideas, the tabula rasa, and other disagreements between the two in *John Locke and the English Literature of the Eighteenth Century* (New York: Russell & Russell, 1962).

32. Watts, *Works*, 4:469. Watts is referring to Locke's *Reasonableness of Christianity* (1695) and his posthumous *Paraphrase and Notes on the Epistles of St Paul* (1705–1707). Watts' reading of Locke's *Paraphrases* is indeed charitable. In the final verse of 2 Corinthians 5, to which Watts refers, the King James Version reads: "For he hath made him to be sin for us, who knew no sin; that we might be the righteousness of God." The disputed phrase is "made him to be sin." Socinians denied that Christ "became sin," a view which Locke seems to share in his notes to 2 Corinthians 5:21: "For god hath made him subject to sufferings and death the punishment and consequence of sin," Locke writes, "*as if he had been a sinner* though he were guilty of [no] sin, that we in and by him might be made righteous by a righteousness imputed to us by god" (emphasis added).

33. As Wolterstorff concludes in his chapter on Locke's philosophy of religion, the "assumed contrast between the epistemic status of natural science and that of religion has not ceased to cast its spell over Western intellectual in the time between us and Locke. Natural science as we know it illustrates responsibly governed belief; religion as we know it represents a failure of responsibly governed belief." Locke regarded the natural science of his day "as a paradigmatic application of his regulative epistemology," Wolterstorff writes, while religious belief represented an epistemological failure (196).

34. Grenz and Franke survey Enlightenment foundationalism with respect to modern theology in chapter two of *Beyond Foundationalism*, including

the modifications by nineteenth-century theologians who promoted "God consciousness" (on the one hand) or an error-free Bible (on the other) as the foundations for religious knowledge.

35. In the broad way he used the term *thinking*, Locke included reasoning, sensing, perceiving, remembering, and imagining. See Roger Woolhouse, "Locke's Theory of Knowledge," in *The Cambridge Companion to Locke*, 152. Locke's description of sensation and reflection as the source of all ideas comes in *Essay*, 105; 2:1.

36. A fourth view of the atonement, "governmental theory," is probably closest to the one found in Locke's *Paraphrase and Notes on the Epistles of St Paul*. In the governmental view, derived from Arminius and developed by Grotius, Christ suffers as an example of both the depths of sin and the lengths to which God will go to uphold the moral order and draw people to himself. Leon Morris discusses these views in his article "Theories of the Atonement" in *Evangelical Dictionary of Theology*, ed. Walter Elwell (Grand Rapids: Baker, 1984), 100–101. Arthur W. Wainwright, editor of Locke's *Paraphrase and Notes on the Epistles of St Paul*, acknowledges the proximity of Locke's view to the governmental theory of the atonement, but denies that he fully developed a theory along these lines (1:37).

37. Locke, *Reasonableness of Christianity*, 205; emphasis added. The other quotations from Locke in this paragraph are from the same location.

38. Noll writes that "[e]vangelicalism at its best is the religion displayed in the classic evangelical hymns" ("Evangelicalism at its Best," *Harvard Divinity Bulletin* 27, no. 2/3 [1998]: 8). In *The Rise of Evangelicalism*, Noll gives the following characteristics of evangelicalism to distinguish it from the dominant forms of Christianity in Europe in the late seventeenth and early eighteenth centuries:

    • from Christian faith defined as correct doctrine toward Christian faith defined as correct living;
    • from godly order as the heart of the church's concern toward godly fellowship as a principal goal;
    • from authoritative interpretation of Scripture originating with ecclesiastical elites toward lay and more democratic appropriation of the Bible;
    • from obedience toward expression;
    • from music as performed by well-trained specialists toward music as a shared expression of ordinary people;
    • from preaching as learned discourses about god toward preaching as impassioned appeals for "closing with Christ."

    Together, writes Noll, these newer emphases have been called "the religion of the heart" (*The Rise of Evangelicalism*, 52).

39. "In fact, it is difficult to discover any significant event, person or structure of early evangelicalism that did not involve the singing of hymns." Noll, *The Rise of Evangelicalism*, 273–74.

40. Chap. 6, Sec. III ("Directions Concerning the Definition of Names") in Watts, *Works* 5:48; emphasis added.

41. See Watts, *The Dissenters*, 1:260–67.

42. Norman Nicholson discusses the Old Testament "national myth" of Puritan England, quoted in Donald Davie, *The Eighteenth-Century Hymn in England*, 147–48.

43. Donald Davie applies the term *tribal* to Watts in *A Gathered Church* (New York: Oxford University Press, 1978), 28–29. In these pages, he also explains the seventeenth-century significance of "plantation" in Watts' popular hymn "We are a Garden wall'd around." The word *saints* appears often in Watts.

44. Watson, *The English Hymn*, 136.

45. Bruce Hindmarsh sees the evangelical stress on experience as a "a robust expression of the Lockean Enlightenment" and goes so far as to call early eighteenth-century evangelicalism "a vector of the Enlightenment." He also emphasizes the role of the community of faith in validating individual testimonies of a personal story that conformed to the larger story of God as seen in the Bible. See "Reshaping Individualism: The Private Christian, Eighteenth-Century Religion and the Enlightenment," in *The Rise of the Laity in Evangelical Protestantism*, ed. Deryck W. Lovegrove (London: Routledge, 2002), 76–80.

46. In Bertrand Bronson, ed., *Selections from Johnson on Shakespeare* (New Haven: Yale University Press, 1986), 8–9.

47. Watts entered these ethical discussions with his essay "Self-Love and Virtue Reconciled only by Religion" (*Works*, 3:725–33). (His nineteenth-century editor fails to give this essay's date.) The title accurately gives the theme of the essay, which does not pursue aesthetic connections to virtue. However, Jonathan Edwards (1703–1758) treats all of these considerations at length in his response to Shaftesbury, Hutcheson, and others in *The Nature of True Virtue*, reprinted in *A Jonathan Edwards Reader*, ed. John E. Smith, Harry S. Stout, and Kenneth P. Minkema (New Haven: Yale University Press, 1995), 244ff., originally published in 1765; also see xxix–xxxii.

48. My version of this account, which rests on hearsay, draws on Benson, *The English Hymn*, 113; Watson, *The English Hymn*, 137; and the article on Watts in the *Dictionary of National Biography*. See also Thomas Milner, *Life, Times and Correspondence of the Rev. Isaac Watts, D.D.* (London, 1834), 176–77, and Thomas Gibbons, *Memoirs of the Rev. Isaac Watts, D.D.* (London, 1780), 254.

49. Johnson, "Watts," in *Lives of the Most Eminent English Poets*, 4:105. Johnson did not like religious verse in general (including that of Watts) primarily because he believed that no human production could possibly exalt the deity. Nevertheless, he insisted on including Watts in this influential work of critical biography.

50. This is the judgment of Glenn C. Wilcox, who edited a reprint of the

1854 edition of William Walker's *Southern Harmony* for the University of Kentucky Press (Lexington, 1987), iii. He goes on to note that about one-fourth of the lyrics in *Southern Harmony* were from Watts (v). *Southern Harmony* uses the tune "Resignation" as the setting for Watts' hymn.

51. See the New International Version and *The NET Bible*, respectively.

52. Locke, *Paraphrase and Notes on the Epistles of St Paul*, 1:226–27 (emphasis added).

53. Wolterstorff writes, more generally of Locke's religious knowledge: "One's *idea*, one's concept, of God is directly present to the mind [in Locke's view]; but not God. The sacramental view, that at least some of us human beings at some points in our lives experience God, was not an assumption Locke made. If asked about it, he would firmly have rejected it" ("Locke's Philosophy of Religion," 186).

54. Watts, *Works*, 4:349. Galatians 6:14 reads, "But God forbid that I should glory, save in the cross of our Lord Jesus Christ, by whom the word is crucified unto me, and I unto the world."

55. Doug Pagitt, *Reimagining Spiritual Formation: A Week in the Life of an Experimental Church* (Grand Rapids: Zondervan, 2004), 17. This phrase is part of the "dream" of the church where Pagitt is the pastor, Solomon's Porch (Minneapolis). One of the more significant cultural statements to come from this movement, *The Church in Emerging Culture: Five Perspectives*, ed. Leonard Sweet (Grand Rapids: Zondervan, 2003) is a conscious attempt to update H. Richard Niebuhr's 1951 classic *Christ and Culture* (New York: Harper).

56. Wuthnow, *All in Sync*, 134. The scope of Wuthnow's book includes more traditional churches and emerging ones.

57. See Pagitt, *Reimagining Spiritual Formation*, 17.

58. Robert Webber recounts the story of a professor who told his class, "'There is only one God-ordained communication, and that is the use of words.' Some time later this professor drew a circle on the board and said, 'This circle represents God.' An astute student seeing the contradiction, said, 'But, professor, you told us that the only God-ordained form of communication is words, and here you are using a symbol.' The professor immediately cleared this throat and said, 'You're right, I did say that.' Then he walked to the blackboard, erased the circle, and said, 'I'm sorry, I'll never do that again.'" See Webber, *Ancient Future Faith*, 112–13.

59. See Grenz and Franke, *Beyond Foundationalism*, 60–63, in which they refer to many major evangelical treatments of Scripture, from B. B. Warfield and Charles Hodge through Carl F. H. Henry and Wayne Grudem.

60. Wuthnow, *All in Sync*, 68–69. See also Steve Scott, *Like a House on Fire: Renewal of the Arts in a Postmodern Culture* (Chicago: Cornerstone, 1997).

61. Leonard Sweet, "A New Reformation," in *Experience God in Worship*,

ed. George Barna (Loveland, Colo.: Flagship Church Resources, 2004), 180.

62. To take just one interesting example of an altered hymn, Watts' hymn on the martyrs of Revelation 7 places them firmly in the Enlightenment: "These glorious *minds*, how bright they shine" (*Works*, 4:266; emphasis added). Most hymnals replace the word *minds* with *spirits*.

63. Johnson, "Life of Gray," in *Lives of the Poets*, 4:184. For a discussion of the "common reader," see Daniel Ritchie, *Reconstructing Literature in an Ideological Age* (Grand Rapids: Eerdmans, 1996), 106–8.

64. As Johnson writes elsewhere, "[a]bout things on which the public thinks long it commonly attains to think right." "Life of Addison," in *Lives of the Poets*, 3:26.

65. Brian McLaren discusses community in *A Generous Orthodoxy: Why I Am a Missional, Evangelical, Post/Protestant, Liberal/Conservative, Mystical/ Poetic, Biblical, Charismatic/Contemplative, Fundamentalist/Calvinist, Anabaptist/Anglican, Methodist, catholic, Green, Incarnational, Depressed-yet-Hopeful, Emergent, Unfinished CHRISTIAN* (Grand Rapids: Zondervan, 2004), 208, 290. Colleen Carroll gives a Catholic view in *The New Faithful* (Chicago: Loyola Press, 2002), 85, 89. Grenz and Franke devote an entire chapter to the issue of community in *Beyond Foundationalism*, 203–38.

66. This is a statement from Solomon's Porch in Pagitt, *Reimagining Spiritual Formation*, 17.

67. The quotation comes from François Lyotard, *The Postmodern Condition*, 9. Lyotard is discussing what gives authority, or legitimacy, to knowledge. That question, he says, "appears in its most complete form, that of reversion, revealing that knowledge and power are simply two sides of the same question: who decides what knowledge is, and who knows what needs to be decided."

68. Eric Reed, "Ministering with 'My Generation,'" *Leadership* (Fall 2000), 52.

69. Watson, *The English Hymn*, 134–36. See also the opening of Bernard Manning's article, "The Hymns of Isaac Watts" (a paper presented to the University Congregational Society in Cambridge, October 17, 1937. www.ccel.org/m/manning/wesleyhymns/htm/vi.htm#vi. Accessed June 1, 2004).

70. To give just four examples of hymns of this sort, consider "I sing the mighty power of God," "Jesus shall reign where'er the sun," "O God, our help in ages past," and "Before Jehovah's Awful Throne" (whose first stanza is actually supplied by John Wesley).

71. Both Watson, *The English Hymn*, 136, and Madeleine Marshall and Janet Todd, *English Congregational Hymns in the Eighteenth Century* (Lexington: University of Kentucky Press, 1982), 33, describe the eclecticism of Watts. Noll describes the cooperation among Protestants at various places in the first chapters of *The Rise of Evangelicalism*, concluding that early evangelicalism was "noteworthy for its massive indifference to the

institutional structures of traditional religion" (101). He describes Isaac Watts' 1737 interaction with Count Zinzendorf, the Moravian nobleman who deeply influenced the Wesleys, and Watts' involvement in the British publication of Jonathan Edwards' *A Faithful Narrative of the Surprizing Work of God* (1737), an account of the revival that led to the First Great Awakening; see Noll, *The Rise of Evangelicalism*, 79–90.

72. Davie, *Eighteenth-Century Hymn*, 30.
73. Wuthnow, *All in Sync*, 76–77; emphasis added.
74. His early education in Latin and Greek poetry, followed by French and Hebrew, is described in Escott, *Isaac Watts*, 19.
75. Watts, preface to *Hymns and Spiritual Songs*, in *Works*, 4:253.
76. Watts describes his reasons for these choices in *Works*, 4:255.
77. McLaren, *A Generous Orthodoxy*, 35.
78. Watts, *Works*, 4:469, 5:501.
79. The quoted phrase, which emerged in the aftermath of the Salter's Hall controversy, diverted the theological controversy from the Trinity to issues of religious liberty. It suggested that one could uphold biblical authority (which was attractive to Trinitarian Dissenters like Philip Doddridge), while allowing leeway on doctrines as essential as the Trinity. See Watts, *The Dissenters*, 1:375–81.
80. See Davis, *Isaac Watts*, 121. In the years following Watts' death, there was much controversy over whether he remained an orthodox Christian or whether he died a Unitarian. Davis notes that Watts never considered himself a Unitarian. Rather, Watts' struggles over the Trinity are "the efforts of a candid and pious soul honestly but hesitantly groping for the truth" (120–26).
81. This is the judgment of Davies, *Worship and Theology in England*, 94–95. Michael Watts finds the cause of the drift toward Unitarianism in the ecclesiastical structure of English Presbyterianism, whereas Congregationalists could insist that individual believers give evidence of their religious experience (377–78). See also Russell Richey, "Did the English Presbyterians Become Unitarian?" *Church History* 42, no. 1 (1973): 58–72.
82. For a measured analysis of recent controversies affecting the emergent church, see Brian McLaren, "Emergent Reactions, Spring 2006" at www.brianmclaren.net/archives/2006/06/emergent_reactions_spring _2006_374.html.

Chapter 3

1. Google, "Company Overview." www.google.com/intl/en/corporate/ index.html, accessed July 7, 2006. In 2005 Google Book Search emerged from Google Print, and adopted the goal of scanning books in the public domain (www.google.com/corporate/history.html).
2. Antoine-Nicolas de Condorcet, *Sketch for a Historical Picture of the Progress of the Human Mind*, trans. June Barraclough (Westport, Conn.:

Hyperion, 1955), 185. The next quotation is from page 184, and the rest of the material from Condorcet comes from 175–201.

3. I will treat the French Revolution in chapter 5. Paul Hollander's *Political Pilgrims: Western Intellectuals in Search of the Good Society* (New Brunswick, N.J.: Transaction Publishers, 2004) surveys the unending quest of Western intellectuals to rationalize Marxist tyrannies, from the Soviet Union and China, through Cuba and Nicaragua. An earlier, incisive description of the dynamics underlying intellectual complicity with Communism is Raymond Aron's *The Opium of the Intellectuals* [1955], trans. Terence Kilmartin (Lanham, Md.: University Press of America, 1985). For material on the involvement of intellectuals with fascism, see Tim Redman, *Ezra Pound and Italian Fascism* (Cambridge: Cambridge University Press, 1991), and Paul Lawrence Rose, *Heisenberg and the Nazi Atomic Bomb Project: A Study in German Culture* (Berkeley: University of California Press, 1998).

4. Lyotard, *The Postmodern Condition*, 4. My next sentence refers to pp. 50 and 53.

5. Despite plentiful scholarship on Swift's critique of the science of his day, there is little sustained writing on Swift and modern technology. The boundaries between science and technology are porous, of course. All discussions of the field acknowledge the 1937 essay by Marjorie Nicolson and Nora Mohler, "The Scientific Background of Swift's *Voyage to Laputa*," in *Science and Imagination*, ed. Marjorie Nicolson, 110–54 (Ithaca: Cornell University Press) and Douglas Lane Patey updated and extended their work in "Swift's Satire on 'Science' and the Structure of *Gulliver's Travels*," *ELH* 59 (1991): 809–39. It is nevertheless striking that scholars have written relatively little on Swift's profound questions regarding the attempts to better human civilization through the use of applied science.

6. *Prose Writings of Jonathan Swift*, ed. Herbert Davis and Harold Williams, vol. 11: *Gulliver's Travels* (Oxford: Blackwell, 1965), 153 (hereafter cited as *Gulliver's Travels*).

7. See Percy G. Adams, *Travel Literature and the Evolution of the Novel* (Lexington: University of Kentucky Press, 1983), and Elizabeth Bohls, "Age of Peregrination: Travel Writing and the Eighteenth-Century Novel," in *A Companion to the Eighteenth-Century English Novel and Culture*, ed. Paula R. Backscheider and Catherine Ingrassia (Malden, Mass.: Blackwell, 2005), 97–116.

8. Nicolson and Mohler, "The Scientific Background of Swift's *Voyage to Laputa*," 124–29.

9. The Royal Society included leading scientists like Isaac Newton, Robert Boyle, and Edmund Halley and philosophers, architects, writers, and other public men, such as John Locke, Christopher Wren, and John Dryden.

10. Nicolson and Mohler, "The Scientific Background of Swift's *Voyage to Laputa*," 140–48.

11. M. H. Abrams, ed. *The Norton Anthology of English Literature*, 6th ed. (New York: W. W. Norton, 2000), 1:2129. This delightful editorial comment appeared only in the sixth (1993) and seventh (2000) editions of the *Norton Anthology*, after which it was eliminated.
12. All quotations in this paragraph are from *Gulliver's Travels*, 185–86.
13. See Claus Westermann's commentary on Genesis 11:1-9 in *Genesis 1–11*, trans. John J. Scullion (Minneapolis: Augsburg, 1984), 553–57.
14. Eighteenth-century scholars use the phrase *print culture* to describe the relationships between the explosion of all kinds of printed material in the Enlightenment with contemporary institutions, industries, scientific developments, and literary styles. See Carey McIntosh, *The Evolution of English Prose, 1700–1800: Style, Politeness, and Print Culture* (Cambridge: Cambridge University Press, 1999), and Roy Porter's chapter, "Print Culture," in his book, *The Creation of the Modern World: The Untold Story of the British Enlightenment* (New York: W. W. Norton, 2000), 72–95.
15. See David J. Gunkel, *"Lingua ex Machina*: Computer-Mediated Communication and the Tower of Babel." *Configurations* 7, no. 1 (1999): 62–63. Norbert Wiener writes, "If I were to choose a patron saint for cybernetics out of the history of science, I should have to choose Leibniz. The philosophy of Leibniz centers about two closely related concepts—that of a universal symbolism and that of a calculus of reasoning." He finds it "not in the least surprising that the same intellectual impulse which has led to the development of mathematical logic has at the same time led to the ideal or actual mechanization of *processes of thought*" (*Cybernetics: Or, Control and Communication in the Animal and the Machine*, 2nd ed. [Cambridge, Mass.: MIT Press, 1961], 12; emphasis added). Wiener is the founder of "cybernetics," which analyzes systems of communication and control through analogies between the brain and the computer. Unfortunately for his readers, Swift himself neglected the work of Leibniz. See Irvin Ehrenpreis, *Swift: The Man, His Works, and the Age* (Cambridge, Mass.: Harvard University Press, 1962–1983), 2:238.
16. Condorcet, *Sketch for a Historical Picture*, 199.
17. Wilkins' topics for theological investigation were recommended to Swift by Archbishop William King in 1711 (Ehrenpreis, *Swift*, 1:74–75). Marjorie Nicolson refers to a number of Wilkins' activities related to the Royal Society in her book, *Science and Imagination*.
18. John Wilkins, "Dedicatory Epistle" to *An Essay Towards a Real Character, and a Philosophical Language*, ed. R. C. Alston (Menston, U.K.: Scolar, 1968).
19. Wilkins, "Epistle to the Reader."
20. Wilkins, *An Essay*, 20. Later in this paragraph, the two quotations from Wilkins' *Essay* regarding the Lord's Prayer come from page 396.
21. This understanding of language is among the insights of Ferdinand de Saussure (1857–1913), one of the founders of modern linguistics. Linguists use the term *signifier* to describe the physical form of

language—usually a printed or vocalized word, or its image—as distinguished from its conceptual meaning (the "signified").

22. Julien Offray de la Mettrie, *Man a Machine*, trans. Gertrude Carman Bussey and M. W. Calkins (La Salle, Ill.: Open Court, 1961), 103–4.

23. Norbert Wiener, *The Human Use of Human Beings: Cybernetics and Society* (New York: Avon, 1967), 45; de la Mettrie, *Man a Machine*, 128.

24. De la Mettrie, *Man a Machine*, 141, 128.

25. Machine translation is the process by which computers translate speech or text without the need of a human translator. It is often faulty, particularly when translating casual or conversational language. For more on machine translation, see *Readings in Machine Translation*, ed. Sergei Nirenburg, Harold Somers, and Yorick Wilks (Cambridge, Mass.: MIT Press, 2003).

26. Gunkel, "*Lingua ex Machina*," 81. See 80–82 for a fuller explanation. Gunkel notes the similarity of this project and that of the three language professors of Lagado.

27. Lanier has received several awards for his work in virtual reality and computation, including an honorary doctorate from New Jersey Institute of Technology in 2006. He discussed the relation of virtual reality to language in a fall 1989 interview with Adam Heilbrun, "Virtual Reality: An Interview With Jaron Lanier," *Whole Earth Review* (108–19). Lanier maintains a website at www.jaronlanier.com, where one may find his claim to have coined the phrase *virtual reality* and the entire interview. The quoted material from Lanier that follows comes from this version of the interview; accessed July 10, 2006. Lanier currently writes a column for *Discover* magazine titled "Jaron's World."

28. Gunkel makes a similar observation in "*Lingua ex Machina*," 82. In his historical survey, Gunkel explains the failed attempts to find a universal language for machine translation. He concludes by questioning the assumption that a universal, transparent language, basic to "mainstream efforts in computer-mediated communication," can be found. See pp. 61–73, 88–89.

29. Wiener's view is evident when he writes, for example: "When I give an order to a machine, the situation is not essentially different from that which arises when I give an order to a person . . . To me, personally, the fact that the signal in its intermediate stages has gone through a machine rather than through a person is irrelevant and does not in any case greatly change my relation to the signal," *The Human Use of Human Beings*, 25.

30. In a significant study of the "information culture" of the literary world of Swift and Alexander Pope, Roger D. Lund looks at satirical treatments of various Enlightenment ways of storing knowledge—prefaces, introductions, footnotes, grammars, keys, digests, concordances dictionaries, and so on. Pope derides these efforts as mere "index learning" (*The Dunciad*, 1:285). See Roger D. Lund, "The Eel of Science: Index Learning, Scriblerian Satire, and the Rise of Information Culture,"

Eighteenth-Century Life 22.2 (1998): 18–42. Accessed through *Project Muse* (www.muse.jhu.edu) August 22, 2003. Kenneth Craven has written a study of Swift's *Tale of a Tub* as satire of information systems (as opposed to technology) in *Jonathan Swift and the Millennium of Madness* (Leiden: Brill, 1992). Swift, he concludes, "argued that *the reduction of learning to the measurable* and of the human only to the virtues—*sans* vices—spelled the doom of art, the humanities, and the *consensus gentium* of the hard-won legacies of time" (6; emphasis added).

31. James O'Donnell, *Avatars of the Word: From Papyrus to Cyperspace* (Cambridge, Mass.: Harvard University Press, 1998), 156. The references in the rest of this paragraph come from pp. 155–62 in O'Donnell's book.

32. See Quentin Schultze, *Habits of the High-Tech Heart: Living Virtuously in the Information Age* (Grand Rapids: Baker, 2002), 32, where he begins raising these and similar questions.

33. Diderot and d'Alembert published the *Encyclopédie* between 1751 and 1772.

34. O'Donnell speculates about the new social and intellectual possibilities of the virtual library in *Avatars of the Word*, 39–43.

35. O'Donnell, *Avatars of the Word*, 41–42.

36. Wendell Berry, *Home Economics* (San Francisco: North Point, 1987), 84, 88–89.

37. Ross Douthat, "The Truth about Harvard," *Atlantic* (March 2005): 95–99. All quotes come from pp. 98 and 99.

38. See Julie Reuben's *The Making of the Modern University* (Chicago: University of Chicago Press, 1996), especially chaps. 1 and 5, and pp. 92–94, 241–43.

39. Reuben, *The Making of the Modern University*, 139.

40. National Association of Scholars, *The Dissolution of General Education: 1914–1993* (Princeton: National Association of Scholars, 1996).

41. Swift, *Gulliver's Travels*, 180. The rest of this paragraph makes use of pages 176–77.

42. Swift, *Gulliver's Travels*, 134.

43. Swift, *Gulliver's Travels*, 136. Swift contrasts the small number of ancient authors to the large number of moderns in *The Battle of the Books* (1704). Treatments of the "ancients and moderns" issue in *Gulliver's Travels* may be found in Robert P. Fitzgerald, "Ancients and Moderns in Swift's Brobdingnag," *Literature in Wissenschaft und Uterricht* (Kiel, Germany) 18 (1985): 89–100; Allan Bloom, "An Outline of *Gulliver's Travels*," in *Ancients and Moderns*, ed. Joseph Cropsey (New York: Basic, 1964), 238–57; and Daniel Ritchie, *Reconstructing Literature in an Ideological Age*, 45–48.

44. Swift, *Tale of a Tub*, 171. The next quotation is from the same passage.

45. Swift, *Gulliver's Travels*, 294.

46. These five final five paragraphs of chapter three of the *Voyage to Laputa* were not included in printed versions of *Gulliver's Travels* until 1899.

Modern versions of the book sometimes reprint them there or in the notes, and sometimes they omit these paragraphs altogether.

47. In previous decades, European countries had frequently debased their currency or introduced coins of lesser metallic value than the ones already in circulation, resulting in economic ruin from the hoarding of gold and silver. For a good overview of the economic issues involved in this controversy, see Patrick Kelly, "Swift on Money and Economics," *The Cambridge Companion to Jonathan Swift*, ed. Christopher Fox (Cambridge: Cambridge University Press, 2003), 128–45.

48. Newton's report to the Treasury is dated in April 1724. Swift, *Prose Writings*, vol. 10: *The Drapier's Letters and Other Works 1724–25*, ed. Herbert Davis (Oxford: Blackwell, 1966), 153–54, 188 (hereafter cited as *Drapier's Letters*). See also Oliver W. Ferguson, *Jonathan Swift and Ireland* (Urbana: University of Illinois Press, 1962), 103.

49. Swift, *Drapier's Letters*, 199–200.

50. Swift, *Drapier's Letters*, 67, 68.

51. Just to take one quote, Bruce Schuman writes, in *Utopian Computer Networking*: "The fabulous resources of human knowledge and wisdom can be combined through modern information science technology to create the most authoritative voice for spiritual truth and insight which has ever existed on this planet," quoted in Gunkel, "*Lingua ex Machina*," 64.

52. Wendell Berry, *What Are People For?* (San Francisco: North Point, 1990), 171.

53. Berry, *Home Economics*, 80.

54. Berry, *Home Economics*, 83.

55. "[I]n the eighteenth century," writes Neil Postman, "information was not always thought of as a commodity to be bought and sold. It was not thought to be useful unless it was imbedded in a context, unless it gave shape or texture or authority to a political or social idea, which itself was required to fit into some worldview. No one was ridiculed more, especially by Jonathan Swift, than the pedant, the person who collected information without purpose, without connection to social life. The idea of a contextless information society would have struck Swift and Voltaire as ludicrous. Information for what? For whom? To advance what idea?" "Building a Bridge to the Eighteenth Century," in *Envisioning the Future*, ed. Marleen S. Barr (Middletown, Conn.: Wesleyan University Press, 2003), 26. Regrettably, Postman does not pursue his analysis of Swift at this point.

56. Jane Smiley satirizes the "student as customer" in her novel, *Moo* (New York: Knopf, 1995). In addition to Postman's critique of the buying and selling of information (see note 55), Sven Birkerts defines "the argument of our time [as] the argument between technology and the soul." The antenna of our race is no longer the poet, he writes, but the dollar: "The dollar is betting, as it always does, against the soul" (*The Gutenberg Elegies* [Boston: Faber & Faber, 1994], 211, 212). Lyotard argues that the

postmodern move away from knowledge as "an end in itself" has redirected education to "professional training," which transmits "an organized stock of essential knowledge." He calls this the "mercantilization of knowledge," whose chief question is "'Is it saleable?'" (*The Postmodern Condition*, 50, 51).

57. By referring to "narrative" rather than theology or history, I hope to emphasize a different side of the picture that has been ably described by Reuben (*The Making of the Modern University*) and George Marsden (*The Soul of the American University*, New York: Oxford University Press, 1994).

58. Birkerts says the collapse of the "'master narratives' (Christian, Marxist, Freudian, humanist . . .)—has all but destroyed the premise of understandability," *The Gutenberg Elegies*, 75. The comparison of the teacher to a memory bank, which follows, comes from Lyotard's analysis of the end of "grand narratives" in *The Postmodern Condition*, 51, 53.

59. Plato, *Phaedrus and the Seventh and Eighth Letters*, trans. Walter Hamilton (Harmondsworth, U.K.: Penguin, 1973), 276a.

60. Jacques Derrida, *Dissemination*, trans. Barbara Johnson (Chicago: University of Chicago Press, 1981), 149. Derrida's entire critique, "Plato's Pharmacy," extends over 100 pages.

61. In this part of Derrida's critique, he focuses entirely on the issue of the "illegitimacy" of writing (with his use of terms like *bastard* and *outside the law* to the exclusion of the term *brother*). He offers a lengthy, subtle treatment of the varieties of meaning of the Greek term *pharmakon*, which is the metonym for writing used by the god who introduces this invention to the Egyptians: "I have discovered a sure receipt (*pharmakon*) for memory and wisdom" (Plato, *Phaedrus*, 274d). Derrida shows how *pharmakon* embraces both positive and negative connotations in Plato's works as a whole, from remedy, prescription ("receipt"), or drug, to magic and poison. Derrida's theoretical prejudices push him to a predictable deconstructive conclusion: the unstable connotations of *pharmakon* subvert the binary opposites that, in his view, are basic to logocentric Western culture: "life/death . . . first/second, legitimate son/ orphan-bastard, soul/body, inside/outside, good/evil, serious/play . . . ," *Dissemination*, 85. In this structure, the deconstructionist inevitably finds that the inferior second term is inscribed in the first, destabilizing the first term and ultimately subverting the entire structure. His theory therefore makes him interested in the "illegitimate" status of writing in Socrates (which is crucial to his argument), but he must ignore the term *brother*, which would complicate—or even deconstruct—his own argument. For other critiques of Derrida's reading of the *Phaedrus*, see chapter two of Stanley Rosen's *Hermeneutics as Politics* (Oxford: Oxford University Press, 1987), and James Risser, *Hermeneutics and the Voice of the Other* (Albany: State University of New York Press, 1997), 174–84.

62. Derrida briefly notes Plato's acknowledgment that some writing rises to the level of the dialectic, but only for the purpose of "teaching the

true as it is *already* constituted," not for any "pathbreaking" inquiry into truth, *Dissemination*, 154; emphasis in original.

63. Plato, *Phaedrus*, 276e–277a.

Chapter 4

1. John Leland, writing as a critic, gives five characteristics of deism: There is one supreme God; he is chiefly to be worshiped; piety and virtue are the principal elements of worship; God will pardon human beings of their sins if they repent; after death, the good will be rewarded and the bad punished, *A View of the Principal Deistical Writers*, 5th ed. (London, 1837), 3.

2. Joseph Addison, *Spectator*, no. 543 (1712).

3. James Boswell, *Life of Johnson*, ed. R. W. Chapman (New York: Oxford University Press, 1980), 281.

4. Arthur Sherbo, *Christopher Smart: A Scholar of the University* (East Lansing: Michigan State University Press, 1967), 115. One of the men associated with St. Luke's Hospital (where Smart was confined), William Battie, defined madness as follows: "'that man alone, is properly mad, who is fully and unalterably persuaded of the existence, or of the appearance, of anything which does not naturally exist, or does not actually appear to him, and who behaves according to such erroneous persuasion'" (Sherbo, *Christopher Smart*, 115). Because Battie administered St. Luke's during Smart's stay and pronounced him "uncured," Sherbo concludes, Smart must have had hallucinations. His mania manifested itself in loud public prayer, in which he often insisted that others participate. Harriet Guest mentions the role of debt in Smart's confinement in *A Form of Sound Words: The Religious Poetry of Christopher Smart* (Oxford: Clarendon, 1989), vii.

5. Although this chapter treats the recent work of John Polkinghorne in more detail, it also refers frequently to the scientist-theologian Ian Barbour. My next sentence draws on terms from Barbour's book *When Science Meets Religion* (San Francisco: HarperSanFrancisco, 2000), 23.

6. Alister McGrath gives a helpful summary of the estrangement of religion from Newtonian physics in *Science and Religion: An Introduction*, (Oxford: Blackwell, 1999), 18–20.

7. The four following approaches form the subject and structure of Barbour's *When Science Meets Religion*. He explains the four approaches in the first chapter of this book. My description in this paragraph and the next applies Barbour's categories, as he explains them in his first chapter, to the eighteenth century.

8. Of d'Holbach's *Système de la nature* (1771), Louis Dupré writes, "Matter is an all-comprehensive, eternal substance that, with the sole support of motion, accounts for the entire scale of the real—from mineral to mind . . . Single-mindedly intent on proving the truth of atheistic naturalism, he borrows from any source like to provide ammunition for his unholy

war" (*Enlightenment and Intellectual Foundations*, 32). In *Moses' Principia* (2nd ed., London 1736), John Hutchinson provides commentary on the scientific implications of various verses from Genesis 1:1 to 8:13. He criticizes Newton's notion of a vacuum on the basis of Genesis 1:2 ("And the Spirit of God moved upon the face of the waters"): "This first Motion is justly attributed to the power of God. And ever since the inspir'd Penmen have, from this Impulse, attributed all the accidents in, and all the operations of this Element upon others, as God's own Acts; and when those Actions are discover'd, It will appear that it deserves a high Title. Here the philosophers must find their Projections, and not in their Vacuum" (14).

9. See Guest, *A Form of Sound Words*, 220–21.
10. James Gleick, *Isaac Newton* (New York: Pantheon, 2003), 100.
11. Sir Isaac Newton, "General Scholium," in *Mathematical Principles of Natural Philosophy*, trans. Andrew Motte, rev. trans Florian Cajori (Berkeley: University of California Press, 1946), 544.
12. Newton, *Mathematical Principles*, 6.
13. Gleick, *Isaac Newton*, 167. Dupré writes that Newton uses the term *sensorium* "in analogy with the sensory apparatus in and through which a remote object becomes present in perception," *Enlightenment and Intellectual Foundations*, 24.
14. Thomas F. Torrance, *Space, Time and Incarnation* (London: Oxford University Press, 1969), 38–39.
15. Newton, "General Scholium," 545; emphasis added. Newton added the "General Scholium" to the second edition of the *Principia*, in 1713.
16. Torrance writes: "In his doctrine of absolute space which is always similar and unmovable without relation to anything, Newton returned to the Aristotelian and medieval notion of a system of reference from a point of absolute rest," *Space, Time and Incarnation*, 39. I shall return to this point later in the chapter when I discuss recent writers on the relationships between physics and theology.
17. Guest, *A Form of Sound Words*, 206. The recent critic she has in mind is John Redwood, whose *Reason, Ridicule and Religion* (London: Thames & Hudson, 1976) makes this point on 169. See also Andrew Pyle, "Introduction," in *The Boyle Lectures 1692–1732* (Bristol: Thoemmes, 2000).
18. The first sentence of *Physico-Theology* (London, 1723) speaks of the design of a creator. Derham proceeds by showing how the construction of the universe is marvelously adapted to life. To give one example, he writes: ". . . behold the Harmony of this lower World, and of the Globes above, and survey GOD's exquisite Workmanship in every Creature" (27). The provision of air, light, the sense of sight, gravity are a few of the other examples that he gives. Joseph Butler's *Analogy of Religion* (1736) is another major work in the tradition of natural religion, but his work is more concerned with moral and strictly epistemological issues than with Smart's main interest, nature. He argues, rather modestly,

that natural evidence suggests the credibility or (at most) probability of revealed truth, and that natural and revealed religion offer equal difficulties. See Earl Wasserman, "Nature Moralized: The Divine Analogy in the Eighteenth Century," *ELH* 20 (1953): 58, and Guest, *A Form of Sound Words*, 96–97, 115, 122.

19. Derham, *Physico-Theology*, 432. My next sentence refers to p. 436.

20. Barbour discusses implications of Newton's view that the world "consists of particles in motion" in *When Science Meets Religion*, 66. See also Fraser Easton, "'Mary's Key' and the Poet's Conception: The Orphic versus the Mimetic Artist in *Jubilate Agno*," in Hawes, *Christopher Smart*, 158: "Smart's ideas about art flow directly from this decentering of the Newtonian lexicon: the premise of Newtonian mechanics (that everything is matter in motion) turns out to be pregnant with a very different message—that matter in motion is the agitated dust of the divine breath. Smart's theory of art is based, then, on this alternative materialism." Although I agree that Smart dissents from Newton, I will try to show that the scope of his poetry (which is by no means materialistic) goes far beyond a theory of art.

21. The best descriptions of Smart's complicated relationship with the thought of John Hutchinson and his followers are in Guest, *A Form of Sound Words*, 207–8; Karina Williamson, "Smart's *Principia*: Science and Anti-Science in *Jubilate Agno*," *Review of English Studies* 30, no. 120 (1979): 412–15; and Karina Williamson, appendix to *Jubilate Agno*, in *The Poetical Works of Christopher Smart*, ed. Williamson and Walsh, I:131–32.

22. See Williamson, "Appendix," 132. See also *Jubilate Agno* B130 and Williamson's notes to B183–86, B195, and B674.

23. The Seatonian Prize was established for a poem by a member of Cambridge University on "the Perfections of Attributes of the Supreme Being." Smart won this prize five times between 1750 and 1755. Smart wrote *Jubilate Agno* between 1758 and 1763, during his confinement. The poem's existence was not publicly known until 1939, when it was published under the title *Rejoice in the Lamb: A Song from Bedlam*, by William Force Stead, the literary clergyman who baptized T. S. Eliot in 1927. Despite the subtitle that Stead chose, there is no evidence that Smart was ever confined in the infamous Bedlam (or Bethlehem) Hospital. "A Song to David" was published by April 6, 1763, about nine weeks after Smart's release from the private madhouse in Bethnal Green, where he spent most of his confinement. It is not known with certainty how much of the latter poem was composed during his confinement. See the remarks of Marcus Walsh in *The Poetical Works of Christopher Smart*, 2:99 and Sherbo, *Christopher Smart*, 114.

24. By Smart's day, "the sublime" was regarded as a psychological law that accounts for the human reactions of terror, astonishment, and awe to an experience that overwhelms one's senses and rationality. Although the sublime has a correlative outside the mind, it cannot be explained apart

from the nature of the mind. Most eighteenth-century writers related the sublime to God through the powerful or transcendent impression made by the experience, although their writing on the subject is not precise. The most significant writers on the subject before 1760 included Boileau (whose *On the Sublime* was translated into English in the late seventeenth century), Addison, Dennis, Hutcheson, Hume, Gerard, Kames, and Blair. Lowth's 1753 lectures (in Latin) had a profound effect on Smart for their description of the sublime poetry of Hebrew Scripture. Edmund Burke's popular *Enquiry into . . . the Sublime and Beautiful* appeared in 1757. Scholarship on this subject is voluminous, beginning with Samuel Holt Monk's *The Sublime: A Study of Critical Theories in XVIII-Century England* (New York: MLA, 1935). Various approaches to the sublime in Smart's poetry are usefully summarized by Hawes in *Christopher Smart and the Enlightenment*, 195–96.

25. By Smart's day, it was conventional to write poetry that harmonized science and theology from within the natural theology framework associated with Derham's *Physico-Theology*. Such poetry—made even more conventional by the establishment of Thomas Seaton's prize—followed in the train of such popular poems as Richard Blackmore's *Creation* (1712), James Thomson's *The Seasons* (1730), and Alexander Pope's *Essay on Man* (1733). The verse forms—heroic couplets or the blank verse used in Smart's Seatonian verse—were conventional as well. (See *The Poetical Works of Christopher Smart*, 3:xxv.) Smart would shortly take more risks, in both form and content, in the more mature works, *Jubilate Agno* and "A Song to David."

26. "Could ought retard / Goodness, that knows no bounds, from blessing ever, / Or keep th' immense Artificer in sloth?" (31–33). La Mettrie's works in the 1740s had made the point that God's role was now little more than to provide a support for physics and morality. See Dupré, *Enlightenment and Intellectual Foundations*, 27.

27. Lines 83–87 refer to recent experiments with electricity. Smart gives a pre-Newtonian, "sympathetic" explanation of magnetism: "Survey the magnet's sympathetic love, / That woos the yielding needle . . ." (80–81). Although his explanation is erroneous, his willingness to question contemporary science and its presuppositions will be important for Smart's later verse.

28. See Marcus Walsh, quoted in *The Poetical Works of Christopher Smart*, 4:xxxii.

29. Williamson, "Smart's *Principia*," 410–11. See also Sherbo, *Christopher Smart*, 149–53.

30. Williamson in the introduction to *The Poetical Works of Christopher Smart*, 1:xxix.

31. See *Jubilate Agno* B284, B213, and B426 for these outdated scientific assertions. Smart claimed to have shown the falsity of inertia at B183.

32. *Two Letters of Sir Isaac Newton to Mr. Le Clerc* (London, 1754). For an estimate of the effect of these letters, see Scott Mandelbrote,

"Eighteenth-Century Reactions to Newton's Anti-Trinitarianism," in *Newton and Newtonianism*, ed. James E. Force and Sarah Hutton (Dordrecht: Kluwer, 2004), 93–112.

33. Sherbo, *Christopher Smart*, 101.

34. *The Oxford English Dictionary* gives "The knowledge or study of nature" as the third definition of the word "philosophy," understood as "natural philosophy." As an example of this usage, it quotes from a 1728 book, titled *Newton's Philosophy*. The *Oxford English Dictionary's* second definition specifically distinguishes this usage of the term from philosophy's moral and metaphysical branches.

35. B1–5; see Williamson's comments on these lines in *The Poetical Works of Christopher Smart*, vol. 1: *Jubilate Agno*, 12.

36. In a short notice written for the first number of *The Universal Visiter and Monthly Memorialist* (January/February 1756), Smart called Lowth's book of lectures "one of the best performances that has been published for a century" (25). Harriet Guest writes that "[t]he influence of Lowth's *Lectures*, or at least of the attitude towards primitive poetry as the expression of a remote and foreign culture which they represent, is everywhere apparent in *Jubilate Agno* . . .," *A Form of Sound Words*, 128. See also Guest, *A Form of Sound Words*, 152–56; James Engell, *The Committed Word* (University Park: Pennsylvania State University Press, 1999), 124; Betty Rizzo, "Christopher Smart's Poetics," in Hawes, 122; and Marcus Walsh "Community of Mind" also in Hawes, 32. The "For" lines of *Jubilate Agno* are conventionally printed in italics.

37. Lowth particularly explores three types of parallelism in Hebrew poetry in Lecture 19. Although Lowth refers to previous writers, his analysis provided the "definitive form" for the modern understanding of parallelism in Hebrew poetry, Robert Lowth, *Lectures on the Sacred Poetry of the Hebrews*, 4th ed., trans. G. Gregory (London, 1839; repr., Whitefish, Mont.: Kessinger Publishing, n.d.), (hereafter cited as Lecture with number). See James Kugel, *The Idea of Biblical Poetry: Parallelism and Its History* (New Haven: Yale University Press, 1981), 287; and Leland Ryken, "The Bible as Literature: A Brief History," in *A Complete Literary Guide to the Bible*, ed. Leland Ryken and Tremper Longman III (Grand Rapids: Zondervan, 1993), 55.

38. See especially Lecture 20. The "expressive" approach to poetry is implicit in a theory of metaphor that emphasizes the sublime, as I will show later.

39. Lowth, Lecture 19, 200–205.

40. Pliny, *Natural History*, 32.69. Loeb Classical Library, vol. 8 of Pliny, *Natural History*, trans. W. H. S. Jones (Cambridge, Mass.: Harvard University Press, 1963).

41. B123–B295; see also Williamson's note to B123 in *The Poetical Works of Christopher Smart*, vol. 1: *Jubilate Agno*.

42. Lowth, Lecture 20, 219.

43. Lowth, Lecture 20, 221. In his *Enquiry*, Burke writes "It is one thing

to make an idea clear, and another to make it *affecting* to the imagination . . . [S]o far is a clearness of imagery from being absolutely necessary to an influence upon the passions, that they may be considerably operated upon without presenting any image at all, by certain sounds adapted to that purpose. . . . In reality a great clearness helps but little towards affecting the passions," his emphasis, Part II, sec. iv; *Writings and Speeches*, 1:232. Sublime poetry, in other words, is more concerned to express the effect of an object on the observer, rather than to represent the object in precise words. Two years later, in the second edition of the *Enquiry* (1759), Burke added a passage stating that a "clear idea is therefore another name for a little idea," and went on to analyze a passage in Job 4:13-17, where Eliphaz expresses the terrifying, sublime effect of a visit from God's spirit, *Writings and Speeches*, 1:235.

44. See *The Poetical Works of Christopher Smart*, vol. 1: *Jubilate Agno*, B195n.

45. Newton wrote: "1. The [word] God is no where in the scriptures used to signify more than one of the three persons at once. 2. The word God put absolutely without particular restriction to the Son or Holy ghost doth always signify the Father from one end of the scriptures to the other. . . .," Quoted in Gleick, *Isaac Newton*, 111.

46. Newton, "General Scholium," 544–45. The next quotation comes from "General Scholium," 545.

47. Torrance, *Space, Time and Incarnation*, 39–40. Torrance's allusion to the *homoousion* is significant: this is the crucial affirmation of the Nicene Creed that Jesus Christ was "of the same substance" with the Father, which Athanasius defended against Arius.

48. Paul is mentioned twice in this portion of the poem (B225, 231), but only in connection with other, more ordinary Christians. The final lines of this section (B239–240) refer to Claudius Lysias, who helped Paul escape an ambush (Acts 23:16-30), and Bernice, the sister of Herod Agrippa II, who ruled parts of Palestine in the second half of the first century A.D. She may be included because, after hearing Paul's testimony she is among those who conclude that Paul deserves neither death nor imprisonment (Acts 26:31). Both Claudius and Bernice, therefore, have supporting roles in the spread of the gospel. Peter was the first apostle mentioned in Fragment B (B123), but his name does not surface again in this portion. However, B214 refers to Simon the Tanner, with whom Peter stayed after receiving the revelation of God's intention to save the Gentiles (see Acts 9:36–11:18).

49. See also Williamson's notes in *The Poetical Works of Christopher Smart*, vol. 1: *Jubilate Agno*, B209–39. My analysis here applies particularly to lines B209–B239. After that point, Smart's biblical names are drawn from the epistles rather than from Acts.

50. The disputes over phlogiston, combustion, and air would continue into the 1770s, which even the controversial discovery of oxygen did not immediately end. Thomas Kuhn uses this controversy to demonstrate the difference between the older view of scientific discovery as proceeding

incrementally from experiment to hypothesis and the actual, historical practice of scientific discovery, in which a new paradigm displaces the expectations of older scientific practices. *The Structure of Scientific Revolutions*, 3rd ed. (Chicago: University of Chicago Press, 1996), 52–56.

51. Let Tryphosa rejoice with Acarne—with such a preparation the Lord's Jubilee is better kept.
    For the rising in the BAROMETER is not effected by pressure but by sympathy (B213)

52. Torrance, *Space, Time and Incarnation*, 19. The next quotation from Torrance comes from the same page.

53. Lowth, Lecture 16, 173.

54. Robert K. Logan, *The Alphabet Effect: The Impact of the Phonetic Alphabet on the Development of Western Civilization* (New York: William Morrow, 1986), 17–24. The next sentences draw on Logan, 18, 23–24.

55. Logan, *The Alphabet Effect*, 19, 24.

56. The Great Chain of Being lost credibility in large part because it could not explain evil adequately. Two different critiques of this concept came from Samuel Johnson (who attacked it in his 1756 review of Soame Jenyns' *Inquiry into the Origin of Evil*) and Voltaire's poem on the 1755 Lisbon earthquake. For Newton, mathematics was the language of God. See Gleick, *Isaac Newton*, 110–11.

57. Smart's use of the alphabet and numbers becomes highly esoteric in Fragment C of *Jubilate Agno*. At these points, his system loses its purchase with the world of nature, in my view, and takes on a life of its own, derived from cabbalistic and Masonic theory rather than serving as an analogy for his experiences with nature.

58. Williamson in the introduction to *The Poetical Works of Christopher Smart*, 1:xxvi.

59. The line that immediately follows the conclusion to this obscure, second abecedarium is: *For Action and Speaking are one according to God and the Ancients* (B562).

60. Williamson in *The Poetical Works of Christopher Smart*, vol. 1: *Jubilate Agno*, B477n.

61. See J. B. Friedman, "The Cosmology of Praise: Smart's *Jubilate Agno*," *PMLA* 82 (1967): 250–56, 251.

62. Scholars have puzzled over this portion of "A Song to David" since its first publication (Walsh, "Introduction," 99–100). In his useful appendix to the poem, Walsh surveys the various theories that account for the particular seven Greek letters used by Smart, as well as their order in the poem. He concludes that all seven of the letters "may be taken to represent names of God" (151). He notes that the association of God's name with creation was a theme Smart had developed elsewhere, including the *lamed* passage from *Jubilate Agno* that I have just discussed.

63. Smart, "A Song to David," 223–24. "Degree" probably alludes to the different degrees within freemasonry. See *The Poetical Works of Christopher Smart*, 2:438.

64. This brief reservation about those who promote the "Anthropic Principle" hardly does justice to the range of thought on this issue. Good introductory descriptions of this idea are found in Barbour, *When Science Meets Religion*, 57–59; and John Polkinghorne, *Belief in God in an Age of Science* (New Haven: Yale University Press, 1998), 6–13.
65. Richard Dawkins, *A Devil's Chaplain* (Boston: Houghton Mifflin, 2003), 117, 151.
66. Dawkins, *A Devil's Chaplain*, 242. My next sentence quotes from Dawkins, 243.
67. Dawkins, *A Devil's Chaplain*, 146.
68. Dawkins, *A Devil's Chaplain*, 11. The next references come from pages 46, 10–11 of the same book.
69. Alister E. McGrath, *Dawkins' God: Genes, Memes, and the Meaning of Life* (Oxford: Blackwell, 2005), 46.
70. Stephen Barr, "The Devil's Chaplain Confounded," *First Things* 145 (2004): 25–31, 28.
71. Barbour's *When Science Meets Religion* treats a number of other scientists who operate under the conflict model, including Carl Sagan, Steven Weinberg, Daniel Dennett, Francis Crick, and Edward O. Wilson.
72. Barbour, *When Science Meets Religion*, 18–19. Stephen Jay Gould explains the phrase "non-overlapping magisteria" in *Rocks of Ages: Science and Religion in the Fullness of Life* (New York: Ballantine, 1999), 49–67.
73. See Barbour, *When Science Meets Religion*, 18.
74. Lyotard, *The Postmodern Condition*, 10.
75. Lyotard, *The Postmodern Condition*, 24; emphasis added.
76. Lyotard, *The Postmodern Condition*, 57.
77. Quoted in Stanley Grenz, "Why Do Theologians Need to be Scientists?" *Zygon* 35, no. 2 (2000): 331–56, 347; emphasis in original.
78. Alan Sokal, "Transgressing the Boundaries: Toward a Transformative Hermeneutics of Quantum Gravity," *Social Text* (Spring/Summer 1996): 217–52. Stanley Fish, executive editor of Duke University Press at the time (which published *Social Text*) attacked Sokal in an Op Ed piece in the May 21, 1996 *New York Times*, "Professor Sokal's Bad Joke," 23. This incident is treated in Alister McGrath, *Scientific Theology*, vol. 2: *Reality* (Grand Rapids: Eerdmans, 2002), 188–91, and John D. Caputo *Deconstruction in a Nutshell* (New York: Fordham University Press, 1997), 72–73.
79. See Alan Sokal and Jean Bricmont, *Fashionable Nonsense: Postmodern Intellectuals' Abuse of Science* (New York: Picador, 1998), 213.
80. Erwin Schrödinger, *Nature and the Greeks and Science and Humanism* (Cambridge: Cambridge University Press, 1996) 95, 97, 98.
81. Barbour, *When Science Meets Religion*, 23.
82. In his book *Scientists as Theologians* (London: SPCK, 1996), Polkinghorne uses the term *consonance* to describe his approach, which is quite similar to what Barbour calls *dialogue*. Polkinghorne distinguishes this approach from one that tries to assimilate (or integrate) scientific and theological

categories by blending them with the minimum possible strain to the secular mind. Consonance "acknowledges that scientific discoveries constrain modes of theological expression, so that they have to be consistent with the truth of what we know about the physical world" (82). Still, it also acknowledges a proper autonomy to theological knowledge: Because God has chosen to act and make himself known in particular ways, our ways of apprehending God must conform to the divine nature. Consonance, then, tries to do justice to both modes of knowledge, while seeking common ground between them.

83. While this element is evident in much of Polkinghorne's work, it is particularly clear in *Faith, Science, and Understanding* (New Haven: Yale University Press, 2000), 86–97. My observation in the next sentence comes from personal experience at two of Barbour's lectures.

84. Polkinghorne, *Belief in God in an Age of Science*, 37–38. The other quotations from Polkinghorne in this paragraph refer to page 38 as well. Polkinghorne names several shortcomings of the "experimentation" analogy: Unlike the objects of the physical world, God cannot be subjected to testing; theology lacks the language of mathematics, which fits the physical world so well; and because language for the divine is ultimately inadequate, theology uses inescapably symbolic terms for God. Kuhn draws an analogy between the creative work of theology and science as well, in *The Structure of Scientific Revolutions*, 136.

85. Barbour, *When Science Meets Religion*, 106; emphasis in original.

86. As he explores the implications of this analogy in chapters 2, 4, and 6 of *When Science Meets Religion*, Barbour refers several times to Polkinghorne's work on the subject.

87. Polkinghorne, *Belief in God in an Age of Science*, 66. The quotation from David Bohm comes from the next page. It should be noted that Bohm's theory remains controversial. Another excellent physicist-theologian, Stephen Barr, provides a critique of it in *Modern Physics and Ancient Faith* (Notre Dame, Ind.: University of Notre Dame Press, 2003), 247–48.

88. Polkinghorne, *Belief*, 72.

89. Polkinghorne, *Belief*, 24.

Chapter 5

1. The meaning of "citizen" is a major theme of Simon Schama's book, *Citizens: A Chronicle of the French Revolution* (New York: Knopf, 1989). He discusses the creation of the citizen explicitly in his first chapter, "New Men," 21–49. See also Gregory Dart, *Rousseau, Robespierre and English Romanticism* (Cambridge: Cambridge University Press, 1999), 5, and Marie-Hélène Huet, *Mourning Glory: The Will of the French Revolution* (Philadelphia: University of Pennsylvania Press, 1997), 24.

2. See François Furet's explanation of this point in his article, "Terror," in *A Critical Dictionary of the French Revolution*, ed. Mona Ozouf and François

Furet, trans. Arthur Goldhammer (Cambridge, Mass.: Harvard-Belknap, 1989), 148–49.

3. Mona Ozouf describes how the new festivals established the permanent fact of the revolution (and their connection to censorship and other forms of control) in the first two chapters of *Festivals and the French Revolution*, trans. Alan Sheridan (Cambridge, Mass.: Harvard University Press, 1988), 13–60, 168–69, and in her article, "Revolutionary Calendar," in *A Critical Dictionary of the French Revolution*, ed. Ozouf and Furet, 544–45. Frank Tallett discusses Robespierre's realization that education and the de-Christianization campaign of 1793, by themselves, had failed to supply the public morality needed by the revolution. See "Robespierre and Religion," in *Robespierre*, ed. Colin Haydon and William Doyle (Cambridge: Cambridge University Press, 1999), 103–5.

4. The term *postmodern* may be unhelpful or even misleading in this chapter. Robespierre, Fabre d'Églantine, and Romme saw further than their contemporaries, but it may be more accurate to think of them as carrying out the implications of enlightened political thinking beyond the imaginations of Locke or Rousseau, rather than questioning the foundations of Enlightenment. Though the ideological movements I will examine later in the chapter often ally themselves with postmodern thought, it may be more precise to think of them as exaggerated or "hyper" modern movements as well, rather than representing a break with enlightened, progressive, or radical political causes.

5. Alexis de Tocqueville discusses the mild despotism of the schoolmaster state in section 2.4.6 of *Democracy in America*, ed. and trans. Harvey C. Mansfield and Delba Winthrop (Chicago: University of Chicago Press, 2000), "What Kind of Despotism Democratic Nations Have to Fear."

6. In his excellent article on Sieyès, Keith Baker traces the thought of the abbé through "What Is the Third Estate" and other writings, including the abbé's departures from Rousseau. See Baker, "Sieyès," in *A Critical Dictionary of the French Revolution*, ed. Ozouf and Furet, 319–20.

7. "To read the principal pamphlets [Sieyès] contributed to the debate over the forms of the convocation of the estates General," Baker writes, "is to follow the creation of revolutionary discourse itself" ("Sieyès," 313–14).

8. Examples from Voltaire's *Philosophical Dictionary* are easily furnished. "It has been very well remarked that the divine writings might, at one and the same time, be sacred and apocryphal; sacred, because they had been undoubtedly dictated by God Himself; apocryphal, because they were hidden from the nations, and even from the Jewish people" ("Apocrypha—Apocryphal"). The next two chapters will give more sustained attention to Voltaire's work.

9. Mona Ozouf describes Voltaire's Pantheonization in her article, "Voltaire," in *A Critical Dictionary of the French Revolution*, ed. Ozouf and Furet, 870–71.

10. As explained in the chapter on Jonathan Swift and technology, Condorcet never lost his faith that political enlightenment would follow philosophical enlightenment, even after a warrant for his arrest was issued early in the Terror. See Huet, *Mourning Glory*, 20–25.

11. Ozouf gives an account of the festivals of reason in *Festivals of the French Revolution*, 97–102. In her article, "Revolutionary Religion," she analyzes F. A. Aulard's influential treatment of this element of the Revolution (in *Le Culte de la Raison et le Culte de l'Etre Suprême, 1793-1794* [Paris: F. Alcan, 1892]). See also Lynn Hunt, *Politics, Culture and Class in the French Revolution* (Berkeley: University of California Press, 2004); and Georges Lefebvre, *The French Revolution: 1793–1799* (New York: Columbia University Press, 1964), 78–79.

12. Robespierre, *Œuvres de Maximilien Robespierre*, 10:196; emphasis in original.

13. For a sustained description of the creation of the new citizen, see Schama's *Citizens*, particularly his first and fourth chapters ("New Men" and "The Cultural Construction of a Citizen").

14. Robespierre, *Œuvres*, 10:197 (November 21, 1793).

15. Robespierre, *Œuvres*, 10:458 (May 7, 1794).

16. Robespierre, *Œuvres*, 10: 451, 452.

17. Robespierre, *Œuvres*, 10:444 (May 7, 1794).

18. Huet discusses the significance of this metaphor for Robespierre and other contemporary figures in considerable detail in the first chapter of *Mourning Glory*, 9–31.

19. See, for instance, Bronislaw Baczko, *Ending the Terror: The French Revolution after Robespierre*, trans. Michel Petheram (Cambridge: Cambridge University Press, 1994) and Furet, "Terror."

20. Ozouf, *Festivals*, 34–36.

21. *The Prelude* (1850), 6:357–58, 352, 371, in *English Romantic Writers*, ed. David Perkins (New York: Harcourt Brace Jovanovich, 1967).

22. Edmund Burke, "A Letter to a Member of the National Assembly," in *Further Reflections on the Revolution in France*, ed. Daniel E. Ritchie (Indianapolis: Liberty Fund, 1992), 46.

23. The "close contact between violence and the festival," as Ozouf writes, is an "enormous problem" in scholarship on the French Revolution. She describes the historiography of Jules Michelet, for instance, who tries to exclude violence from his description of true revolutionary festivals. See *Festivals*, 18–21, 11.

24. Burke, *Letters on a Regicide Peace* [1796], in *Writings and Speeches*, 9:241, 242; emphasis in original.

25. See Paine, *The Rights of Man* [Part I, 1791], 71–72, 79.

26. The material in the rest of this paragraph is indebted to Ozouf, *Festivals* 11, 96, 111, 112.

27. See the editors' notes to the speech in Robespierre, *Œuvres*, 10:443.

28. Ozouf, *Festivals*, 59–60, and Albert Mathiez, *The Fall of Robespierre, and Other Essays* (New York: Knopf, 1927), 103. The rest of the paragraph

relies on Ozouf's treatment at 111, 115–17, and 12 and J. M. Thompson, *Robespierre*, vol. 2 (New York: Appleton-Century, 1936) 191.

29. The quoted phrase comes from Pierre Nora's general introduction to *Realms of Memory*, in vol. 1, *Conflicts and Divisions*, trans. Arthur Goldhammer (New York: Columbia University Press, 1996), 15.

30. See Ozouf's discussion in her article, "Revolutionary Calendar," 540–46. She concludes:

> The dream of a new man, so central to revolutionary thought, presupposed freeing the old man from his moorings in order to make him a citizen and then surrounding him with a dense network of luminous images, disciplining rituals, and instructive habits. In order to make this positive pedagogy possible, time had to be restructured in such a way that the regular occurrence of special days with their attendant emotions would forge new habits. The republican calendar was thus conceived as an instrument, whose content was to have engendered the new loyalties of the citizen and whose form was to have been a "mold" to shape an obedient nation.

31. *Procès-Verbaux du Comité d'Instruction Publique de la Convention Nationale*, ed. M. J. Guillaume (Paris, 1894), 2:696.

32. Ozouf, "Revolutionary Calendar," 544–45. The observations after the quotation from Burke are indebted to these pages as well.

33. Burke, "Letter to William Elliott," in *Further Reflections*, 266–67.

34. Romme makes these connections in his speech of September 20, 1793. See *Procès-Verbaux*, 440–46.

35. Bentabole's remarks (October 5, 1793) are recorded in the *Procès-Verbaux*, 585.

36. Ozouf, "Revolutionary Calendar," 543–44.

37. *Procès-Verbaux*, 697–713. The quote in the next paragraph comes from 699.

38. Ozouf, "Revolutionary Calendar," 545.

39. See Furet, "Terror," 143–45.

40. The quotation is from Robespierre's speech of 18 Floréal (May 7, 1794; *Œuvres*, 10:457). A month earlier, on April 5 (16 Germinal), Danton, Demoulins, Fabre d'Églantine, and Hérault de Séchelles had all been executed.

41. Robespierre uses this expression in the same speech (18 Floréal; *Œuvres*, 10:457). See Furet, "Terror," 144–45.

42. The speech is found in Robespierre, *Œuvres*, 10:350–67. The references here and in the succeeding sentences of this paragraph are from 10:352.

43. Robespierre, *Œuvres*, 10:356–57.

44. Dart, *Rousseau, Robespierre and English Romanticism*, 38. See also Huet, *Mourning Glory*, 50; and Baczko, *Ending the Terror*, 24.

45. Robespierre, *Œuvres*, 10:366. Speech of 17 Pluviôse.

46. Huet, *Mourning Glory*, 50–51. I refer as well to Huet's observation that "Language is suspect, and the Law of 22 Prairial is also a law against words" (51).

47. Charles Péguy put it best: "Everything begins in mysticism and ends in politics." "Notre Jeunesse," *Œuvres en Prose* (Paris: Bibliotheque de la Pleiade, 1961), 518.

48. These points are made in Richard Bernstein's *Dictatorship of Virtue* (New York: Knopf, 1994) and Diane Ravitch's *The Language Police* (New York: Knopf, 2003). Ravitch details successful efforts by the right to pressure publishers into eliminating references to abortion, evolution, witchcraft, and sexual expression—or entire literary works that deal with such matters—in books for K–12 students.

49. This paragraph's description of the curriculum's reception in Queens comes from Bernstein, *Dictatorship of Virtue*, 164–68. The quoted material at the end of this paragraph comes from 168.

50. In addition to the books by Richard Bernstein and Diane Ravitch, mention should be made of Alan Charles Kors and Harvey A. Silvergate, *The Shadow University* (New York: Free Press, 1998) and Neil W. Hamilton, *Zealotry and Academic Freedom: A Legal and Historical Perspective* (New Brunswick, N.J.: Transaction Publishers, 1995). A more recent book is Donald Alexander Downs, *Restoring Free Speech and Liberty on Campus* (Cambridge: Cambridge University Press, 2006).

51. The details on Timothy George's 1990 experience at Cornell are from Bernstein, *Dictatorship of Virtue*, 88–91. The quoted material is from 90–91.

52. Out of the work of Kors and Silverglate, The Foundation for Individual Rights in Education was formed to defend students and faculty who run afoul of campus codes. Information on such cases may be found at the FIRE Web site, www.thefire.org.

53. A recent study of the Higher Education Research Institute at University of California at Los Angeles reports that about two-thirds of U.S. students socialize frequently with members of another racial/ethnic group and over a third said that promoting racial understanding was "essential" or "very important." See "The American Freshman: Forty Year Trends, 1966–2006," www.gseis.ucla.edu/heri/40yrtrends.php, accessed July 1, 2009.

54. Furet, "Terror" 147–48.

55. Fish's most concentrated discussion of this matter is found in the eighth chapter of his book, *There's No Such Thing as Free Speech and It's a Good Thing Too* (New York: Oxford University Press, 1994). The quoted material comes from 114; emphasis in original.

56. Fish, *There's No Such Thing as Free Speech*, 102. Any edition of Boswell's *Life of Johnson* will have Johnson's remark, "Patriotism is the last refuge of a scoundrel" (April 7, 1775). The next quotation is from Fish, *There's No Such Thing as Free Speech*, 111.

57. In more recent years, Christian groups at Tufts, Middlebury, Williams, Whitman, and Grinnell, among others, have had to fight school authorities for the right to elect leaders who accept biblical teachings on sexuality. Students at Rutgers, North Carolina, and Ball State have fought for similar rights, often having to oppose suspension (from official recognition, the right to meeting space, etc.) by threatening their own institutions with lawsuits. See documentation of these cases at www.thefire. org.

58. Fish, *There's No Such Thing as Free Speech*, 111.

59. See the treatment of Alan Sokal's parody of postmodern physics in the previous chapter and Fish's, "Professor Sokal's Bad Joke," *The New York Times*, May 21, 1996, 23.

60. Ozouf, *Festivals*, 28–29.

61. E. G. Richards writes: "[C]alendars are religious objects; they define the times of rites and fasts and festivals. Where there is a calendar there is a religion more often than not; where there is a religion, there is a calendar." See Richards, *Mapping Time: The Calendar and Its History* (New York: Oxford University Press, 1998), 110.

62. Information on Vagina day comes from Sommers and the Vagina Day Web site (www.vday.org/). More recent updates to the Web site says that the *V* may stand for vagina, valentine, or victory. In Eve Ensler's *The Vagina Monologues: The V-Day Edition* (New York: Villard, 1998) the director of the Vagina Day College Initiative does not use the term *victory* in her description of the event (129–44). Much of my description of the events at Roger Williams University comes from Sommers' article in National Review Online. More recently, Sommers has applauded the work of Eve Ensler, author of *The Vagina Monologues*, on behalf of women brutalized in Afghanistan. However, even left-leaning commentators are put off by Ensler's assertion that "Afghanistan is everywhere" and for equating sex with violence. See Sommers, "The Subjection of Islamic Women and the Fecklessness of American Feminism," *The Weekly Standard*, May 21, 2007, 14–20; Janelle Brown, "Eve Ensler: 'Afghanistan is Everywhere,'" interview with Eve Ensler, November 26, 2001, http://archive.salon.com/people/feature, accessed October 4, 2008; and Camille Paglia, "Our Unimpressive President," http://archive.salon.com/people, April 11, 2001, accessed October 4, 2008.

63. Calendars of Anglican and Catholic saints emphasize SS. Cyril and Methodius on February 14, not St. Valentine.

64. See Ensler, *The Vagina Monologues*, 129–77.

65. Its mission statement describes Roger Williams University as "a respectful, diverse, and intellectually vibrant university community." See www. rwu.edu/about/mission/, accessed October 4, 2008.

66. Monique Stuart, e-mail message to author, July 10, 2006.

67. Christopher Kempling was suspended from his post in 2003 when the British Columbia College of Teachers decided his newspaper letter was

"derogatory and demeaning." He appealed to the British Columbia Supreme Court, arguing that the Canadian Charter of Rights protected him, but the Court upheld the discipline in 2004 and the Court of Appeal rejected his suit in June 2005. The British Columbia Civil Liberties Association argued against Kempling (Canadian Press NewsWire, 14 June 2005. Accessed June 30, 2005). In June 2003 the Rev. Ake Green preached that homosexuality was "a deep cancerous tumor in [Sweden's] entire society" and linked it to pedophilia and bestiality. He was convicted of violating the country's 2002 hate speech law, but his conviction was overturned in February 2005 (*Washington Post*, February 12, 2005).

68. Alexis de Tocqueville, *Democracy in America*, 243. The quoted material in the next lines is from 662, 663.

69. Details on Black History Month may be found in Raphael Cassimere, "Frederick Douglass and the Origin of Black History Month," *Crisis* 102, no. 2 (1995): 18–19.

70. "About Kwanzaa." http://melanet.com/kwanzaa/whatis.html#history. June 2, 2005. In more recent years, this Web site has become inaccessible.

71. Karenga, Maulana (Ron), see www.officialkwanzaawebsite.org/celebrating.html. The wording on this page has changed somewhat since my original June 2, 2005 accession date. Tony Snow's comments appeared in "The Truth About Kwanzaa," *Jewish World Review*, December 31, 1999. www.jewishworldreview.com, accessed June 2, 2005.

72. The more successful, rival group associated with Earth Day, the "Earth Day Network," which promotes the more common April 22 date, has much less grandiose goals for the holiday (www.earthday.net). Still, even this group's Web site advertises Earth Day as the largest "secular holiday in the world, celebrated by more than a half billion people."

73. John McConnell, "Earth's Resurrection," March 20, 2005. International Earth Day Official Site, www.earthsite.org, accessed April 26, 2005.

74. This and the following two sentences refer to Eviatar Zerubavel, *Hidden Rhythms: Schedules and Calendars in Social Life* (Chicago: University of Chicago Press, 1981), 101–5, 111. Zerubavel's principal source is Émile Durkheim's *Elementary Forms of Religious Life* (1912).

75. Zerubavel, *Hidden Rhythms*, 103.

76. For the French background described in this and the following two paragraphs, see Ozouf, *Festivals*, 21, 45, 47, 57, 88–89. The recent examples come from personal observation at a couple of Minneapolis marches.

77. The Web site for V-Day has an entire page dedicated to "resistance" to the festival. See www.vday.org/contents/resistance, accessed July 1, 2009.

78. Two examples chosen almost at random, one on feminism, the other on feminism and multiculturalism, may serve as examples of how student disagreement is treated as "resistance." Each is filled with references to previous scholarship on the same issue: Melanie Moore, "Student Resistance to Course Content: Reactions to the Gender of the

Messenger," *Teaching Sociology* 25, no. 2 (2004): 128–33. Anne Donadey, "Negotiating Tensions: Teaching about Race Issues in Graduate Feminist Classrooms," *National Women's Studies Association Journal* 14, no. 1 (2002): 82–102. This article argues against allowing both sides of an issue to be expressed in class, for doing so only "privileg[es] dominant power relations" (87).

Chapter 6

1. This particular description, typical of many that deal with Western culture, comes from the introduction to the "World Heritage Course" Millsaps College in Jackson, Mississippi (IDS 1118–1128, fall 2000). "Effective reasoning," it continues, "requires thinking logically and reflectively, analyzing critically and constructively." Although this is a course in Western culture, the description contains nothing about the value of the traditions represented by that culture.

2. Harry R. Lewis, a former dean of Harvard College, provides a valuable examination of his school's embrace of globalism at the expense of a curricular commitment to educate its students in the American tradition. See *Excellence without A Soul: How a Great University Forgot Education* (Cambridge: Perseus-Public Affairs, 2006), 59–72.

3. Edward Shils analyzes the tension between traditionalism and Enlightenment thought in *Tradition* (Chicago: University of Chicago Press, 1981), esp. 21–23.

4. The "hermeneutics of suspicion" is derived from Paul Ricoeur's description of Marx, Freud, and Nietzsche as three "masters of suspicion" in *Freud and Philosophy*, trans. Denis Savage (New Haven: Yale University Press, 1970), 33.

5. Jean Grondin discusses the problem of considering Gadamer a postmodern thinker in the introduction to *The Philosophy of Gadamer*, trans. Kathryn Plant (Montreal: McGill-Queens University Press, 2003). Grondin maintains that Gadamer distances himself from postmodern thinkers, for they still follow Descartes in their reliance upon method to "exercise a monopoly on the notion of truth," 3. Stanley Grenz, by contrast, argues that Gadamer "prefigures the postmodern philosophers" for his critique of a faith in objective methodology as such in *A Primer on Postmodernism* (Grand Rapids: Eerdmans, 1996), 108–12. Catherine Zuckert includes Gadamer in *Postmodern Platos* because, like the other major figures in her book, he begins his dialogue with Plato "on the basis of a conviction that modern rationalism has exhausted its promise and its possibilities" (Chicago: University of Chicago Press, 1996), 1.

6. Edmund Burke, *The Correspondence of Edmund Burke*, ed. Thomas W. Copeland (Chicago: University of Chicago Press, 1958–1978), 6:85–87. For the sake of convenience, I will generally refer to the "Glorious Revolution" of 1688–1689, as it is known in the United States, as the Revolution of 1688.

7. Burke, *Reflections on the Revolution in France* [1790], in *Writings and Speeches* 8:126. (All subsequent quotations from the *Reflections* are drawn from this edition.) Burke's 1773 visit to France is described in F. P. Lock, *Edmund Burke* (Oxford: Clarendon, 1998), 1:342–43.

8. French pornography had been comparing Marie Antoinette to sexual profligates for many years. See Schama, *Citizens*, 203–27.

9. Burke, *Correspondence*, 6:90. The word *dramatically* is printed as "systematically" in the 1844 edition of Burke's correspondence. The manuscript is difficult to decipher. However, as Burke's thought moves from classical history to classical and Renaissance drama in this passage, the word "dramatically" seems the better choice.

10. Alasdair MacIntyre wrongly accuses Burke of thinking that tradition was "essentially unitary" in "Epistemological Crises, Dramatic Narrative, and the Philosophy of Science," (*Why Narrative?* 151). Burke's arguments with Francis and others over historical traditions show his awareness of the multiplicity of traditions that one partly inherits, partly creates.

11. For an unsympathetic reading of Burke's response to Francis, see Tom Furniss, "Stripping the Queen: Edmund Burke's Magic Lantern Show," in *Burke and the French Revolution: Bicentennial Essays*, ed. Steven Blakemore (Athens: University of Georgia Press, 1992), 69–96.

12. Burke, *Reflections*, 129. "It is not enough for poems to be beautiful," quotes Burke from Horace. "They must be sweet."

13. See Chapter 4, "Allusion," in Robert Alter, *The Pleasures of Reading in an Ideological Age* (New York: Simon & Schuster, 1989), esp. 112–16.

14. Christopher Reid explains that the "beautiful" qualities in Burke's aesthetic and political vocabulary—sympathy, affection, friendship—are those that enable society to cohere. As the 1790s went on, Burke drew more and more on sublime imagery, which inspires dread, terror, and uncertainty, to convey his perception of the tragic elements of revolutionary politics that, he believed, were overwhelming Europe. See "The Politics of Taste," chap. 3 in Christopher Reid, *Edmund Burke and the Practice of Political Writing* (Dublin: Gill & Macmillan, 1985).

15. Referring to an earlier work by Ernest Barker, Allen Guttman writes: "In his contempt for the theory of natural rights, Burke 'bows before the pageant of history and worships its sanctities.'" *The Conservative Tradition in America* (New York: Oxford University Press, 1967), 10. In their generally excellent treatments of Burke, James Schmidt and J. G. A. Pocock, "Burke and the Ancient Constitution," in *Politics, Language, and Time* (New York: Atheneum, 1971), sometimes incline to this view as well.

16. Paine, *The Rights of Man*, Part I, 81. The quotation from the next sentence is from page 71.

17. Paine, *The Rights of Man*, Part I, 72. The quotation from the next sentence is from page 94. J. T. Boulton also notes Paine's rhetorical ploy of opposing "truth and fiction, reality and art, reason and imagination" in these passages. See *The Language of Politics in the Age of Wilkes and Burke* (Toronto: University of Toronto Press, 1963), 144–46.

18. Paine, *The Rights of Man*, Part I, 79; emphasis added. Paine's assumption about the certainty of his historical writing is by no means unusual. Over a hundred years before, the great popularizer of Enlightenment thought, Fontenelle (1657–1757), urged that geometrical thinking serve as the model for our understanding of the arts and politics. He chose geometry precisely because it is abstract and can be recreated out of a few simple axioms by any logical thinker. See the treatment of Fontenelle in Joseph Levine, *The Battle of the Books*.
19. Paine, *The Rights of Man*, Part I, 83.
20. Paine, *The Rights of Man*, Part I, 84, 87.
21. Burke, *An Appeal from the New to the Old Whigs*, in *Further Reflections*, 168–69. All quotations from the *Appeal* come from this edition.
22. Similar points are made by Peter Stanlis, *Edmund Burke and the Natural Law* (Ann Arbor: University of Michigan Press, 1958), 125–27, and Joel Weinsheimer, "Burke on Taste," in *Eighteenth-Century Hermeneutics: Philosophy of Interpretation in England from Locke to Burke* (New Haven: Yale University Press, 1993), 220.
23. See Steven Blakemore, *Burke and the Fall of Language* (Hanover: University Press of New England, 1988), 98–99. Boulton shows how Paine consciously embraced a "vulgar" style in opposition to Burke's rhetoric. See Boulton, *The Language of Politics in the Age of Wilkes and Burke*, 139–50.
24. Burke frequently uses insulting terms such as these to refer to the new rulers of France. See *Reflections*, 93, 100, for instance. Although it may be easy to assume simple class bias on Burke's part, Robert Darnton's careful historical work has demonstrated there was indeed a large number of literary mediocrities in France on the eve of the Revolution. Many were eager for power. Darnton quotes Antoine Rivarol (1753–1801) on the influence of "the dullest spirits of literature" that occupied the National Assembly. See "The Literary Revolution of 1789," *Studies in Eighteenth-Century Culture* 21 (1991): 3–26.
25. It should be admitted, however, that the density of Burke's allusions is greater in his antirevolutionary writings.
26. Nicholas Robinson discusses the abundance of literary allusions in the satirical prints directed against Burke in *Edmund Burke: A Life in Caricature* (New Haven: Yale University Press, 1996), 8–9. Rousseau's allusions to Sparta and Jacques-Louis David's artistic allusions to republican Rome are very well known to students of this period.
27. Burke never knew Hebrew and his allusions to Greek (which he mostly forgot) are rare. (See Lock, *Edmund Burke*, 1:35–37). Frans de Bruyn has some excellent remarks on Burke's use of biblical allusion throughout *The Literary Genres of Edmund Burke* (Oxford: Clarendon, 1996). In the 1789 sermon that so irritated Burke, Richard Price's praise of the French Revolution alludes to the prayer of Simeon, on the sight of the infant Jesus: "Lord now lettest thou thy servant depart in peace, for mine eyes have seen thy salvation," Luke 2:29–30; see Burke, *Reflections*, 115. This

prayer, the "nunc dimittis," had been part of the Anglican liturgy of Evening Prayer since the sixteenth century. Price's allusion immediately put Burke in mind of its use during trial and execution of King Charles I in 1648–1649 by the radical preacher, Hugh Peter (1598–1660), who was later hanged, drawn, and quartered.

28. Burke, *Reflections*, 147.

29. See Shils, *Tradition*, 21–27, for a discussion of the differences among the scientific, artistic, and literary traditions.

30. Burke, *Appeal*, 159, 160. The allusion is to the *Aeneid*, 1:542–43: "If you have no respect for the human race and mortal arms, / Yet beware the gods who remember right and wrong."

31. Paine, *The Rights of Man*, Part I, 67.

32. Richard Price, "A Discourse on the Love of our Country," in *Political Sermons of the American Founding Era, 1730–1805*, ed. Ellis Sandoz (Indianapolis: Liberty Press, 1991), 1005–28, esp. 1021–24.

33. Montesquieu's praise for Britain's balance of powers and for its constitutional prudence are among the elements of his analysis that Burke refers to toward the end of his *Appeal*, 196–201.

34. This group is actually the last of three items in Price's list, although he gives special weight to it. The first two items are (1) the right to liberty of conscience in religious matters; and (2) the right to resist power when abused. See "A Discourse on the Love of our Country," 1021.

35. Pocock describes Locke's role in the debates over the relations between the English, American and French revolutions in the introduction to his edition of Burke's *Reflections* (Indianapolis: Hackett, 1987), xii–xv. He is careful to note that eighteenth-century legal and historical writers as different as William Blackstone and David Hume denied the validity of Locke's *Second Treatise* as an account of the events of 1688–1689. For a more recent study of the relation between the English and American revolutions, see Michael Barone, *Our First Revolution* (New York: Crown, 2007).

36. In the debate on the Quebec Government Bill (May 6 and 11, 1791), Burke's alienation from his Whig party became irreparable. "[N]ot one of the party spoke one conciliatory word" to me, Burke wrote his patron, Earl Fitzwilliam. In the *Appeal*, Burke quotes the following report from the May 12 *Morning Chronicle*: "The great and firm body of the Whigs of England, true to their principles, have decided on the dispute between Mr. Fox and Mr. Burke; and the former is declared to have maintained the pure doctrines by which they are bound together, and upon which they have invariably acted. The consequence is, that Mr. Burke retires from Parliament." See Burke, *Appeal*, 76n and Burke, *Correspondence of Edmund Burke*, 6:271–75. In addition to analyzing the Sacheverell trial, the *Appeal* quotes from Paine, Mary Wollstonecraft, and others who participated in the huge pamphlet war that followed Burke's *Reflections* the previous November. See Gayle Trusdel Pendleton, "Towards a

Bibliography of the *Reflections* and *Rights of Man* Controversy," *Bulletin of Research in the Humanities*, 82 (1982): 65–103.

37. Burke, *Appeal*, 147.

38. Burke, *Appeal*, 71, 137.

39. Throughout this chapter I use the word *nature* advisedly and with reference to Burke's use of the term. Burke's richest use "nature," at *Reflections*, 83–85, will be examined, along with his view of history. It is important to distinguish Burke's view from the "Whig interpretation of history," in which Britain's achievement of liberty and prosperity, may be predicted at any given historical moment, as the providential or necessary outcome of history. Burke does believe in a discernible nature of the Constitution, but he is too aware of the role of particular individuals, and of the contingencies and tragic possibilities of history to promote a "Whig interpretation."

40. *Fourth Letter on a Regicide Peace* in *Writings and Speeches*, 9:82.

41. T. B. Macaulay, "Warren Hastings," in *Critical, Historical, and Miscellaneous Essays* (New York, 1897), 5:111.

42. Burke, *Reflections*, 83–84; emphasis in original.

43. David Harvey reproduces two contrasting maps of France, one from 1780, the other from 1789, to complement his excellent discussion of the Enlightenment efforts to impose a rationalistic vision on physical space. See *The Condition of Postmodernity*, 255–59.

44. Burke, *Reflections*, 244.

45. The *Oxford English Dictionary* gives the legal definition of *mortmain* as "the condition of lands or tenements held inalienably by an ecclesiastical or other corporation."

46. See Joel Weinsheimer, "Burke on Taste," 196, for a similar discussion.

47. In *Candide* (1759) and his poem on the disastrous Lisbon earthquake (1755), Voltaire is good at excoriating theologians and philosophers who attempt to explain away evil with reference to a providential system, but incapable of exploring the tragic dimensions of suffering.

48. The remarks here and in the next paragraph draw on the analyses of Hartmut and Gernot Böhme, "The Battle of Reason with Imagination," in Schmidt, *What Is Enlightenment?* 432; Kneller, "The Failure of Kant's Imagination," in *What Is Enlightenment?* 459–60; and Weinsheimer, "Burke on Taste," 198–99. See Kant, *Critique of Judgment*, sec. 50. The most profound analysis of Kant's significance for these issues comes in Gadamer's *Truth and Method*, 2nd rev. ed., trans and rev. Joel Weinsheimer and Donald G. Marshall (New York: Continuum, 1994), 38–55) which I will discuss.

49. In addition to Weinsheimer's essay, this relationship is the focus of books by Christopher Reid and Frans De Bruyn, both previously cited. One of the first works to raise this issue to attention in more recent times is Ronald Paulson's "Burke's Sublime and the Representation of Revolution," in *Culture and Politics from Puritanism to the Enlightenment*,

ed. Perez Zagorin (Berkeley: University of California Press, 1980), 241–69.

50. Paine, *Rights of Man*, Part I, 72.

51. Peter Stanlis argues for the significance of natural law to Burke's thought in *Edmund Burke and the Natural Law*. Although Stanlis' view was controversial when it appeared, its importance is more generally accepted today. See Lock, *Edmund Burke*, 1:37, 194, 495–96; and R. B. McDowell's introduction to Burke's Irish writings in *Writings and Speeches*, 9:411.

52. Paine writes: "From these premises [regarding natural rights], two or three certain conclusions will follow. 1st, that every civil right grows out of a natural right; or, in other words, is a natural right exchanged . . ." *Rights of Man*, Part I, 87.

53. Burke, *Appeal*, 91.

54. Burke, *Appeal*, 196.

55. Burke, "Thoughts on the Present Discontents," in *Writings and Speeches*, 2:317.

56. See Stanlis, *Edmund Burke*, 113–24.

57. The leader of the Whig Party, Charles James Fox, dismissed as "mere madness" Burke's *Letter to a Member of the National Assembly* (May 1791), which contrasts at length the taste formed by classical writers from that formed by Rousseau. Mary Wollstonecraft accused Burke of a "moral antipathy to reason." Isaac Kramnick's psycho-biography concludes that Burke longed "for the elimination of rational thought from politics." See *The Rage of Edmund Burke* (New York: Basic Books, 1977), 23.

58. See Weinsheimer, "Burke on Taste," 221–25.

59. Burke, *Reflections on the Revolution in France*, 293.

60. Burke explains his "inconsistency" in defending the different parts of Britain's mixed Constitution in the *Appeal*. See *Further Reflections*, 101.

61. See Weinsheimer, "Burke on Taste," 209.

62. Burke, *Appeal*, 147; emphasis in original.

63. Burke, *Appeal*, 193.

64. Burke, *Reflections*, 138.

65. Schmidt, *What Is Enlightenment?* 5.

66. Voltaire, *Philosophical Dictionary*, 12:289; emphasis added.

67. Repeated in Schmidt, *What Is Enlightenment?* 170.

68. Schmidt, *What Is Enlightenment?* 18; emphasis in original. The second half of this introduction contains many excellent connections between the Enlightenment and Gadamer's work.

69. "Speech on a motion made in the House of Commons, the 7th of May 1782 for a committee to inquire into the state of the representation of the commons in Parliament," in *The Works of the Right Honourable Edmund Burke* (London: Bohn, 1861), 6: 147.

70. Pocock begins his essay "Burke and the Ancient Constitution" with a good summary of Burke's traditionalism, along these lines.

71. Gadamer, *Truth and Method*, 277. The next sentences quotes are from p. 273.
72. Harold Bloom, *The Western Canon* (New York: Harcourt Brace, 1994), 371. I do not wish to judge the degree to which Bloom himself has changed his critical approach, only that his emphasis on older authors, as opposed to the various critical theories that have gained control of literary studies, has been striking to many who followed his career in light of professional literary studies.
73. Frank Lentricchia, "Last Will and Testament of an Ex-Literary Critic," *Lingua Franca* (September-October 1996): 63.
74. *Practicing New Historicism* (Chicago: University of Chicago Press, 2000), 210. Gallagher and Greenblatt refer to the Nietzschean roots of New Historicism, as mediated by Michel Foucault (see chapter 2, "Counter History and the Anecdote"). They deny that New Historicism is a methodology or a program for literary criticism (19). See, however, the significant critique of the assumptions and tactics of New Historicism in Paul Cantor's essay, "Stephen Greenblatt's New Historicist Vision," *Academic Questions* 6, no. 4 (1993): 21–36. See also Cantor's "Shakespeare—For All Time?" *The Public Interest* 110 (1993): 34–48.
75. Gadamer, *Truth and Method*, 293. This comes at the end of one of Gadamer's most extended discussions of "the hermeneutic circle," which affirms that belonging to a tradition is a precondition for all interpretation. Roger Lundin, writing on Gadamer, modifies the image somewhat by calling it a "hermeneutical spiral." A circle suggests a "self-enclosed finality" to one's experience with a text, Lundin writes, which would distort Gadamer's theory. See Roger Lundin, Clarence Walhout, and Anthony C. Thistleton, eds., *The Promise of Hermeneutics* (Grand Rapids: Eerdmans, 1999), 57.
76. Several writers have noted the similarities between Gadamer and Burke. In his famous debate with Gadamer, Jürgen Habermas mentions Burke in the context of criticizing the relationship between prejudice and knowledge in Gadamer. See Habermas' 1970 review of *Truth and Method*, in *The Hermeneutic Tradition*, ed. Gayle L. Ormiston and Alan D. Schrift (Albany: State University of New York Press, 1990), 236. James Schmidt addresses the same issue in *What Is Enlightenment?* 16–20, 28–29. Special mention should be made of the work of Joel C. Weinsheimer, who helped translate the second edition of Gadamer's *Truth and Method* and wrote a major analysis of the philosopher, *Gadamer's Hermeneutics*. Weinsheimer's work on the role of taste in Burke shows the deep, fruitful influence of Gadamer's thought.
77. "Hermeneutic work is based on a polarity of familiarity and strangeness," Gadamer writes. "[T]here is a tension . . . in the play between the traditionary text's strangeness and familiarity to us, between being a historically intended, distanciated object and belonging to a tradition," *Truth and Method*, 295.

78. Gadamer, *Truth and Method*, 10. The next quoted phrases come from page 14. Gadamer's translators generally translate *Bildung* by "culture," and give a useful history of the word in their preface, xii–xiii.

79. Gadamer refers to Bacon's role in the critique of prejudice in *Truth and Method*, 348–50.

80. Gadamer, *Truth and Method*, 357. The next sentence is indebted to Weinsheimer, *Gadamer's Hermeneutics: A Reading of Truth and Method* (New Haven: Yale University Press, 1985), 13. The issue under discussion in this paragraph is Gadamer's difficult (yet central) concept of *wirkungsgeschichtliches Bewusstein*. It is translated as "historically effected consciousness" in the second edition of *Truth and Method*, which implies that our consciousness is brought into being by history. I have tended to emphasize this connotation of Gadamer's term. Gadamer's usage of the term also implies that our consciousness is "affected by" history in a weaker sense. In both cases, however, Gadamer's usage stresses that we have a relationship of "belonging" to the past. See *Truth and Method*, xv–xvi.

81. Gadamer, *Truth and Method*, 245, 302.

82. Gadamer, *Truth and Method*, 298–99.

83. In various places in *Truth and Method*, Gadamer criticizes Schleiermacher for this approach to hermeneutics.

84. Gadamer, *Truth and Method*, 268. The following quotation comes from page 269.

85. Gadamer, *Truth and Method*, 293. The rest of this explanation has been drawn from pp. 306–7.

86. Gadamer, *Truth and Method*, 43; emphasis in original.

87. Gadamer, *Truth and Method*, 36; emphasis in original.

88. This discussion of Gadamer is based on *Truth and Method*, 36–39, 277, 289. Part of the weakness of Burke's early *Enquiry into . . . the Sublime and Beautiful* was precisely its attempt to find universal aesthetic principles for judging art. This approach is contrary to Burke's later practice of political judgment. See Weinsheimer, "Burke on Taste," 198–99.

89. Taste is distinguished from fashion, Gadamer explains, by demanding that the individual exercise his or her judgment about the worth of a particular trend. Unlike fashion, therefore, taste is not subservient to the community. Gadamer, *Truth and Method*, 37.

90. Burke's *Letter to Sir Hercules Langrishe* (1792), for instance, argues that many of the disabilities suffered by Irish Catholics were counter to the British constitutional tradition. See *Writings and Speeches*, 9:594–638.

91. With the exception of Sir William Blackstone (1723–1780), the English jurists named here were seventeenth-century figures whose writings and actions helped create the constitutional tradition that became part of Burke's historical imagination. He mentions Matthew Hale in his *Letter to a Member of the National Assembly* (1791), and the other three in the *Reflections* (*Writings and Speeches*, 8:302–3, 81–82). Pocock discusses their

significance to "Burke and the ancient constitution" throughout his essay of that name.

92. Gadamer, "Reply to My Critics," in *The Hermeneutic Tradition from Ast to Ricoeur*, ed. Gayle L. Ormiston and Alan D. Schrift (Albany: State University of New York Press, 1990), 288. To maintain that Burke or any other significant constitutional intepreter modifies the Constitution is by no means a radical statement—indeed it is almost tautological. All living traditions with a significant body of interpretation—the British or American Constitutions, the Bible, Shakespeare—are modified by their interpreters.

93. This paragraph draws on Gadamer, *Truth and Method*, 281–82.

94. Habermas makes this criticism of Gadamer in *The Hermeneutic Tradition*, 237. James Schmidt has a similar critique of Burke in *What Is Enlightenment?* 17–20.

95. Schmidt, *What Is Enlightenment?* 20.

96. Burke, *Reflections*, 138.

97. See Gadamer, *Truth and Method*, 168–69, for similar phrasing.

Chapter 7

1. Michael Polanyi, *Personal Knowledge: Towards a Post-Critical Philosophy* (Chicago: University of Chicago Press, 1962), 135.

2. See Polkinghorne, *Faith, Science, and Understanding*, 34–35, for a discussion of how Polanyi's approach differs from efforts to attain a mode of scientific or logical reasoning that would be valid in all possible worlds.

3. The parallels between Polanyi's work and Cowper's poetry are, of course, completely my own. There is no evidence Polanyi, a scientist and philosopher, was familiar with the eighteenth-century poet.

4. In his memoir *Adelphi* (written in about 1767), just after recounting his suicide attempts, Cowper names his "neglect to improve the mercies of God" as the unpardonable sin, *Letters and Prose Writings of William Cowper*, ed. James King and Charles Ryskamp (Oxford: Clarendon, 1979–1986), 1:27. Later, he considered his failure to commit suicide (during his climactic depression in 1773) to be unpardonable. See "Cowper's Spiritual Diary, June–July 1795," reprinted in *Letters and Prose Writings* 4:467–70. In the 1780s, Cowper hints that God may accept him after all, but nothing comes from these suggestions. See, for instance, *Letters and Prose Writings*, 2:412.

5. Cowper, *Letters and Prose Writings*, 1:39–40.

6. On February 26, 1791, Boswell records that a Mr. Sharpe attributes to Cowper "at bottom a deep religious melancholy," which came from apprehending "himself to be in a state of reprobation, being impressed with the most dismal doctrines of Calvinism." See *The Journals of James Boswell, 1762–1795*, ed. John Wain (New Haven: Yale University Press, 1991), 372. G. K. Chesterton, never able to resist a well-balanced

witticism, wrote that Cowper was driven mad by the ugly logic of predestination: "He was damned by John Calvin; he was almost saved by John Gilpin"—the comic horseman of his extraordinarily popular poem of 1785. See *Orthodoxy* (San Francisco: Ignatius Press, 1995), 21. Among more recent authors, Roy Porter wrongly says that Cowper had been "brought up a Calvinist" and had thought himself a reprobate "[f] rom early youth." *Mind Forg'd Manacles* (Cambridge, Mass.: Harvard University Press, 1987), 265, 266. For a brief, accurate discussion of Cowper's depression, madness, and suicide attempts, see James King, *William Cowper: A Biography* (Durham, N.C.: Duke University Press, 1986), 57–58.

7.   Cowper, *Letters and Prose Writings*, 1:25.

8.   Cowper, *Letters and Prose Writings*, 1:15.

9.   Susanna Unwin was married in 1774. Newton said the engagement of Mary Unwin and Cowper was "well known" to most of their friends. See King, *William Cowper*, 86–88. King argues that Cowper's 1773 madness was brought on primarily by the prospect of losing Mary Unwin as a mother figure. The editors of Cowper's *Poems* also note the conflict between an engagement to Mrs. Unwin and Cowper's earlier pledge of lifelong fidelity to Theodora Cowper, *The Poems of William Cowper*, 1:xix.

10. The account of Cowper's nightmare, found in a number of biographical treatments, is largely pieced together from his letters. See Cowper, *Letters and Prose Writings*, 1:509–10, 2:127; 2:385; 2:454–55; 4:466–67.

11. See Cowper, *The Poems of William Cowper*, 1:xx–xxi. Cowper wrote some Latin verse during these years, but apart from his despairing "Hatred and Vengeance," discussed below, nothing in English until 1778 or 1779.

12. Cowper also shrank from displaying himself to the wider public as a poet. Only after he had published a poetic satire under the secure cover of anonymity (*Antithelyphthora*, 1781) was Cowper willing to proceed with his first solo book of verse. My speculation on self-exposure as the thread that links Cowper's mental illnesses does not explain his severe depression later in life (1787), which was brought on, in part, by the untimely death of his good friend William Unwin. By this time, I believe, Cowper's mental condition had assumed a pattern from which it never recovered, despite his sometimes courageous struggles against it. Other elements that connect Cowper's periods of insanity are his self-loathing and his sense of abandonment. His self-loathing is evident in his conviction that he was damned for having committed the unforgivable sin, Cowper, *The Poems of William Cowper*, 1:xx, and King, *William Cowper*, 7–8, 86. His sense of abandonment was of long standing, stemming from the death of his mother in 1737, a couple of days before his sixth birthday. "In his imagination," writes biographer King, Cowper "clung relentlessly to his mother" (7, see also 57–58). As late as 1790, Cowper wrote an elegy "On the Receipt of My Mother's Picture" that begins: "Oh that those lips had

language! Life has pass'd / With me but roughly since I heard thee last" (*The Poems of William Cowper*, 3:56).

13. October 27, 1782: "I have not even asked a blessing upon my food these ten years, nor do I expect that I shall ever ask it again," Cowper, *Letters and Prose Writings*, 2:84. The same year saw the publication of a major collection of new poems by Cowper, many of which satirize contemporary culture from a Calvinist perspective. See the editor's introduction to *The Poems of William Cowper*, 1:xix–xxi.

14. "Truth," lines 254, 271. The next quotation is from lines 450–52, *The Poems of William Cowper*, 1:286-92. The modes of the suicide described by Cowper, by drowning and stabbing, are among the ones he contemplated or attempted in 1763.

15. Cowper, *Letters and Prose Writings*, 4:93.

16. Cowper, *The Poems of William Cowper*, 1:209. This is the single English poem attributed to Cowper between 1773 and at least 1777.

17. Cowper, *The Poems of William Cowper*, 3:214.

18. Cowper, *Letters and Prose Writings*, 2:455.

19. *Biographia Literaria*, ed. George Watson (New York: Dutton, 1965), 13. Coleridge is referring specifically to *The Task* here. The passage also credits William Lisle Bowles with achieving this reconciliation. Coleridge called Cowper the best modern poet in a 1798 conversation with William Hazlitt. See "My First Acquaintance with Poets," in *The Collected Works of William Hazlitt*, ed. William Henley (London: Dent, 1904), 12:273.

20. Cowper, *The Poems of William Cowper*, 1:xvi. His friend William Bull, who became a good friend of Cowper's after their 1780 meeting, disagreed with Lady Hesketh, saying that the project conformed to his tastes and religious sympathies. King, *William Cowper*, 82–86, gives a fuller consideration of this issue.

21. *Olney Hymns* was extremely popular in the evangelical revivals around the turn of the nineteenth century. It went through thirty-seven editions in the first fifty years. When I refer to this work, I will have in mind only the contributions of Cowper, not Newton. See King, *William Cowper*, 83; and Cowper, *The Poems of William Cowper*, 1:xxix–xxx, 479–80, 483.

22. Cowper, *Letters and Prose Writings*, 1.104. Another possible explanation for Cowper's rationalism in this letter is that the recipient, Harriot Cowper (Lady Hesketh), was unsympathetic to evangelical religious expression. In this letter, Cowper places almost equal importance on Scriptural proof of the falsity of Roman Catholicism. His attitude toward Catholicism changed because of his growing friendship with, and ultimate dependence upon, the Catholic Throckmorton family (1786 and later). His attitude toward Catholicism thus provides another example of the significance of personal commitments—friendship, in this case—to knowledge.

23. *The Task* (1785), 3:108–23, in *The Poems of William Cowper*, 2:165–66.

24. Hymn 3, lines 6–12, in *The Poems of William Cowper*, 1:141–42.

25. "A Song of Mercy and Judgment," lines 67–76, in *The Poems of William Cowper*, 1:137. See also 1:xxx.

26. Hymn 35, "Light Shining Out of Darkness," lines 13–16 in *The Poems of William Cowper*, 1:175.

27. Hymn 49, "Joy and Peace in Believing," lines 1–8 in *The Poems of William Cowper*, 1:188.

28. *The Oxford Book of Christian Verse* (New York: Oxford University Press, 1981), xxv.

29. See, e.g., Hymn 9 ("The Lord will happiness divine"), Hymn 39 ("God of my life, to thee I call"), Hymn 41 ("When darkness long has veil'd my mind"), all in *The Poems of William Cowper*, 1:148-49, 178-79, 180-81.

30. Hymn 1, "Walking with God," lines 5–8 in *The Poems of William Cowper*, 1:139-40.

31. Donald Davie notes that in Cowper's "most poignant hymns [the word] 'we' stands for the dispersed company of hesitant and demoralized worshippers like himself. . . ." *The Eighteenth-Century Hymn in England*, 149. Cowper's well-known hymn "There is a Fountain fill'd with blood" is unusual among these works, both for its rich imagery and its lack of any such diffidence.

32. This particular way of phrasing the relation between doubt and knowledge comes from Richard Gelwick's discussion of Michael Polanyi: "Doubt and skepticism, instead of being expurgated from knowing, have to be included in a wider framework of understanding . . . Since belief is inherent in knowing, so also is doubt. These components of belief and of doubt do not undermine the process that leads to discovery and the acquisition of knowledge," *The Way of Discovery: An Introduction to the Thought of Michael Polanyi* (New York: Oxford University Press, 1977), 151.

33. "Truth," lines 175–78 in *The Poems of William Cowper*, 1:284.

34. "Conversation," lines 707–8, 715–18 in *The Poems of William Cowper*, 1:372.

35. Cowper, *Letters and Prose Writings*, 2:44. In this letter of April 1, 1782 to William Unwin, Cowper refers to the reviewers as "fiery Socinians."

36. Cowper, *Letters and Prose Writings*, 2:246.

37. "Expostulation," lines 107–8 in *The Poems of William Cowper*, 1:299-300. The next quotation is from line 118.

38. "The Progress of Error," lines 496–501 in *The Poems of William Cowper*, 1:276.

39. "The Progress of Error," lines 594–95 in *The Poems of William Cowper*, 1:279.

40. "Hope," lines 423–24 in *The Poems of William Cowper*, 1:327.

41. The quoted phrase is from Cowper, *Letters and Prose Writings*, 2:41.

42. Voltaire, *Philosophical Dictionary*, "Solomon" 236, 237, 241–42.

43. "Truth," lines 315–16 in *The Poems of William Cowper*, 1:288.

44. He uses the phrase twice in "Retirement," lines 747, 765 in *The Poems of William Cowper*, 1:397.

45. David is the last of a number of figures who appear in "Retirement," lines 767–83 in *The Poems of William Cowper*, 1:397.

46. Newton's preface is reprinted in *The Poems of William Cowper*, 1:567–70. My quotations in this paragraph are from pages 569, 570. The italicized words are emphasized in Newton's original. Interestingly, Cowper's publisher, the radical Unitarian Joseph Johnson, worried about the effect of Newton's preface and (after printing a few copies with the preface) received Cowper's permission to cancel it. He believed the preface would "recommend the volume to the Religious, [but] it would disgust the profane." Only if "a purchaser looked serious and methodistical" was he shown a copy of the Poems with Newton's preface. He didn't want to narrow the appeal of his product by marketing its use to only one side in the culture war of his own day.

47. Cowper, *Letters and Prose Writings*, 1:59.

48. "Table Talk," lines 733, 734–35 in *The Poems of William Cowper*, 1:260–61. The poet's imagined song, he continues, is to "tell the world . . . That he who died below, and reigns above / Inspires the song, and that his name is love," lines 736, 738–39.

49. The phrase appears in Newton's Preface to the 1782 edition of Cowper's *Poems*. See *The Poems of William Cowper*, 1:569.

50. April 17, 1786. In a letter of May 12, 1783 to William Unwin, Cowper writes that "Creation is a work for which mere mortal man, is very indifferently qualified." See Cowper, *Letters and Prose Writings*, 2:523, 132.

51. Laplace's "ideal of universal knowledge" is an object of criticism throughout Michael Polanyi's epistemology in *Personal Knowledge*, which I will presently discuss.

52. *The Task* 6:1–5, *The Poems of William Cowper*, 2:237.

53. *The Task* 6:77–91, *The Poems of William Cowper*, 2:239.

54. *The Task* 6:177–85, *The Poems of William Cowper*, 2:241.

55. *The Task* 3:361, 373–76. *The Poems of William Cowper*, 2:172 and notes at 2:369. The phrase "studious of laborious ease" alludes to Virgil's *Georgics* 4:561 and Horace's *Epistles* 1:11:28. The literary sources of this aspect of *The Task* include georgic poetry, which is examined by Dustin Griffin, particularly with regard to its socio-political significance, in "Redefining Georgic: Cowper's Task," *ELH* 57, no. 4 (1990): 865–79. Tim Fulford widens the discussion to include Cowper's poem "Yardley Oak" in his chapter "Wordsworth, Cowper and the Language of Eighteenth-Century Politics," in *Early Romantics*, ed. Thomas Woodman, 117–33 (New York: St. Martin's Press, 1998). James Sambrook also has an excellent discussion of georgic and *The Task* in *William Cowper: The Task and Selected Other Poems*, ed. James Sambrook (London: Longman, 1994). Sambrook emphasizes Cowper's acute powers of observation, in combination with his self-reflection and even eighteenth-century scientific writing. None of these critics, however, connects these elements with Cowper's critique of Enlightenment approaches to knowledge.

56. *The Task* 5:841. Cowper explicitly names "[t]he time of rest, the promised sabbath" in an apocalyptic vision near the end of the poem (6:733),
The Poems of William Cowper, 2:232, 255.
57. *The Task* 5:842–49, *The Poems of William Cowper*, 2:232. Without explicitly alluding to Milton, these lines suggest a contrast with the fruitless
intellectual and physical exploration of the fallen angels "in wandering
mazes lost . . . [who] found no rest" in *Paradise Lost* (2:556–618).
58. *The Task* 3:355–56, *The Poems of William Cowper*, 2:172.
59. Voltaire's entries in the *Philosophical Dictionary* on "Theism" and
"Theist" describe a religion of "good sense not yet instructed by revelation," compared to "other religions [which] are good sense perverted
by superstition." The closest he comes to describing a relationship
between God and man is the human capability of performing good and
evil act, and humanity's "good sense . . . on which the law of nature is
founded."
60. *The Task* 6:198–210, *The Poems of William Cowper*, 2:242.
61. *The Task* 3:229–32. The "philosophic tube" is a telescope. The next
reference comes from line 238, *The Poems of William Cowper*, 2:168–69.
62. *The Task* 5:538–39. The next quotation comes from line 545, *The Poems
of William Cowper*, 2:224–25.
63. *The Task* 3:243–60, *The Poems of William Cowper*, 2:169.
64. Polanyi called the weekly seminar at the University of Berlin's Physics
Colloquium "the most glorious intellectual memory of my life." In addition to the three physicists I have mentioned, the participants included
Lise Meitner, Otto Hahn, and Max von Laue. See William Taussig Scott
and Martin X. Moleski, *Michael Polanyi: Scientist and Philosopher* (New
York: Oxford University Press, 2005), 85–86.
65. Polanyi's *Science, Faith, and Society* (Chicago: University of Chicago
Press, 1964) begins by recounting a number of incidents during the
1930s that caused his increasing concern, notably a meeting with
Bukharin in Moscow in 1935. Another crucial event in Polanyi's turn to
a career in philosophy was his review of J. D. Bernal's *The Social Function
of Science* (1939), in which he rejected Bernal's view that the worker's
state should serve as the arbiter of truth. See Scott and Moleski, *Michael
Polanyi*, 174–75. Polanyi mentions Bernal along with Sartre and Picasso
as men who surrendered "to a philosophy which denied the very existence of their intellectual pursuits," Polanyi, *Personal Knowledge*, 237.
66. Polanyi's essay, "Why did we destroy Europe?" which appeared in 1970,
is reprinted in *Society, Economics, & Philosophy* (New Brunswick, N.J.:
Transaction Publishers, 1997), 107–15. See Scott and Moleski, *Michael
Polanyi*, 211 and 216, for details on Polanyi's departure from chemistry
and his earlier shock over the destruction of World War I.
67. Gelwick talks about these elements of Polanyi's critique in the introduction and first part of his book, *The Way of Discovery*, xi–20.
68. Polanyi, *Personal Knowledge*, vii. Charles Taylor writes that "much of the
most insightful philosophy of the twentieth century has gone to refute

this picture of the disengaged subject." *Sources of the Self: The Making of the Modern Identity* (Cambridge, Mass.: Harvard University Press, 1989), 514. Although Polanyi begins by saying his book is "primarily an enquiry into the nature and justification of scientific knowledge," he immediately goes on to state that its purpose is "to establish an alternative ideal of knowledge, quite generally." Biology, psychology, and sociology are the fields mentioned in his preface, but the book gives significant attention to religion, aesthetics, and politics as well.

69. Polanyi describes the "ecstatic communion" that was central to Kepler's astronomic discoveries and the intuitions of relativity that Einstein began to have in his teen years. Polanyi, *Personal Knowledge*, 7, 10.

70. Polanyi, *Personal Knowledge*, 16.

71. Polanyi, *Personal Knowledge*, 252. The next quotations are from pp. 132 and 135.

72. Polanyi, *Personal Knowledge*, 27.

73. Polanyi, *Personal Knowledge*, 60.

74. Polanyi, *Personal Knowledge*, 53.

75. Polanyi, *Personal Knowledge*, 133.

76. Polanyi, *Personal Knowledge*, 148, 144. The next quotation is from p. 15.

77. Polanyi, *Personal Knowledge*, 43–44. Polanyi's conclusion, which I refer to next, is on p. 48.

78. Polanyi, *Personal Knowledge*, 5–6.

79. Polanyi, *Personal Knowledge*, 266. Polanyi's references to Augustine come from the same page.

80. Polanyi, *Science, Faith, and Society*, 32. The next sentence refers to the same page, as well as to Polanyi, *Personal Knowledge*, 267.

81. "The past four or five centuries . . . have enriched us mentally and morally to an extent unrivalled by any period of similar duration. But its incandescence had fed on the combustion of the Christian heritage in the oxygen of Greek rationalism, and when this fuel was exhausted the critical framework itself burnt away," Polanyi, *Personal Knowledge*, 265–66.

82. Polanyi, *Personal Knowledge*, 268.

83. Polanyi, *Personal Knowledge*, 315.

84. Polanyi, *Personal Knowledge*, 312. The next sentence refers to *Science, Faith, and Society*, 31–32.

85. Polanyi, *Science, Faith, and Society*, 34.

86. Polanyi, *Personal Knowledge*, 105, 194 n. 272.

87. Andrew Witmer, *Tacit Knowing, Truthful Knowing: The Life and Thought of Michael Polanyi* (Mars Hill Audio Report 2, 1999).

88. Polanyi, *Personal Knowledge*, 64. See also 201–2.

Conclusion

1. Burke, *Writings and Speeches*, 8:128.

SELECTED BIBLIOGRAPHY

I list here primarily the works I refer to multiple times. I have included several works, even if I refer to them only once, by virtue of their importance to eighteenth-century studies.

Baczko, Bronislaw. *Ending the Terror: The French Revolution after Robespierre.* Translated by Michel Petheram. Cambridge: Cambridge University Press, 1994.

Baird, John D., and Charles Ryskamp. "Cowper and His Poetry, 1731–1782." In Cowper, *The Poems of William Cowper*, 1:ix–xxv.

Baker, Keith M. "Sieyès." In Ozouf and Furet, *A Critical Dictionary of the French Revolution*, 313–23.

Barbour, Ian. *When Science Meets Religion.* San Francisco: HarperSanFrancisco, 2000.

Bennington, Geoffrey. *Lyotard: Writing the Event.* New York: Columbia University Press, 1988.

Benson, Louis F. *The English Hymn: Its Development and Use in Worship.* Philadelphia: Presbyterian Board of Publication, 1915. Reprint, Richmond, Va.: John Knox, 1962.

Bernstein, Richard. *Dictatorship of Virtue.* New York: Knopf, 1994.

Berry, Wendell. *Home Economics.* San Francisco: North Point, 1987.

———. *What Are People For?* San Francisco: North Point, 1990.

Birkerts, Sven. *The Gutenberg Elegies.* Boston: Faber & Faber, 1994.

Borges, Jorge Luis. "The Library of Babel." In *Collected Fictions*, translated by Andrew Hurley, 112–18. New York: Viking, 1998.

Boswell, James. *Life of Johnson.* Edited by R. W. Chapman. New York: Oxford University Press, 1980.

Boulton, J. T. *The Language of Politics in the Age of Wilkes and Burke.* Toronto: University of Toronto Press, 1963.

Burke, Edmund. *The Correspondence of Edmund Burke.* Edited by Thomas W. Copeland. 10 vols. Chicago: University of Chicago Press, 1958–1978.

———. *Further Reflections on the Revolution in France.* Edited by Daniel E. Ritchie. Indianapolis: Liberty Fund, 1992.

———. *Reflections on the Revolution in France,* vol. 8 of *The Writings and Speeches of Edmund Burke.*

———. *The Writings and Speeches of Edmund Burke.* Edited by Paul Langford and P. J. Marshall. 12 vols. Oxford: Clarendon, 1981–.

Chappell, Vere, ed. *The Cambridge Companion to Locke.* Cambridge: Cambridge University Press, 1994.

Condorcet, Antoine-Nicolas de. *Sketch for a Historical Picture of the Progress of the Human Mind.* Translated by June Barraclough. Westport, Conn.: Hyperion, 1955.

Cowper, William. *The Letters and Prose Writings of William Cowper.* Edited by James King and Charles Ryskamp. 5 vols. Oxford: Clarendon, 1979–1986.

———. *The Poems of William Cowper.* Edited by John D. Baird and Charles Ryskamp. 3 vols. Oxford: Clarendon, 1980–1995.

Dart, Gregory. *Rousseau, Robespierre and English Romanticism.* Cambridge: Cambridge University Press, 1999.

Davie, Donald. *The Eighteenth-Century Hymn in England.* Cambridge: Cambridge University Press, 1993.

Davies, Horton. *Worship and Theology in England.* Vol. 3: *From Watts and Wesley to Maurice, 1690–1850.* Princeton: Princeton University Press, 1961.

Davis, Arthur Paul. *Isaac Watts: His Life and Works.* London: Independent Press, 1943.

Dawkins, Richard. *A Devil's Chaplain.* Boston: Houghton Mifflin, 2003.

Defoe, Daniel. "The Family Instructor." In *Daniel Defoe,* edited by James T. Boulton, 196–207. New York: Schocken Books, 1965.

———. *The Works of Daniel Defoe.* Edited by G. H. Maynadier. Vol. 2: *The Farther Adventures of Robinson Crusoe.* New York: George D. Sproul, 1903.

———. *The Life and Strange Surprizing Adventures of Robinson Crusoe.* Edited by J. Donald Crowley. New York: Oxford University Press, 1981.

———. *The Works of Daniel Defoe.* Edited by G. H. Maynadier. Vol. 3: *Serious Reflections during the Life and Surprising Adventures of Robinson Crusoe.* New York: George D. Sproul, 1903.

———. *The Works of Daniel Defoe.* Edited by G. H. Maynadier. 16 vols. New York: George D. Sproul, 1903.

Derham, William. *Physico-Theology.* London, 1723.

Derrida, Jacques. *Dissemination.* Translated by Barbara Johnson. Chicago: University of Chicago Press, 1981.

Dupré, Louis. *The Enlightenment and the Intellectual Foundations of Modern Culture.* New Haven: Yale University Press, 2004.

Ehrenpreis, Irvin. *Swift: The Man, His Works, and the Age.* 3 vols. Cambridge, Mass.: Harvard University Press, 1962–1983.

Ensler, Eve. *The Vagina Monologues: The V-Day Edition.* New York: Villard, 1998.

Escott, Harry. *Isaac Watts, Hymnographer.* London: Independent, 1962.

Fish, Stanley. *There's No Such Thing as Free Speech and It's a Good Thing Too.* New York: Oxford University Press, 1994.

Frei, Hans W. *The Eclipse of Biblical Narrative: A Study in Eighteenth and Nineteenth Century Hermeneutics.* New Haven: Yale University Press, 1974.

———. *Theology and Narrative: Selected Essays.* Edited by William C. Placher and George Hunsinger. New York: Oxford University Press, 1993.

Furet, François. "Terror." In Ozouf and Furet, *A Critical Dictionary of the French Revolution,* 137–50.

Gadamer, Hans-Georg. *Truth and Method.* 2nd rev. ed. Translated and revised by Joel Weinsheimer and Donald G. Marshall. New York: Continuum, 1994.

Gelwick, Richard. *The Way of Discovery: An Introduction to the Thought of Michael Polanyi.* New York: Oxford University Press, 1977.

Gleick, James. *Isaac Newton.* New York: Pantheon, 2003.

Green, Garrett. "'The Bible As. . .' Fictional Narrative and Scriptural Truth." In *Scriptural Authority and Narrative Interpretation,* edited by Garrett Green, 79–96. Philadelphia: Fortress Press, 1987.

Grenz, Stanley J., and John R. Franke. *Beyond Foundationalism: Shaping Theology in a Postmodern Context.* Louisville, Ky.: Westminster John Knox, 2001.

Guest, Harriet. *A Form of Sound Words: The Religious Poetry of Christopher Smart.* Oxford: Clarendon, 1989.

Gunkel, David J. "*Lingua ex Machina*: Computer-Mediated Communication and the Tower of Babel." *Configurations* 7, no. 1 (1999): 61–89.

Habermas, Jürgen. "A Review of Gadamer's *Truth and Method.*" In *The Hermeneutic Tradition,* edited by Gayle L. Ormiston and Alan D. Schrift, 213–41. Albany: State University of New York Press, 1990.

Harvey, David. *The Condition of Postmodernity.* Cambridge, Mass.: Blackwell, 1990.

Hawes, Clement, ed. *Christopher Smart and the Enlightenment.* New York: St. Martin's Press, 1999.

Horkheimer, Max, and Theodor Adorno. *Dialectic of Enlightenment.* Translated by John Cumming. New York: Herder & Herder, 1972.

Huet, Marie-Hélène. *Mourning Glory: The Will of the French Revolution.* Philadelphia: University of Pennsylvania Press, 1997.

Hunter, J. Paul. *The Reluctant Pilgrim: Defoe's Emblematic Method and Quest for Form in "Robinson Crusoe."* Baltimore: The Johns Hopkins University Press, 1966.

"Hymn." In *The New Grove Dictionary of Music and Musicians*, 2nd ed., edited by Stanley Sadie and John Tyrrell, 12:29–31. New York: Grove's Dictionaries, 2001.

Johnson, Samuel. *A Dictionary of the English Language* [1755]. A facsimile of the first edition. New York: Arno Press, 1979.

———. *Lives of the Most Eminent English Poets; With Critical Observations on their Works*. Edited by Roger Lonsdale. 4 vols. Oxford: Clarendon, 2006.

King, James. *William Cowper: A Biography*. Durham, N.C.: Duke University Press, 1986.

Kors, Alan Charles, and Harvey Silverglate. *The Shadow University*. New York City: Free Press, 1998.

Kreiswirth, Martin. "Trusting the Tale: The Narrativist Turn in the Human Sciences." *New Literary History* 23, no. 3 (1992): 629–57.

Levine, Joseph. *The Battle of the Books*. Ithaca: Cornell University Press, 1991.

Lock, F. P. *Edmund Burke*. Vol. 1: *1730–1784*. Oxford: Clarendon, 1998.

Locke, John. *An Essay Concerning Human Understanding*. 4th ed. Edited by Peter H. Nidditch. Oxford: Clarendon, 1975.

———. *A Paraphrase and Notes on the Epistles of St Paul to the Galatians, 1 and 2 Corinthians, Romans, Ephesians*. Edited by Arthur W. Wainwright. 2 vols. Oxford: Clarendon, 1987.

Logan, Robert K. *The Alphabet Effect: The Impact of the Phonetic Alphabet on the Development of Western Civilization*. New York: William Morrow, 1986.

Lowth, Robert. *Lectures on the Sacred Poetry of the Hebrews*. 4th ed. Translated by G. Gregory. London, 1839. Reprint, Whitefish, Mont.: Kessinger Publishing, n.d.

Lyotard, Jean-François. *The Postmodern Condition: A Report on Knowledge*. Minneapolis: University of Minnesota Press, 1984.

MacIntyre, Alasdair. "Epistemological Crises, Dramatic Narrative, and the Philosophy of Science." In *Why Narrative? Readings in Narrative Theology*, edited by Stanley Hauerwas and L. Gregory Jones, 89–110. Grand Rapids: Eerdmans, 1989.

McKeon, Michael. *The Origins of the English Novel, 1600–1740*. Baltimore: The Johns Hopkins University Press, 1987.

McLaren, Brian. *A Generous Orthodoxy: Why I Am a Missional, Evangelical, Post/Protestant, Liberal/Conservative, Mystical/Poetic, Biblical, Charismatic/ Contemplative, Fundamentalist/Calvinist, Anabaptist/Anglican, Methodist, catholic, Green, Incarnational, Depressed-yet-Hopeful, Emergent, Unfinished CHRISTIAN*. Grand Rapids: Zondervan, 2004.

Mettrie, Julien Offray de la. *Man a Machine*. Translation by Gertrude Carman Bussey and M. W. Calkins. La Salle, Ill.: Open Court, 1961.

Newton, Sir Isaac. "General Scholium." In *Mathematical Principles of Natural Philosophy*, translated by Andrew Motte, 543–47. Revised translation by Florian Cajori. Berkeley: University of California Press, 1946.

Nicolson, Marjorie, and Nora Mohler. "The Scientific Background of Swift's *Voyage to Laputa.*" In Nicolson, *Science and Imagination.* Ithaca: Cornell University Press, 1956, 110–54.

Noll, Mark. *The Rise of Evangelicalism: The Age of Edwards, Whitefield and the Wesleys.* Downers Grove, Ill.: InterVarsity, 2003.

O'Donnell, James. *Avatars of the Word: From Papyrus to Cyberspace.* Cambridge, Mass.: Harvard University Press, 1998.

Ozouf, Mona. *Festivals and the French Revolution.* Translated by Alan Sheridan. Cambridge, Mass.: Harvard University Press, 1988.

———. "Revolutionary Calendar." In Ozouf and Furet, *A Critical Dictionary of the French Revolution,* 538–47.

Ozouf, Mona, and François Furet, eds. *A Critical Dictionary of the French Revolution.* Translated by Arthur Goldhammer. Cambridge, Mass.: Harvard-Belknap, 1989.

Pagitt, Doug. *Reimagining Spiritual Formation: A Week in the Life of an Experimental Church.* Grand Rapids: Zondervan, 2004.

Paine, Thomas. *The Rights of Man, Parts I and II.* In *Political Writings,* edited by Bruce Kuklick. Cambridge: Cambridge University Press, 1989.

Patey, Douglas Lane. "Swift's Satire on 'Science' and the Structure of *Gulliver's Travels.*" *ELH* 59 (1991): 809–39.

Placher, William C. "Introduction." In Frei, *Theology and Narrative: Selected Essays,* 3–25.

Plato. *Phaedrus and the Seventh and Eighth Letters.* Translated by Walter Hamilton. Harmondsworth, UK: Penguin, 1973.

Pocock, J. G. A. "Burke and the Ancient Constitution." In his *Politics, Language, and Time.* New York: Atheneum, 1971, 202–32.

Polanyi, Michael. *Personal Knowledge: Towards a Post-Critical Philosophy.* Chicago: University of Chicago Press, 1962.

———. *Science, Faith and Society.* Chicago: University of Chicago Press, 1964.

Polkinghorne, John. *Belief in God in an Age of Science.* New Haven: Yale University Press, 1998.

———. *Faith, Science, and Understanding.* New Haven: Yale University Press, 2000.

Price, Richard. "A Discourse on the Love of Our Country." In *Political Sermons of the American Founding Era, 1730–1805,* edited by Ellis Sandoz, 1005–28. Indianapolis: Liberty Press, 1991.

Procès-verbaux du Comité d'Instruction Publique de la Convention Nationale. Edited by M. J. Guillaume. Vol. 2. Paris, 1894.

Reuben, Julie A. *The Making of the Modern University.* Chicago: University of Chicago Press, 1996.

Ritchie, Daniel. *Reconstructing Literature in an Ideological Age.* Grand Rapids: Eerdmans, 1996.

Robespierre, Maximilien. *Discours.* Edited by Marc Bouloiseau and Albert Soboul. Vol. 10 of *Œuvres de Maximilien Robespierre,* edited by E.

Déprez and E. Lesueur. 10 vols. Paris: Presses Universitaires de France, 1910–1967.

Rogers, Pat, ed. *Daniel Defoe: The Critical Heritage*. London: Routledge, 1972.

Rorty, Richard. *Contingency, Irony, and Solidarity*. Cambridge: Cambridge University Press, 1989.

———. *Philosophy and the Mirror of Nature*. Princeton: Princeton University Press, 1979.

———. *Objectivity, Relativism, and Truth: Philosophical Papers Volume One*. Cambridge: Cambridge University Press, 1991.

Sambrook, James. "Introduction." In *William Cowper: The Task and Selected Other Poems*, edited by James Sambrook, 27–31. London: Longman, 1994.

Schama, Simon. *Citizens: A Chronicle of the French Revolution*. New York: Knopf, 1989.

Schmidt, James, ed. *What Is Enlightenment? Eighteenth-Century Answers and Twentieth-Century Questions*. Berkeley: University of California Press, 1996.

Scott, William Taussig, and Martin X. Moleski. *Michael Polanyi: Scientist and Philosopher*. New York: Oxford University Press, 2005.

Sherbo, Arthur. *Christopher Smart: Scholar of the University*. East Lansing: Michigan State University Press, 1967.

Shils, Edward. *Tradition*. Chicago: University of Chicago Press, 1981.

Stanlis, Peter. *Edmund Burke and the Natural Law*. Ann Arbor: University of Michigan Press, 1958.

Stroup, George W. *The Promise of Narrative Theology: Recovering the Gospel in the Church*. Atlanta: John Knox, 1981.

Swift, Jonathan. *Prose Writings of Jonathan Swift*. Edited by Herbert Davis and Harold Williams. 16 vols. Oxford: Blackwell, 1939–1974.

———. *A Tale of a Tub*. 2nd ed. Edited by A. C. Guthkelch and D. Nichol Smith. Oxford: Clarendon, 1958.

Tocqueville, Alexis de. *Democracy in America*. Translated and edited by Harvey C. Mansfield and Delba Winthrop. Chicago: University of Chicago Press, 2000.

Torrance, Thomas F. *Space, Time and Incarnation*. London: Oxford University Press, 1969.

Voltaire. *Philosophical Dictionary*. Vols. 5–14: *The Works of Voltaire*. Translated by William Fleming. Paris: E. R. Dumont, 1901.

Walsh, Marcus. "Introduction to *A Song to David*." In Williamson and Walsh, *The Poetical Works of Christopher Smart*, 2:99–126.

———. "Appendix to *A Song to David*." In Williamson and Walsh, *The Poetical Works of Christopher Smart*, 2:148–55.

Watson, J. R. *The English Hymn: A Critical and Historical Study*. Oxford: Clarendon, 1997.

Watt, Ian. "*Robinson Crusoe* as a Myth." *Essays in Criticism* (April 1951): 95–119.

Watts, Isaac. *The Works of the Reverend and Learned Isaac Watts, D.D.* Edited by David Jennings and Philip Doddridge. 6 vols. London, 1810–1811.

Watts, Michael. *The Dissenters: From the Reformation to the French Revolution.* Vol. 1. Oxford: Clarendon, 1978.

Webber, Robert. *Ancient Future Faith: Rethinking Evangelicalism for a Postmodern World.* Grand Rapids: Baker, 1999.

Weinsheimer, Joel C. *Eighteenth-Century Hermeneutics: Philosophy of Interpretation in England from Locke to Burke.* New Haven: Yale University Press, 1993.

———. *Gadamer's Hermeneutics: A Reading of Truth and Method.* New Haven: Yale University Press, 1985.

Wiener, Norbert. *The Human Use of Human Beings: Cybernetics and Society.* New York: Avon, 1967.

Wilkins, John. *An Essay Towards a Real Character, and a Philosophical Language.* Edited by R. C. Alston. Menston, U.K.: Scolar, 1968.

Williamson, Karina. Appendix to *Jubilate Agno.* In Williamson and Walsh, *The Poetical Works of Christopher Smart,* 1:131–32.

———. "Smart's *Principia*: Science and Anti-Science in *Jubilate Agno.*" *Review of English Studies* 30, no. 120 (1979): 409–22.

Williamson, Karina and Marcus Walsh, eds. *The Poetical Works of Christopher Smart.* 6 vols. Oxford: Clarendon, 1980–1996.

Wilson, William. *Memoirs of the Life and Times of Daniel Defoe.* 3 vols. New York: AMS Press, 1973.

Wolterstorff, Nicholas. "Locke's Philosophy of Religion." In Chappell, *The Cambridge Companion to Locke,* 172–98.

Wuthnow, Robert. *All in Sync: How Music and Art are Revitalizing American Religion.* Berkeley: University of California Press, 2003.

Zerubavel, Eviatar. *Hidden Rhythms: Schedules and Calendars in Social Life.* Chicago: University of Chicago Press, 1981.

INDEX

academic freedom, 144–45, 149

Adorno, Theodor, 2, 5

Aristotle, 159

Auerbach, Erich, 30

Augustine, 20, 34

authority, 10, 21, 34, 206; grand narratives, 34; little narratives, 26–27; narrative theology, 35; *see also* Enlightenment; epistemology

Barbour, Ian, 123–25

Barr, Stephen, 120

Baxter, Richard, 38

beauty, 76, 212; *see also* epistemology, beauty; hymnody

Berry, Wendell, 68, 83, 90–91, 213

Bible, 13, 105, 124, 160, 173; grand narrative, 27; higher criticism, 10–11, 13, 30; pre-critical reading, 30–31; post-critical reading, 32; *see also* language, alphabet; Locke; nar-

rative theology; science; Smart, use of Bible

Bohm, David, 124

Borges, Jorge Luis, 82

Boswell, James, 96, 145

Boyle, Robert, 63; Boyle lectures, 100–101

Bunyan, John, 13, 51; *The Pilgrim's Progress*, 11, 13, 14, 53

Burke, Edmund, 1, 2, 7, 107, 155–83, 186; allusion, 159–65; British Constitution, 166–71, 181–82; prejudice, 155, 156, 175–83, 214; revolutionary festivals, 133–34, 136; social contract, 164; sublime, 107, 160, 172, 243; taste, 159, 161, 171–75; tradition, 158–77; *see also* Gadamer

calendar, 128, 146–48; reform, 147–53; *see also* French Revolution, revolutionary calendar

277